AF658100

SOIL ECOSYSTEM AND LITHOSPHERE

ENV BOOKS SERIES

SOIL ECOSYSTEM
AND
LITHOSPHERE

Editors

Dr. Abhishek Swami
Associate Professor
Department of Environmental Sciences
SGT (Shree Guru Gobind Singh Tricentenary) University
Gurugram (HR), (India)

Dr. Prasann Kumar
Division of Research and Development
Lovely Professional University
Jalandhar - 144 411 (Punjab)
(India)

&

Dr. Pawan Kumar 'Bharti'
Society for Environment, Health Awareness of
Nutrition & Toxicology (SEHAT)
B-225/5D, Top Floor, Subhash Gali, Road No. 7, Block B
Ashok Nagar, Shahdara, Delhi - 110 093
(India)

DPH

DISCOVERY PUBLISHING HOUSE PVT. LTD.
INDIA

Published by:
Namit Wasan
DISCOVERY PUBLISHING HOUSE PVT. LTD.
4383/4B, Ansari Road, Darya Ganj
New Delhi-110 002 (India)
Phone : +91-11-23279245; 23253475; 43596065
E-mail : discoverybooksindia@gmail.com
discoverypublishinghouse@gmail.com
namitwasan9@gmail.com
web : www.discoverypublishinggroup.com

First Edition: **2020**

ISBN: 978-93-88854-50-4

Soil Ecosystem and Lithosphere

© Editors

All rights reserved. No part of this publication should be reproduced, stored in a retrieval system, or transmitted in any form or by any means: electronic, mechanical, photocopying, recording or otherwise, without the prior written permission of the author and the publisher.

This book has been published in good faith that the material provided by authors/editors is original. Every effort is made to ensure accuracy of material, but the publisher and printer will not be held responsible for any inadvertent error(s). In case of any dispute, all legal matters are to be settled under Delhi jurisdiction only.

Printed at:
Infinity Imaging Systems
Delhi

M.S. Swaminathan Research Foundation

M. S. Swaminathan
Founder chairman
Ex-Member of Parliament (Rajya Sabha)

Foreword

I am very glad to know that a several books are being edited under the aegis of ENVBOOKS series, Delhi, India on various sub-themes of Agriculture and environment like:

'Cultivation Techniques for Agriculture Crops'

'Air Pollution and Control'

'Seed and Food Storage Technologies'

'Heavy Metals and Impacts on Plants'

'Climate Change and Agriculture Production'

'Scientific Writing and Research Methodology'

'Laboratory Management'

'Statistical Tools in Science'

'Advances in Chemistry and Chemical Sciences'

'Irrigation Techniques in Crop Management'

'Waste Management Practices'

'Vermitechnology, Farm and Fertilizers'

'Animal Science and Pest Control'

'Recent Research in Biochemistry and Molecular Biology''

'Water Management and Sustainability'

'Soil Quality and Agriculture'

I am very happy to learn that a number of editors and authors from different institutions and university of different nations are involved in editing these books. The books are the compendium of screened-in manuscripts received from different countries like UK, Canada, Egypt, Nigeria, Ghana, Ethiopia, China, South Africa, Japan, Guyana, PNG, Nepal, South America, and various parts of India. I am feeling delighted in writing forward to these books and congratulate to Dr. Pawan Kumar Bharti, Editor-in-Chief and founder of ENVBOOKS series and of course his team for their tenacity and hard work in compiling these valuable compendiums.

I hope these books will be beneficial for academician, researchers, industrialist, policy makers and students as study material and will work as reference for further research work.

M.S. Swaminathan

PREFACE

Soil and its microorganisms and plants are vital for each other's composition. Acidic, sandy soil can only support hardy species or species with traits that make them able to absorb the limited nutrients in these ecosystems. These species may include plants like sundew, which gets its nutrients by catching insects, or heather, which gets its nutrients by growing with (symbiosis) fungi in the soil, which enables the heather to use the soil's organic nitrogen. This enables dwarf shrubs like crowberry and common heather (in dry soils) and bell heather (in moist soils) to dominate the plant community and, thus, be the species that create the ecosystem (ecosystem creators). In areas richer in nutrients, more species are able to survive. In such areas, species are able to outperform by growing so large that they shade out the other species. These species include meadowsweet and mercury, but can also include forest trees such as ash and elm. Plants may use chemical warfare in all types of soil, and these consist of plants secreting chemical compounds into the soil that make it difficult for other species to germinate and grow or that the plants contain chemical compounds, such as polyphenols, that make them unpalatable to animals and, in turn, contribute to slowing down the rate of degradation and in this way forming a moor layer. The fact that the species are competing for exclusive rights to the nutrients in the soil affects the soil's appearance, composition and chemical properties, including its buffer system.

The present book updates the subject content of Soil Quality Assessment; Soil Erosion, Phytoremediation of Contaminated Soil; Soil Amendments; Metal Extraction from Soil; Sheet and Rill Erosion; Restoration of Contaminated Areas.

Thanks are due to publisher and contributors from various institutions and universities.

The book will be helpful for the researchers, academia working in the field of Soil Quality Assessment; Soil Erosion, Phytoremediation of Contaminated Soil; Soil Amendments techniques; Metal Extraction from Soil by Microorganism-Assisted Plant; Forecasting Productivity Losses Cost by Sheet and Rill Erosion; Restoration of Contaminated Areas and Assessment of Agricultural soil variables.

Editors
(envbooks@gmail.com)

CONTENTS

Soil Ecosystem and Lithosphere **Pages 1-11**
Edited by: Dr. Abhishek Swami, Dr. Prasann Kumar and Dr. Pawan Kumar 'Bharti'
ISBN: 978-93-88854-50-4
Edition: 2020
Published by: Discovery Publishing House Pvt. Ltd., New Delhi (India)

1 Introduction

The soil environment consists of a variety of physical, biological and chemical factors that affect the abundance and diversity of microbes found in the soil. At its basic level, the soil environment consists of a solid and porous fraction. Within these fractions, a variety of chemical and physical factors are affected by and and affect microbes. These include, but are not limited to texture, temperature, pH, oxygen, cation exchange capacity and redox reactions.

The soil environment directly affects the types of microbes, as well as the rates of processes they perform. For example, microbial activity increases with temperature, which in turn affects rates of decomposition. On the other hand, microbial processes directly affect their environments as well, contributing to the carbon and nitrogen cycles, which are important for microbial and plant health. At the micro scale, bacteria and other microbes participate in a variety of reactions that affect nutrient cycling, pH, as well as oxygen and CO_2 content. At the macro scale, these processes can change the landscape in drastic ways, assisting in weathering of the soil and development of soil layers.

The principal environmental variables affecting life in soils include moisture, temperature, pH, aeration (i.e. presence or absence of sufficient oxygen), organic matter, and inorganic nutrients such as nitrogen and phosphorus. The balance of these factors controls the abundance and activities of the microbes and larger animals in soils which in turn have a marked influence on the critical processes of soil aggregation and degradation of plant and animal residues and the nutrient cycling that accompanies this latter process.

To understand life in the soil, the soil is best viewed as an extremely heterogeneous collection of microhabitats. The soil is a matrix of solids including sand, silt, clay, and organic matter particles as well as aggregates of various sizes formed from them, and pore space, which may be filled with air or water. Thus, depending on the mix of environmental variables, prevailing conditions can vary quite markedly over distances on the order of a few millimeters (1 inch = 25.4 millimeters).

Soil Water

Soil water is usually derived from rainfall or some other form of overland flow. The amount of water that enters the soil is a function of soil structure which in turn is a function of texture and higher-order structure i.e. aggregation (e.g. well-aggregated, porous soils allow greater infiltration). Larger pores created by root channels and animal burrows (ant tunnels, crayfish tunnels and worm holes) as well as other types of macropores also greatly facilitate movement of water into and through the soil profile. This is why these soil animals are usually regarded as highly beneficial in soil and why some scientists often use the abundance of earthworms as an indicator of a "healthy soil", though it should be remembered that highly fertile, productive soils do not always contain large numbers of earthworms and other soil animals.

Water moves through soil by mass flow (i.e. fluid movement through larger channels) and by capillary action, the slower movement through the highly tortuous network of very small channels and pores. Most soil water is held in this system of capillary pores and channels and can be held quite firmly through physical interactions with the solid components of the soil matrix. Matric water is held in small (usually microscopic) pores and is often adsorbed onto particle surfaces that can be held rather tightly. Because these interactions with the soil matrix essentially bind the soil water, energy on the part of plants and microbes is required to extract water. These forces are usually given as a matric potential or pressure and they indicate how tightly the water is held. These values are usually expressed as a negative value because they are a measure of the amount of suction required to extract water from the soil. It is this adsorption of water to soil solids that explains why plants can wilt in a soil having substantial clay content, even when some matric water is still present. Beyond a certain point, the water is held too tightly for the plants to extract and the so-called wilting point is reached. An often-stated value for the matric potential at the permanent wilting point is approximately -15 bars (-1.5 mPa). Plants exposed to lower matric (more negative) potentials may wilt and not recover. It should be stressed that the matric potential is a function of soil texture and that fine-textured soils (silts and clays) can contain moisture at very low matric potentials because of the much greater numbers of small particles (greater surface area) and the finer pore network which adsorbs and retains water. Thus in clayey soils, water is not as biologically available as it is in coarser-textured soils. A corollary, however, is that coarse-textured soils do not retain as much water because the larger particles do not adsorb water as well and the larger pores drain more rapidly? Thus, nutrients and other chemicals may be retained in a clay soil whereas they may leach, i.e. move downward, with water more rapidly through sandy soils. These textural concerns are of extreme importance to our understanding of the movement of materials into ground water.

Water occupying the pore network in soil is often called the soil solution. It is never pure water but rather it is a solution containing dissolved salts and gases. This is the solution which is most available to plants and microbes and provides some of the nutrients needed for growth. Many nutrients actually reach the roots of plants through mass flow of the water to the vicinity of the roots. Too much water in the soil disrupts the ideal balance between air-filled and water-filled pores, i.e. soil aeration (discussed below). Salts dissolved in the soil solution give rise to an osmotic pressure or potential which can be measured. The osmotic potential can influence the movement of water into and out of cells and therefore it is important that the soil solution not be allowed to become too saline (salty) as it might in a soil experiencing increased salinity due to prolonged irrigation and poor drainage. Under low osmotic (high negative) potentials (salty or sugary solutions), water is actually drawn out of cells resulting in physiological impairment, that is, being dehydrated beyond some critical point. This is the basis of preserving foods by adding high concentrations of salt.

Osmotic and matric potentials are the two major factors controlling the availability of water to soil life and of these two, it is the matric potential which most affects soil microbes. As a soil dries, life in the soil must work harder to extract water against ever increasing matric and osmotic potentials. For these reasons, adequate soil moisture is required for maximum rates of plant growth and to maintain the vital soil microbial processes essential for life on earth.

Soil Atmosphere

The soil atmosphere is the mixture of gases occupying that portion of the pore network that is not filled with water. It is derived from the overlying air but differs in a few prominent ways. Most notably, the soil atmosphere contains less oxygen than the overlying air and typically has 10- to 100-fold more carbon dioxide. You might surmise, and you would be correct, that these changes are driven by the aerobic respiration of the organisms inhabiting the soil. These changes are also a result of the physical characteristics of the soil environment. Generally, the rate of movement of oxygen back into the soil is not sufficient to keep up with all the respiratory demand because movement of gases is restricted by the highly elaborate network of fine pores and capillaries. Filling pores with water restricts the movement of gases even further, and it is for this reason that waterlogged soils often become anaerobic (i.e. depleted of molecular O). This condition should be avoided because it gives rise to a number of negative consequences, not the least of which is that plant roots are injured or killed, not just due to lack of O_2, but to the accumulation of toxic products such as organic acids (e.g. acetic acid) or hydrogen sulfide (rotten egg gas) arising from anaerobic activities of soil bacteria.

Most soil organisms are aerobic, i.e. they require O_2 to grow. However, some soil bacteria do not require O_2 and in fact may be killed or inhibited by it. These bacteria are called anaerobes and they function when there are low concentrations of soil O_2, for example, during periods of prolonged waterlogging. Still other bacteria, called facultative anaerobes, can grow in the presence or absence of O_2.

This discussion of soil water and the soil atmosphere reveals why it is so desirable to maintain a soil in a highly aggregated state. Aggregation is indispensable for maintaining the balance between air- and water-filled pores that is essential for the maintenance of aerobic, beneficial microbes and soil animals.

Soil Temperature

Soil temperature is controlled by a number of factors not the least of which is the amount of sunlight incident upon it and the amount of water it contains. Soils are warmed by solar radiation. For this reason, dark-colored soils tend to absorb more heat and warm earlier in the spring than light-colored soils do. Obviously, vegetative cover plays an important role in controlling the amount of solar radiation that reaches the soil surface. We all know the value of a good shade tree on a hot summer afternoon. Because the soil can become quite warm in the surface few centimeters, particularly when free of vegetation, it is not surprising that numbers of microbes and soil animals are lower near the immediate surface. It is frequently just too hot and too dry in this narrow band of soil. Deeper in the solum the soil warms according to its moisture content and the amount of irradiance received on the surface.

Temperature affects soil life in several ways. First, all organisms exhibit preferences for certain temperature ranges; the so-called minimum, maximum and optimum temperatures. Soil microbes can grow across a very wide range of temperatures so that some portion of the population may be active nearly year round. At the lower extremes of temperature (near freezing) are microbes called cryophiles which actually require or prefer these cold temperatures. At the other extreme are thermophiles, organisms which thrive in high-temperature environments like the boiling geothermal hot springs of Yellowstone National Park at temperatures near 94°C (water boils below 100°C because of the lower atmospheric pressure at the higher altitude). Thermophiles are also critical components of composting systems designed to accelerate the conversion of municipal refuse, paper etc. into compost for use in gardens and for disposal onto land. In the middle temperature range (15 to 40°C) we find the mesophiles and, not surprisingly, ourselves (humans) and most other life forms. Most soil microbes are mesophiles. Most of life's important biological processes operate best in the mesophilic range and we find special adaptations in those organisms that live in colder or hotter environments.

Temperature affects soil microbes and microbial processes in another fundamental way. Namely, it governs the rate of chemical and biological reactions. Thus, biological reactions and processes tend to occur more rapidly as temperature rises to some point where some vital function (perhaps an important enzyme) of the cell is impaired or destroyed and the organism is killed. At colder temperatures, reaction rates slow down and may almost completely stop. This is the well-known basis for preserving food from spoilage by keeping it cold in the freezer or refrigerator. We mentioned above that temperature controls biological processes in soil. One can easily see the value of early warming of soils in the spring for germination of seed and an early start of a crop growth cycle. One can also look at maps of soil organic matter content and easily ascertain the combined effects of soil moisture and temperature on maintenance of organic matter in the soil. In warm, moist climates, soil organic matter is difficult to maintain because the conditions for growth of soil microbes are favorable for longer periods of the year. In colder climates, soil organic matter can accumulate because of prolonged periods when the soil is very cold or even frozen in the near surface layers where most microbes reside.

Soil and its microorganisms and plants are vital for each other's composition. Acidic, sandy soil can only support hardy species or species with traits that make them able to absorb the limited nutrients in these ecosystems. These species may include plants like sundew, which gets its nutrients by catching insects, or heather, which gets its nutrients by growing with (symbiosis) fungi in the soil, which enables the heather to use the soil's organic nitrogen. This enables dwarf shrubs like crowberry and common heather (in dry soils) and bell heather (in moist soils) to dominate the plant community and, thus, be the species that create the ecosystem (ecosystem creators). In areas richer in nutrients, more species are able to survive. In such areas, species are able to outperform by growing so large that they shade out the other species. These species include meadowsweet and mercury, but can also include forest trees such as ash and elm. Plants may use chemical warfare in all types of soil, and these consist of plants secreting chemical compounds into the soil that make it difficult for other species to germinate and grow or that the plants contain chemical compounds, such as polyphenols, that make them unpalatable to animals and, in turn, contribute to slowing down the rate of degradation and in this way forming a moor layer. The fact that the species are competing for exclusive rights to the nutrients in the soil affects the soil's appearance, composition and chemical properties, including its buffer system.

Soil Environment Overview

Solid Fraction

The solid fraction of the soil consists of mineral and organic matter, which is typically about 50% of the soil by volume, and it has a dominant influence on heat, water, and chemical transport and retention process. Most of the solid particles are derived from mineral sources such as decomposed rocks or sediments. Soil organic matter (SOM) consists of all of the organic components of a soil, including living biomass, decomposing tissue, and fully decomposed tissue called humus. The rate and pathway of carbon decomposition and SOM formation directly affects the carbon cycle. Texture can also influence chemical properties such as cation exchange capacity (CEC). Finer textured soils with high clay content will have great CEC than soils with low clay content.

Soil pores consist of the air and water filled fractions of the soil, and together they make up about 50% of the soil by volume. Pore space is largely determined by size and arrangement of aggregates and affects the movement of water, air, and organisms in soil. Soil pores are typically classified based on size: Macropores (>75 μm) Mesopores (30-70 μm) Micropores (5-30 μm) Ultramicropores (0.1-5 μm) Cryptoporus (<0.1 μm).

The air filled pores of the soil typically have a similar distribution of gases as the atmosphere above the soil, with slightly lower oxygen and slightly more CO_2 due to the respiration of microorganisms. The soil atmosphere consists of about 18-20% oxygen near the surface, which decreases with depth. CO_2 is around 1%, and N_2 is about 78% of the soil air filled pore space. Oxygen content will be lower when available carbon is high (demand for high O_2 to utilize carbon). Soil that is high in clay content and/or compacted may have trouble exchanging gases to the atmosphere. Soil air generally has a very high moisture content when compared to the atmosphere (~100% unless the soil is very dry). The amount and composition of air in a soil is largely determined by the water content in the soil.

The main source of soil water is rainfall and overland flow. The amount of water that enters the soil is a function of soil structure and texture. Water moves in soil through mass flow and capillary action. The water in soil is often called the soil solution, which can move nutrients from the surface through the soil column. The water fraction of the pores is typically between 20% to 30% but can vary depending on precipitation, soil texture, and soil structure. The water content of a soil influences gas exchange, nutrient movement and concentrations of nutrients, and buffers the temperature of the soil.

Soil Aggregates & Structure

Soil aggregates are groups of soil particles that bind to each other more strongly than to adjacent particles. The space between the aggregates provide pore space for retention and exchange of air and water. Aggregation affects erosion, movement of water, and plant root growth. Polysaccharides produced by soil bacteria, and humic substances and hyphae produced by fungi improve aggregation.

Soil structure is the arrangement of primary soil particles into aggregates which describes the arrangement of the solid parts of the soil and the pore spaces between them. Soil structure has a major influence on water movement, SOM leaching, and gas exchanges of the soils. The water movement, affected by structure can bring SOM in the surface to deep inside the soil. Soil with high clay content and/or poor structure, may have reduced infiltration and will cause runoff, erosion and surface crusting. This can cause nutrient loss and increase the potential of desertification.

Factors affecting Soil Environment

Texture

Soil texture is defined as the distribution of sand (0.05-2.0 mm), silt (0.002-0.05mm), and clay (< 0.002 mm) in soil. Soil texture indirectly influences properties such as: water holding capacity, porosity, aeration and nutrient availability. Clay particles have a very high surface to volume ratio, which makes them very chemically active and have high nutrient availability. Due to the adhesion of water, soils high in clay will also have a high water holding capacity. Soils with a high clay content will often have a very active microbial community, especially in areas of the rhizosphere.

One study by Hamarshid found that CO_2 production rates were greatest in fine textured soil compared to coarse textured soil. This was due to finer textured soils' greater ability to hold nutrients and water, allowing microbial populations to thrive. However, this is not always the case, as other chemical or physical properties may affect the ability of microbes to perform processes such as carbon decomposition. (e.g. temperature, pH and quality of substrate).

Temperature

Soil temperature changes with depth: the surface soil (~0-20 cm) is highly affected by the solar radiation. Moving deeper (~below 27 cm) temperatures are very stable over time. This is because heat moves in soil mainly by conduction, which does not allow much heat to reach deep in the soil profile. Soil temperature is also affected by the soil color, soil cover, and the water content of the soil. A darker soil can absorb more heat compared to lighter color soil. A dry soil is more easily heated than a wet one due to the higher heat capacity of water. Heat moving in soil is analogous to the movement of water. Generally, the higher the temperature, the more active microbes are, with microbial activity typically doubling with a 10° rise in temperature. However, some bacteria thrive at very low temperatures (psychrophiles) and very high temperatures (extremophiles).

pH change in soils is due to both biotic and abiotic processes. Microbes consume and release H+ through redox reactions and fermentation. Abiotic processes such as rainfall can also affect the pH of the soil. In areas of high rainfall, acidic soils can be created through leaching of bases from the soil, while more basic soils are typically located in arid environments. One study by Fierer et al, found that pH was the single most important factor influencing microbial diversity at the continental scale. The study used 98 samples from across North and South America, and found that the greatest microbial diversity coincided with a neutral pH, even between two soil from the same forest.

pH affects microbial diversity because many microbial species cannot tolerate extreme levels of pH (high or low). Alterations in pH can render essential microbe enzymes inactive and/or denature proteins within the cells and prevent microbial activity from occurring. However, there are microbes that can withstand extreme pH environments. At pH below 5, fungi and acidophilic bacteria have a competitive advantage over other bacteria that thrive at a more neutral pH.

pH can also affect the availability of nutrients in this soil. Below a pH of 5, essential plant nutrients such as phosphorous, calcium and magnesium are not available. Low pH can also cause aluminum (Al^{3+}) to be released from soil minerals. Al^{3+} in soil solution is not only toxic to plants and microbes, it can combine with OH^- ions causing the free H^+ ions to lower the pH further. The effect of pH on nutrient availability and microbe survivability can be seen in figure 1.7.

Oxygen

Oxygen (O_2) is a very important component of the productivity of both microbes and plant roots. Oxygen has a very high electrical potential (Eh), meaning that it has a lot of potential to produce energy when used as an electron acceptor in an oxidation-reduction reaction. An example oxidation-reduction reaction can be seen in equation 1, where glucose is being oxidized, and oxygen is being reduced.

$$6O_2 + C_6H_{12}O_6 \rightarrow 6CO_2 + 6H_2O \qquad \text{[eq. 1]}$$

The amount of oxygen available in a soil depends on a number of factors, including soil porosity, water content, and consumption by respiring organisms. If soil pores are large and interconnected, oxygen can flow easily. However, even in a well aerated soil, micro-aggregates may contain anaerobic zones in which oxygen flow is very limited. In a flooded soil environment oxygen content will be very limited because oxygen diffuses about 10,000 times more slowly through water than through air.

In areas where oxygen is not present, soil microbes may use alternative electron acceptors such as nitrate, manganese, iron, sulfate, and carbon dioxide.

Cation Exchange Capacity

Cation exchange capacity (CEC) is the ability of a soil to hold and exchange cations. The amount of CEC in soil is highly dependent on the texture and organic matter of the soil. The high surface area and negative charge of clay allows it to bind and exchange with soil solution, which contains cations that are important for plant and microbial health.

For many soils, especially those with low clay and organic carbon content, CEC is dependant upon soil pH (see figure 1.9). As pH decreases , an increasing amount of H^+ ions are attracted to negatively charged clay particles and functional groups in SOM. This causes other cations, that were attached to these surfaces to fall off into the soil solution. CEC will increase as pH increases as less cations are being pushed out by H^+ ions.

At typical soil pH values (5-8), microbes and clay particles are both negatively charged, but microbes still to bind to clay. This binding could be due van der waals, hydrogen bonding, sharing electrons and ion exchange.

Redox Reactions

Reduction-oxidation (redox) reactions are chemical reactions in which reactants experience a change in oxidation number (which means these reactants either gain or lose electrons). Many reactions in the soil involve the gain or loss of electrons, obtaining or releasing energy. Redox reactions are important in the soil, because microbes obtain energy through redox reactions for their metabolism, and the redox state can also determine the microbial processes that will occur.

Redox reactions include anabolism and catabolism process, both of which play important roles in microbial metabolism. Anabolism is the biosynthesis of cellular components, linked to energy requirements, while catabolism is the the biochemical processes leading to breakdown of organic substances, linked to energy production. For example, the photosynthesis and respiration processes are the coupled reactions in the soil, where plants required energy from light and reduce carbon dioxide to glucose, which then be used by microbes in the soil as the energy for their metabolism.

The tendency of compounds to accept or donate electrons is expressed as "redox potential". Redox potential (Eh), determined from the concentration of oxidants and reductants in the environment, is to measure the oxidation-reduction status and electron availability within this system. Electrons are essential to all inorganic and organic chemical reactions. Redox potential measurements allow for rapid characterization of the degree of reduction and for predicting stability of various compounds that regulate nutrients and metal availability in soil and sediment. The inorganic oxidants include oxygen, nitrate, nitrite, manganese, sulfate, and CO_2, while the reductants include various organic substrates and reduced inorganic compounds (NH^{4+}, Fe^{2+}, Mn^{2+}, S_2^-, CH_4, and H_2).

The redox potential of a substance depends on Affinity of molecules for electrons and Concentration of reductants and oxidants (referred to as redox pair) Anaerobic environments such as wetland soils and flooded soils are usually limited by electron acceptors and have an abundant supply of electron donors. In this case, most microbes' activity is limited, and facultative and obligate microbes reduce the minerals following the electron tower. Aerated soils are usually limited by electron donors and have an abundant supply of electron acceptors (primarily O_2).

Salinity

Soil salinity refers to the salt content in the soil. The concentrations and types of ions in solution in the soil can cause modifications in the dispersion of the clay fraction, degrading the original soil fraction. The sodium ion, being monovalent, increases the width of the diffuse double layer on the surface of the clays, reducing the attractive forces between them with a consequent increase in particle dispersion. The consequence of this dispersion of the clay is also shown by a reduction in stability of the soil aggregates, which are thus easily transported by rain or irrigation.

Soil salinization is a big problem for soils in arid or semi-arid regions and agricultural soils throughout the world. Salts can adversely affect plant and microbial growth, due to destruction of the soil structure and its consequent compacting. The stress of high salt concentration can be detrimental for sensitive microorganisms and decrease the activity of surviving cells, due to the metabolic load imposed by the need for stress tolerance mechanisms.

Bioavailability

Bioavailability assesses what proportion of a contaminant present at a contaminated site is available for uptake by organisms. Bioavailability processes are the biological, chemical and physical processes that result in an organism being exposed to a contaminant present in the soil. These processes are: release of the contaminant from the solid phase, transport of the contaminant to and across a biological membrane and, incorporation into a living organism.

Bioavailable molecules must cross a biological membrane, which means the molecules have to interact with the aqueous phase. Therefore, soil properties which control partitioning between the solid phase in soil and the pore water, such as pH, organic matter content, Eh, cation exchange capacity (CEC), and the concentration of clay minerals, have a significant impact on bioavailability. Increasing exchange sites aids the retention of molecules in the pore water in a bioavailable form, but molecules sorbed strongly to surfaces or in solid form are generally not bioavailable.

REFERENCE

Brady, Nyle C., and Ray R. Weil. Elements of the Nature and Properties of Soils. Upper Saddle River, NJ: Pearson Prentice Hall, 2010. Print.

"BIO 212 Study Guide". Iowa State University. <https://www.studyblue.com/notes/note/n/bio-212-study-guide-2012-13-yin/deck/9716305>

Delaune, R. D., and Reddy, K. R., Encyclopedia of Soils in the Environment. 2005, Elsevier Ltd.

"Soil_Microaggregate_and_bacteria." UC Berkeley, n.d. Web. 25 Feb. 2016. <http://em-lab.berkeley.edu/EML/images/TEM-Gallery1/pages/Soil_Microaggregate_and_bacteria.htm>.

"Electron Tower Theory." Bioremediation Specialists, n.d. Web. 14 Mar. 2016. <http://Bioremediation-specialists.com/Electron-Tower-Theory.php>.

Fierer, N., and R. B. Jackson. "The Diversity and Biogeography of Soil Bacterial Communities." Proceedings of the National Academy of Sciences 103.3 (2006): 626-31. Web.

Hamarshid N.H., Othman M.A., and Hussain M.-A.H., 2010. Effects of Soil Texture on Chemical Compositions, Microbial Populations and Carbon Mineralization in Soil. Egypt. J. Exp. Biol. (Bot.), 6(1), 59-64. Kabala C. and Zapart J., 2012.

Hodson, M. E., Vijver, M. G. and Peijnenberg, W. J. G. M. (2011) Bioavailability in Soils. In: Swartjes, F. A. (ed.) Dealing with Contaminated Sites: From Theory Towards Practical Application. Springer, pp. 721-746. ISBN 9789048197569 doi: 10.1007/978-90-481-9757-6 Available at http://centaur.reading.ac.uk/20839/.

https://microbewiki.kenyon.edu/index.php/Soil_Environment

http://organiclifestyles.tamu.edu/soilbasics/soilenvironment.html

https://bios.au.dk/en/about-bioscience/organisation/plant-and-insect-ecology/effects-of-farming/soil-environment/

Munkholm, L. J., Heck, R. J., Deen, B., & Zidar, T. (2016). Relationship Between Soil Aggregate Strength, Shape and Porosity for Soils Under Different Long-term Management. Geoderma, 26852-59. doi:10.1016/j.geoderma.2016.01.005

Moravec, C., Whiting, D., and Reeder, J. "Introduction to Soils." CMG GardenNotes. Colorado State University Extension. Oct. 2015. <http://www.cmg.colostate.edu/>

Maganhotto, C. M.,and Francisconi Fay,E., (2012). Effect of Salinity on Soil Microorganisms, Soil Health and Land Use Management, Dr. Maria C. Hernandez Soriano (Ed.), InTech, Available from: http://www.intechopen.com/books/soil-health-and-land-usemanagement/Effect-of-salinity-on-soil-microorganisms.

"PH and Organic Substrate Nutrients." N.p., n.d. Web. 13 Mar. 2016. <http://organicsoiltechnology.com/ph-and-organic-substrate-nutrients.html>.

Provin, T., and Pitt, J. L. "Managing Soil Salinity". Texas AgriLife Extension Service. March, 2012. <http://soiltesting.tamu.edu/publications> Edited by Students of Kate Scow.

"Soil Reaction (pH)." University of New South Wales, n.d. Web. 25 Feb. 2016. <http://www.terragis.bees.unsw.edu.au/terraGIS_soil/sp_soil_reaction_ph.html>.

"Soil Images - Redoximorphic Features." New England Soil, n.d. Web. 25 Feb. 2016. <http://nesoil.com/images/redox.htm>.

Sylvia, D. M. Principles and Applications of Soil Microbiology. Upper Saddle River, NJ: Pearson Prentice Hall, 2005. Print.

"Soil Structure and Macropores." Soil Quality: Indicators:. NRCS, n.d. Web. 13 Mar. 2016. <http://soilquality.org/indicators/soil_structure.html>.

Todar, Kenneth. "Nutrition and Growth of Bacteria." N.p., n.d. Web. 13 Mar. 2016. <http://textbookofbacteriology.net/nutgro_5.html>.

Soil Ecosystem and Lithosphere **Pages 12-21**
Edited by: **Dr. Abhishek Swami, Dr. Prasann Kumar and Dr. Pawan Kumar 'Bharti'**
ISBN: 978-93-88854-50-4
Edition: **2020**
Published by: **Discovery Publishing House Pvt. Ltd., New Delhi (India)**

2

Soil Erosion
The Matter of Overview

Jagdish Chand[1] & Prasann Kumar[1, 2*]

ABSTRACT

As we know that soil erosion is termed as the detachment of soil particles from one place to another place by action water, wind, airmainly. Along with soil, nutrients and soil microorganisms are also transported from one place to another place results in the loss of soil fertility, physical and chemical properties. On the other hand in case of formation of soil take many years i.e. (for formation 1 cm of it will take 200-400 years). Thus if erosion of soil is increasing day by day without any check so we lose the fertile portion of soil and soil finally loses the capacity to produce something then we only left with barren land or dead soil. So to avoid this situation of soil erosion we have to check the various factors of soil erosion and adopt the new methods of cultivations which reduce the impact of soil erosion. A good knowledge of soil erosion is a key factor to save the soil from the erosion. By virtue of that we can save the soil for our future generation.

Keywords: *Agriculture, Barren, Crop, Erosion, Fertile, Knowledge*

Introduction

Soil erosion is be called as the form of soil degradation, which degrade the soil quality to produce something the rate of soil degradation is increases day by day due to the human interference. There are different types and agents which are responsible for causing the soil erosion."Soil Erosion is a process of detachment and transportation of soil materials by erosive agents" (Ellison, 1946).

Types of Soil Erosion

It is generally divided into two different types.

1. **Natural erosion:** Which is naturally occurred in nature at very slow rate having least bed effect on the environment and mankind this natural

[1] Department of Agronomy, School of Agriculture, Lovely Professional University, Jalandhar, Punjab, India, 144411
[1, 2] Division of Research and Development, Lovely Professional University, Jalandhar, Punjab, India, 144411

process seems important sometime for occurrence of new things having positive effects.

2. **Accelerated erosion:** This type of problem occurs when the speed of the natural erosion is increases at very fast rate due to the interference of human activities. The rate of this erosion is greater than the rate of the soil formation. India's total geographical area of 328.73 million hectare and reporting area is 304.89 million hectare. Soil degradation in India is estimated on 147 mha of land which includes 94 mha under water erosion, 9 mha under wind erosion, 16 mha under salinity, and 14 mha under flooding. Along with soil erosion loss of nutrients also occurs i.e. According to central soil and water conservation and research institute (ICAR) provided the data on an average 0.8 M tons of nitrogen, 1.8 M tons of phosphorus, and 26.3 M tons of potassium. This is very serious situation because on an average India constitutes 18% of world population and 15% of world livestock populationonly having 2.4% of world land area (Bhattacharyya *et.al.* 2015).

Agents of Soil Erosion

There are four types of soil erosion

1. Water Erosion
2. Wind Erosion
3. Gravity Erosion
4. Glacier Erosion

1. **Water Erosion:** Water erosion is very serious problem over large part of the world. Water erosion occurs in different steps i.e. Rainfall, Detachment, transportation, translocation, and deposition of soil particles with water.

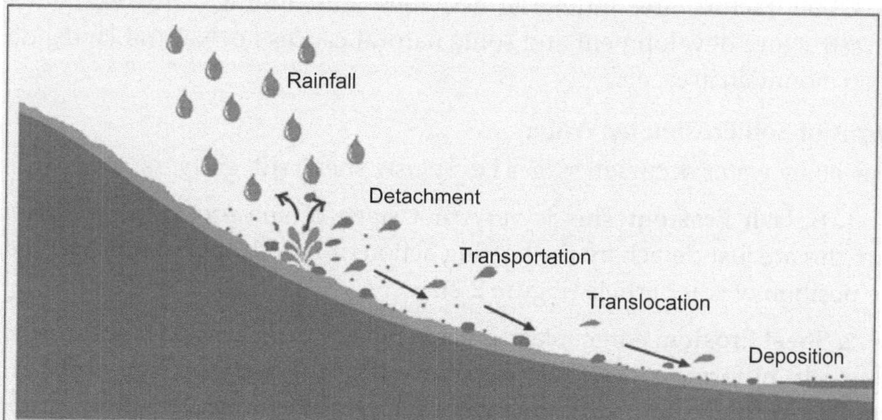

Fig. 2.1: Steps of soil erosion with water

(**Source:** http://www.google.co.in/imgres)

Causes of Water Erosion

Human activities and natural causes may lead to soil degradation. There are different types of activities that increases the rate of soil erosion and degradation i.e.

1. **Agriculture causes:** Main cause of the soil erosion by agriculture is improper management of soil cultivated land, improper use of the land, sometimes we can cultivate the sloppy land along the slope without opting any conservation practices and keeping land unprotected and subjected it directly to the action of rain.
2. **Deforestation and removal of natural vegetation:** This is the era of commercialization as the rate of commercialization is increases day by day it may leads to the rapid deforestation of forest and natural vegetation, arable land are easy to convert the site for commercialization though land for agriculture is decreases this leads to the shifting cultivation by cutting the forest cover and expose more area under erosion.
3. **Over exploitation of vegetation for domestic use:** Over exploitation of natural resources like wood from forests, Fodder, timber etc. may increase the rate of soil erosion by removing the soil vegetative cover.
4. **Overgrazing:** Overgrazing is the process in which animals are aloe to graze again and again on the same piece of land this many result in the complete removal of soil cover compaction of soil surface by hooves animals it does reduce the infiltration rate and thus could affect the ground water.

Other factors are: Industrial activities and mining, Urbanization and infrastructure development and some natural causes i.e. Natural landslide in steep mountain area, etc.

Forms of Soil Erosion by Water

Erosion by water occurs in stages i.e. Splash, sheet, rill, gully, ravine.

1. Splash Erosion: This is very first stage of soil erosion in which soil particles are just detach by the beating action of rain drop and little change in the position of soil particle (Figure 2.2).

2. Sheet Erosion: After splash erosion next stage of erosion is sheet erosion in which uniform layer of soil is removed by the action of raindrops. This type of erosion occurs on those areas having gentle slope. The flowing water moves in the form of a thin sheet over the soil surface, called as "sheet flow" (figure 2.3).

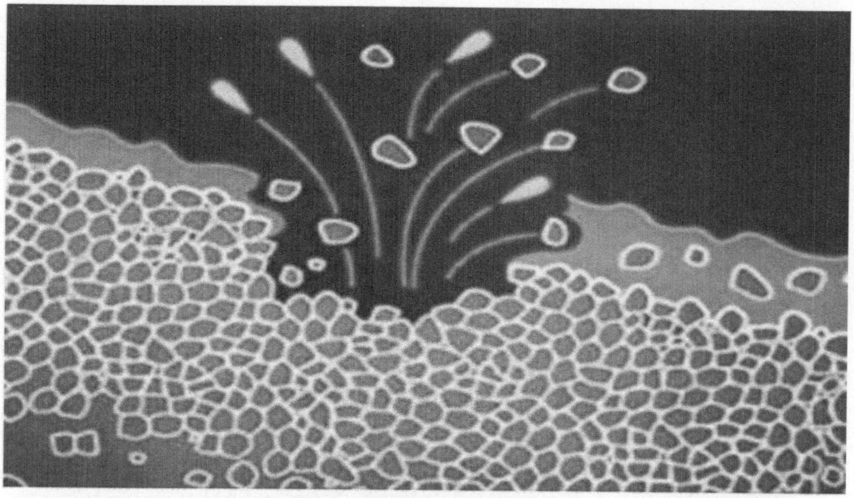

Fig. 2.2: Splash Erosion

(**Source:** http://www.google.co.in/imgres?imgurl)

Fig. 2.3: Sheet Erosion

(**Source:** http://www.google.co.in/imgres)

The occurrence of sheet erosion in a given field can be identified by the following changes on that place (Suresh, 2004).

- Change in soil color.
- Expansion of depression size.
- Presence of coarse sand particles (gravel like) on the soil surface.
- Enlargement of rills.
- Exposure of unproductive sub soil or bed rock.

3. Rill Erosion: After the sheet erosion the velocity of the flowing water increases leads to formation of small channel. The channels are of the size that they can be easily removed from site by manual intercultivation or tillage. Rill erosion is much serious on the soils highly susceptible to erosion. i.e., loose shallow top soil. Rill erosion is identified by the finger like projections on the entire fieldin the direction of flowing field (Figure 2.4).

Fig 2.4: Rill Erosion

(**Source:** http://www.google.co.in/imgres?)

4. Gully Erosion: When rill erosion is neglected not controlled timely then the width as well as the depth of the small rills gets wider and deeper day by day by the action of flowing water may form the large gullies. This is also known as advanced form of rill erosion. It is very difficult to cover those gullies manually they need some mechanical instruments to cover them (Figure 2.5).

Fig. 2.5: Gully Erosion

(**Source:** http://www.google.co.in/imgres?)

The development of gullies takes place in four stages given by (Schwab *et.al.* 1981)

Step 1: Formation stage: Downward scouring of the top soil lead to channel erosion. At this stage the of formation of gully is much slower where the top soil is firmlyresistant to erosion.

Step 2: Development stage: It consist the upstream movement of the gully in width and depth. As the gully cuts deep in the 'C' horizon, the weak parent material is moved quickly. A waterfall developed and falls from the upstream portion of the eroded channel below.

Step 3: Healing stage: Vegetation starts growing in the gully which initiates healing of the gully. During this stage, there is no appreciable erosion this gully section.

Step 4: Stabilization stage: Stabilization takes place when gully reaches a stable gradient. The gully walls reach a stable slope and vegetative cover spread widely over the gully surface.

5. Ravine Erosion: Advanced stage of gully erosion is ravine erosion it is typically found in deep alluvial soils. Deeper and wider gullies indicating the ravine erosion causing then very bad effects on the soil and very difficult to cure. In monsoon season final result of these erosion is land slide on erosion permitting areas causing great loss of economy and human life.

2. Wind Erosion: Wind erosion is defined as the detachment of soil particles by the action of wind. It may occurs almost in all parts of world in India maximum of wind erosion occurs in hot deserts and semi-arid regions located in different states i.e., Rajasthan, Gujarat, Haryana, Punjab, Andhra Pradesh, Karnataka and Maharashtra (Mukherjee *et.al.*, 1985). In desert areas the is the maximum of probability of occurring wind storms they may transport large amount of soil along with and deposited those soil at another place sometimes the site of deposition is miles away depending upon the speed of the storm (Figure 2.6).

Fig. 2.6: Dust storm in Bikaner (Rajasthan)

(**Source:** India today)

According to (Chepil, 1945), Stated that the soil erosion occurs in different steps these steps are:

- Soil loosing, disintegration, and denudation
- Initiation of movement
- Transportation
- Elutriation (sorting)
- Abrasion
- Avalanching
- Deposition
- Soil consolidation and deposition etc.

Forms of Soil Erosion

When soil erosion occurs due to wind the soil particles transport from one place to another place by three forms i.e. Suspension, Saltation and creeping etc.

1. **Suspension:** This occurs when very fine soil particle like dirt and dust particles once into the air by the action of air then they can travel very long distances. When soil is carried by the suspension can easily identified and recognized.
2. **Saltation:** Through this process major portion of soil is transported from one place to another. Soil particle transported from one place to another can cause severe damage to soil surface and vegetation.
3. **Creeping:** Heavy particles which are not transported through suspension and saltation are carried away by the process of creeping. In this process soil particles are rolled across the soil surface (figure 2.7).

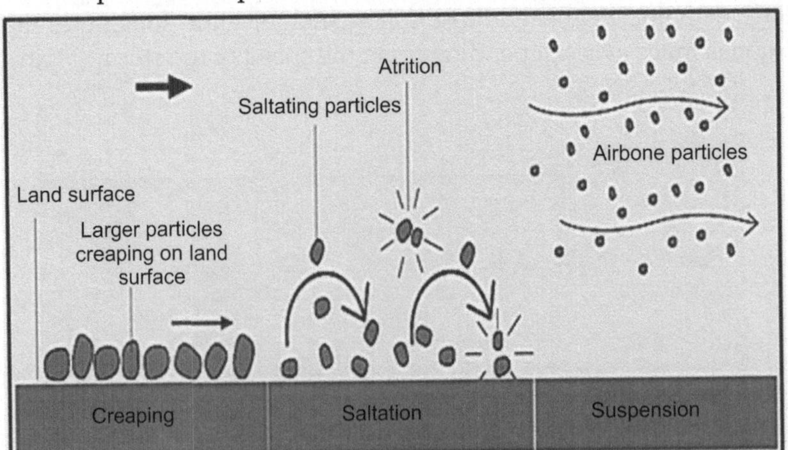

Fig. 2.7: Forms of transportation of soil particles

(**Source:** http://www.google.co.in/imgres)

3. Gravity Erosion: In this type of erosion materials are transported from higher elevation to lower elevations by the action of gravity, Along with the movement of those materials soil particles are also carried with these materials (like rocks) in very huge amount (Figure 2.8).

Fig. 2.8: Erosion by gravity

(**Source:** http://www.google.co.in/imgres?)

4. Glacier Erosion: When glacier moves down the slope in the sloppy areas the also carried soil and bed rocks along with and sometimes the speed of movement of glacier is too fast then they carry large amount of upper layer of soil. In this process gravity play an important role for the movement down the slope (figure 2.9).

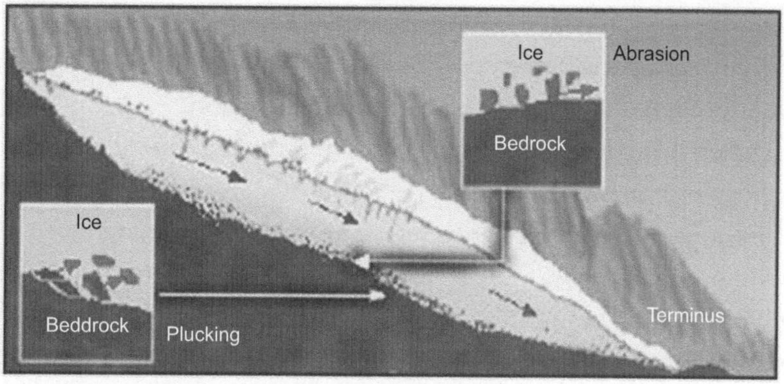

Fig. 2.9: Glacier Erosion

(**Source:** http://www.google.co.in/imgres)

Effect of Soil Erosion

Soil erosion causes many bad effects on the agriculture as well as environment also i.e.

- **Loss of Arable Land:** Soil erosion removes fertile top layer of soil along with essential nutrients important for plant growth. This finally results in low crop productivity.

- **Air pollution:** When dust particle uplift in the air resulting in air pollution. Sometimes fumes of some toxic substances like pesticides and herbicides are transported from one place to another and inhaled inside.
- **Clogging of waterways:** In the process of erosion soil I transported from one place other and finally deposited in the water bodies and clog the water bodies and raise the level of water bodies and increases the chances of flooding in nearby areas .
- **Desertification:** In erosion the fertile portion of soil is washed away and soil loses the capacity to produce something and arable soil turns into barren soils leads to desertification.
- Sometimes wind exposes the plant roots and damages the crop completely.
- Dust Storms along with the soil particles can destroy the homes/shelter of poor people and other properties. Storms sometimes take place of cyclone that is very dangerous.
- Sometimes heavy winds also damage the crop by uprooting them.
- The population of soil microorganism also affected by the soil erosion etc.

Some Preventive Measure for Soil Erosion

Following are the some methods which can reduce the soil erosion.

- By covering the barren portion of soil by planting the trees on it.
- Adopt mulching practices to reduce the erosion.
- Across the row planting also helps in reducing the soil erosion.
- Strip row planting.
- In sloppy area adopt bench terracing, contour bunding etc.
- Reforestation.
- Vertical mulching.
- Avoid to grow the erosion primitive crops in those areas which are prone to erosion.
- Construction of check dames to deduce the speed of flowing water in streams etc.

Conclusion

There are different type of soil erosion which leads to transportation of soil from one place to another place and causing loss if fertile upper layer of soil. Along with soil large amount of nutrients, microorganisms get also lost through this. This process of erosion is increasing day by day which may results in the desertification of arable land. If all the fertile portion of soil is lost through erosion so soil can't able to produce something. If we want to provide good life for over future generation then we have to save the soil don't promotes any negative thing which harm the soil and leads to soil erosion, We have to adopt the soil conservation practices like covering the open soil area, mulching, reforestation and many more to avoid soil water, wind, gravity, and glacier erosion etc.

REFERENCES

Bagnold, R.A. 1943. "The Physics of Blown Sand and Desert Dunes". Morrow, New York.

Bennett, H.H. 1939. Soil Conservation, McGraw Hill, New York.

Chepii, W.S. 1945b, Soil sci, 60:397-411.

Carter, D.L. 1983, Erosion and Sediments Losses in Furrow Irrigation Land, In: Soil Erosion and Conservation.

Ellison, W.D. 1946. "Soil Detachment and Transportation."

Haigh, M. J. (1984), Ravine Erosion and Reclamation in India, Geoform, Vol. 15, No. 4, pp. 543-561.

https:wwwc worldwildlife.org.in

Mukherjee, B.K., Das., Singh, Shamsher. Prasad, C.S. and Samuel, J.C. 1985.

Singh, H.P. 1977. A Review-The Problem of Wind Erosion and Its Control.

Soil Ecosystem and Lithosphere **Pages 22-35**
Edited by: Dr. Abhishek Swami, Dr. Prasann Kumar and Dr. Pawan Kumar 'Bharti'
ISBN: 978-93-88854-50-4
Edition: 2020
Published by: Discovery Publishing House Pvt. Ltd., New Delhi (India)

3 Soil Quality Assessment in Bhutan

Pawan Kumar 'Bharti'

Introduction

The Bhutan Environment Outlook finds that Bhutan has 72 per cent forest coverage, and that 20 per cent of its land is designated as protected areas, while the cultivated area accounts for only 8%. Pastures account for nearly 4% of the total land. Usable land is severely limited due to rugged and mountainous terrain and vast areas of snow and rocks. As in other parts of the world, Bhutan is also experiencing land use changes due to a number of activities - both man-made as well as natural. Land degradation in the country is mostly manifested in the displacement of soil material through water erosion and internal biophysical and chemical deterioration. The rising population has aggravated the situation and will further worsen it if timely counter measures are not taken. Soil quality is simply defined as "the capacity of a specific kind of soil to function", i.e. mainly to provide nutrition to plants and absorb the drain water. The different properties of soil are - texture, moisture, fertility (level of nitrogen, phosphorus, potassium) and pH level. The pH is the measure of a soil's acidity or alkalinity. Each of these properties depends on different factors. For example, soil moisture depends on climate, topography and other soil characteristics. The temperatures of soils vary depending on their water holding capacity. Soils with low water holding capacity are warm. The most significant environmental problems in Bhutan were soil erosion and water pollution. The erosion of the soil occurs because 50% of the land in Bhutan is situated on mountainous slopes, which are subject to landslides during the monsoon season. Soil represents the loose and unconsolidated materials derived through the breaking down of rocks. The soil is a natural body of animal, mineral and organic constituents differentiated into horizons of variable depth, which differ from the material below in morphology, physical make up, chemical properties and composition and biological characteristics. The comprehensive study of soil system in terms of its contamination with a toxic chemical is of vital significance because it is an integral part of the bio-geographic system. Land environment study is an important study for prediction of various impacts due to industrialisation and urbanisation. The impact of pollutants on soil quality may be a rather slow process but it can sometimes cause concern in the long run. The fall out of heavy metals and other pollutants present in the smoke and dust emitted from industries, traffic and other sources may get accumulated in the soil and ultimately affect the trace metal concentration. Such accumulation could also prove to be beneficial to plant growth but beyond a certain limit, the pollutant concentration may be deleterious to the vegetation. Studies were carried out in the study area, for estimation of Physico – chemical characteristics of the soil.

Pollutant Migration Potential

The migration of pollutants released in an environment in the land occurs through the ground & when it interacts with the water table, it can pollute the ground making it unsuitable for domestic and agricultural use. Part of pollutants may be transported during monsoon floods when water flows as sheet run off. As no major polluting industries are present in the study area, only the domestic effluents which seep through the local streams runs and get dried in a open land which is not used for cultivation.

Study Area Description

The study area considered for REIA studies is an area covering 5 kms radial distance from proposed plant site. The area has an undulating topography is a pediplain with number of residual hills which have steep slopes.

Soil Description

Two different types of soil have been observed and are classified according to texture as sandy silt and silty sand. Results of analysis indicated that the soil is neutral to alkaline in nature. All the parameters, especially heavy metals were found to be present in very less concentration.

Selection of Sampling Location

Analysing the soil samples collected from 6 locations in the study area has assessed the soil characteristics in the study area, especially the extent of pollution undergone by the soils due to various sources and reasons. Sampling locations were chosen to represent the soil quality of the study area. Details of the soil sampling locations are given in the following table.

Table 3.1

S. No.	Station	Station Code	Location	Direction w.r.t. the project site	Distance from the Central site (Km)	No. of Samples Taken/ Season
1	Project Site	SQ – 1	Near DCPA Site Office	---	--	1
2	Menchu	SQ – 2	Drujay's Garden	SSE	2.4	1

3	Nganglam	SQ – 3	Thring Chojaoy's Land, Near Lower Sec. School	S	3.5	1
4	Gacheri	SQ – 4	Tashis's Orchards	WSW	1.5	1
5	Kangrizhe Mines	SQ – 5	Mines Area	NNW	1.7	1
6	Marung Ri Mines	SQ – 6	Mines Area	NNE	3.1	1

Sampling and Analysis Methodology

A preliminary reconnaissance survey was made to get a general picture of the area's land use. The activities around the sampling sites were also taken into consideration to learn the sources of pollution if any or factors governing the Physico-chemical properties of the soil.

To analyse the soil quality of the area and to assess the impact of industrial / urban activities on land environment with respect to any specific contamination.

(*a*) **Sampling:** Our team visited the site and identified the exact locations for soil sampling. At each location the sample was collected by hand-driven sampling augers from sub-surface region. Topsoil samples from all six locations at depth of 15 cm. (sub surface) region of the soil profile were collected for Physico-chemical analysis.

(*b*) **Analysis:** Attention was paid to collect adequate amount of composite samples for analysis with the standard methods. Samples were homogenised before testing. The samples were packed in dependable, waterproof containers. They were marked accurately and distinctly, brought to the SRI laboratory for testing and analysed there as per ASTM, USEPA, IS: 2720, M.L. Jeckson (Soil Chemical Analysis). A brief methodology of each parameter is as under:

Parameters and methods for analysis of soil samples are given in following table:

Table 3.2

S.No.	Parameters	Method	Protocol
1.	pH (30 gms/ 75 ml)	pH meter	IS:2720 (Pt.-26)
2.	E. conductivity, µmho/cm (1:5 with water)	Conductivity meter	Handbookof Soil Chemical analysis by ML Jackson
3.	Moisture, % by mass	Oven dry	Oven dry
4.	Texture	Grain size analysis	IS:2720(Pt.-4)

5.	Particle Size Distribution	Sieve analysis	IS:2720(Pt.-4)
6.	Water Holding Capacity	Mechanical	Mechanical
7.	Alkalinity as $CaCO_3$	Titrimetric	APHA, 21th Ed.
8.	Organic Carbon	Titrimetric	IS:2720 (Pt.-22)
9.	Chlorides as Cl, % by mass	Volhard's method	Volhard's method
10.	Sulphates as SO_4, % by mass	Gravimetric method	IS:2720 (Pt.-27)
11.	Avialable Nitrogen as N, mg/kg	Kjeldhal's method	Titrimetric
12.	Avialable Potassium as K, mg/kg ass	AAS	AAS
13.	Avialable Phosphorus as P, mg/kg	Gravimetric	Handbookof Soil Chemical analysis by ML Jackson
14.	Sodium as Na_2O, % by mass	AAS	AAS
15.	Copper as Cu	AAS	APHA, 21th Ed.
16.	Zinc as Zn	AAS	APHA, 21th Ed.
17.	Lead as Pb	AAS	APHA, 21th Ed.
18.	Iron as Fe_2O_3	AAS	APHA, 21th Ed.
19.	Cadmium as Cd	AAS	APHA, 21th Ed.
20.	Chromium as Cr	AAS	APHA, 21th Ed.
21.	Sodium absorption ratio	By calculation	By calculation

Soil Quality-Data

Table 3.3

S. No.	Parameters	Unit	Winter	Summer	Monsoon	Post-Monsoon	Avg. Results
Physical Parameters							
1.	pH (30 gm in 75 ml water)	---	5.6	7.1	4.5	5.3	5.6
2.	E. Conductivity (1: 5 ratio)	µ mho/ cm	99	918	170	78	316.3
3.	Moisture Content	% by mass	7	11.9	9.3	7.0	8.8
4.	Texture	---	Sandy Silt	Sandy Silt	Sandy Silt	Sandy Silt	Sandy Silt

5.	Particle Sizes Sand Silt Clay	% by mass	 66 33 01	 62 47 01	 59 40 01	 46 51 03	 58.3 42.7 1.5
6.	Water Holding Capacity	% by mass	49.1	48.2	47.6	47	48
Chemical Characteristics							
1.	Alkalinity as $CaCO_3$	% by mass	Nil	Nil	Nil	Nil	Nil
2.	Organic Carbon	% by mass	0.10	0.15	0.15	0.66	0.27
3.	Chlorides as Cl	% by mass	0.12	0.14	0.08	0.03	0.09
4.	Sulphates as SO_4	% by mass	<0.01	<0.01	<0.01	<0.01	<0.01
5.	Available Nitrogen as N	mg/kg	98.1	219	220	201	184.5
6.	Available Potassium as K	mg/kg	31.3	102	105	103	85.3
7.	Available Phosphorus as P	mg/kg	31.1	7.6	7.9	9.3	14
8.	Sodium as Na_2O	% by mass	0.8	0.8	1.9	1.0	1.1
9.	Copper as Cu	mg/kg	11.6	30	17	40	24.7
10.	Zinc as Zn	mg/kg	44.4	39.7	77	136	74.3
11.	Lead as Pb	mg/kg	4.9	81	51	410	136.7
12.	Iron as Fe_2O_3	% by mass	3.6	3.1	2.8	6.7	4.1
13.	Cadmium as Cd	mg/kg	1.1	2.0	1.4	0.7	1.3
14.	Chromium as Cr	mg/kg	21.8	26	28	103	44.7
15.	Sodium absorption ratio (SAR)	-	3.1	3.5	12.7	5.2	6.1

Table 3.4

S. No.	Parameters	Unit	Winter	Summer	Mon-soon	Post-Monsoon	Avg. Results
Physical Parameters							
1.	pH (30 gm in 75 ml water)	---	5.0	6.3	4.9	5.4	5.4
2.	E. Conductivity (1: 5 ratio)	µ mho/ cm	225	353	209	62	212.3
3.	Moisture Content	% by mass	5	8.2	9.1	6.3	7.2
4.	Texture	---	Silty sand	Silty sand	Silty Sand	Sandy Silt	Silty Sand
5.	Particle Sizes Sand Silt Clay	% by mass	 47 52 02	 51 47 02	 46 50 04	 39 66 06	 45.7 53.8 3.5
6.	Water Holding Capacity	% by mass	48.7	49.2	50.1	51	49.8
Chemical Characteristics							
1.	Alkalinity as $CaCO_3$	% by mass	Nil	Nil	Nil	Nil	Nil
2.	Organic Carbon	% by mass	0.26	0.21	0.21	0.64	0.33
3.	Chlorides as Cl	% by mass	0.10	0.11	0.04	0.01	0.07
4.	Sulphates as SO_4	% by mass	<0.01	<0.01	<0.01	<0.01	<0.01
5.	Available Nitrogen as N	mg/kg	147.1	237	234	216	208.5
6.	Available Potassium as K	mg/kg	320.5	96	85	70	142.9
7.	Available Phosphorus as P	mg/kg	262.2	8.1	8.5	8.9	71.9
8.	Sodium as Na_2O	% by mass	0.6	0.9	0.7	0.7	0.7
9.	Copper as Cu	mg/kg	8.7	25	25	26	21.2
10.	Zinc as Zn	mg/kg	107.6	90	84	53	83.7
11.	Lead as Pb	mg/kg	31.1	32	114	331	127
12.	Iron as Fe_2O_3	% by mass	7.92	2.7	4.5	5.9	5.3

13.	Cadmium as Cd	mg/kg	1.22	0.4	0.3	1.1	0.75
14.	Chromium as Cr	mg/kg	75.02	61	57	72	66.3
15.	Sodium absorption ratio (SAR)		2.8	4.8	3.9	3.8	3.8

Table 3.5

S. No.	Parameters	Unit	Winter	Summer	Mon-soon	Post-Monsoon	Avg. Results
Physical Parameters							
1.	pH (30 gm in 75 ml water)	---	3.8	5.7	7.1	5.2	5.5
2.	E. Conductivity (1: 5 ratio)	µ mho/ cm	100	280	140	60	145
3.	Moisture Content	% by mass	6	7.5	7.1	6.7	6.8
4.	Texture	---	Sandy Silt	Sandy Silt	Silty Sand	Sandy Silt	Sandy Silt
5.	Particle Sizes Sand Silt Clay	% by mass	 51 47 02	 53 46 01	 47 50 03	 41 64 05	 48 51.8 2.8
6.	Water Holding Capacity	% by mass	48.4	48.2	53.5	54	51
Chemical Characteristics							
1.	Alkalinity as $CaCO_3$	% by mass	Nil	Nil	Nil	Nil	Nil
2.	Organic Carbon	% by mass	0.24	0.14	0.24	0.60	0.31
3.	Chlorides as Cl	% by mass	0.13	0.10	0.05	0.03	0.08
4.	Sulphates as SO_4	% by mass	<0.01	<0.01	<0.01	<0.01	<0.01
5.	Available Nitrogen as N	mg/kg	109	199	285	234	206.8
6.	Available Potassium as K	mg/kg	76.4	58	32	41	51.9
7.	Available Phosphorus as P	mg/kg	88.2	7.5	7.8	8.2	27.9
8.	Sodium as Na_2O	% by mass	1.1	0.8	0.8	0.2	0.7

9.	Copper as Cu	mg/kg	15.2	31	25	28	24.8
10.	Zinc as Zn	mg/kg	56	74	302	53	121.3
11.	Lead as Pb	mg/kg	24.2	32	95	292	110.8
12.	Iron as Fe_2O_3	% by mass	3.1	4.4	3.5	3.7	3.7
13.	Cadmium as Cd	mg/kg	1.5	1.0	0.1	0.5	0.8
14.	Chromium as Cr	mg/kg	22.1	24	102	61	52.3
15.	Sodium absorption ratio (SAR)		6.8	4.1	2.3	1.5	3.7

Table 3.6

S.No.	Parameters	Unit	Winter	Summer	Monsoon	Post-Monsoon	Avg. Results
Physical Parameters							
1.	pH (30 gm in 75 ml water)	---	5.0	5.2	5.6	5.7	5.4
2.	E. Conductivity (1: 5 ratio)	µ mho/ cm	131	241	296	53	180.3
3.	Moisture Content	% by mass	5	10.5	10.4	4.9	7.7
4.	Texture	---	Silty sand	Sandy Silt	Sandy Silt	Sandy Silt	Sandy Silt
5.	Particle Sizes Sand Silt Clay	% by mass	 46 52 02	 45 52 03	 53 44 03	 44 64 02	 47 53 2.5
6.	Water Holding Capacity	% by mass	49.4	50.4	50.1	52	50.5
Chemical Characteristics							
1.	Alkalinity as $CaCO_3$	% by mass	Nil	Nil	Nil	Nil	Nil
2.	Organic Carbon	% by mass	0.28	0.17	0.17	0.63	0.31
3.	Chlorides as Cl	% by mass	0.14	0.16	0.03	0.02	0.09
4.	Sulphates as SO_4	% by mass	<0.01	<0.01	<0.01	<0.01	<0.01
5.	Available Nitrogen as N	mg/kg	132.4	214	218	187	187.9

6.	Available Potassium as K	mg/kg	348.3	31	98	62	134.8
7.	Available Phosphorus as P	mg/kg	116.3	7.4	8.5	7.6	34.9
8.	Sodium as Na_2O	% by mass	0.5	1.2	0.4	0.5	0.65
9.	Copper as Cu	mg/kg	17.0	19	16	12	16
10.	Zinc as Zn	mg/kg	86.3	62	66	41	63.8
11.	Lead as Pb	mg/kg	7.7	28	69	262	91.7
12.	Iron as Fe_2O_3	% by mass	6.6	2.0	3.1	2.6	3.6
13.	Cadmium as Cd	mg/kg	0.9	2.3	<0.1	0.6	1.0
14.	Chromium as Cr	mg/kg	108.4	109	64	32	78.4
15.	Sodium absorption ratio (SAR)		2.7	7.8	2.7	3.4	4.2

Table 3.7

S. No.	Parameters	Unit	Winter	Summer	Monsoon	Post-Monsoon	Avg. Results
Physical Parameters							
1.	pH (30 gm in 75 ml water)	---	6.6	4.5	5.9	5.3	5.6
2.	E. Conductivity (1: 5 ratio)	μ mho/ cm	119	184	356	58	179.3
3.	Moisture Content	% by mass	7	8.4	7.5	4.7	6.9
4.	Texture	---	Silty sand	Silty sand	Silty Sand	Silty Sand	Silty Sand
5.	Particle Sizes Sand Silt Clay	% by mass	 45 52 3	 47 51 02	 45 53 02	 52 47 01	 47.3 50.8 2.0
6.	Water Holding Capacity	% by mass	52.4	51.2	52.0	52	51.9
Chemical Characteristics							
1.	Alkalinity as $CaCO_3$	% by mass	Nil	Nil	Nil	Nil	Nil

2.	Organic Carbon	% by mass	0.22	0.24	0.24	0.69	0.35
3.	Chlorides as Cl	% by mass	0.05	0.10	0.04	0.01	0.05
4.	Sulphates as SO_4	% by mass	<0.01	<0.01	<0.01	<0.01	<0.01
5.	Available Nitrogen as N	mg/kg	93.4	232	236	244	201.4
6.	Available Potassium as K	mg/kg	51.9	65	63	89	67.2
7.	Available Phosphorus as P	mg/kg	68.7	9.2	9.5	8.6	24
8.	Sodium as Na_2O	% by mass	0.6	0.2	0.4	0.7	0.48
9.	Copper as Cu	mg/kg	8.65	14	32	21	18.9
10.	Zinc as Zn	mg/kg	49.5	29	89	89	64.1
11.	Lead as Pb	mg/kg	14.32	33	85	238	92.6
12.	Iron as Fe_2O_3	% by mass	4.1	0.5	3.5	3.3	2.9
13.	Cadmium as Cd	mg/kg	1.6	1.6	<0.1	0.2	0.9
14.	Chromium as Cr	mg/kg	26.8	31	33	47	34.5
15.	Sodium absorption ratio (SAR)		2.5	1.6	2.1	3.9	2.5

Table 3.8

S. No.	Parameters	Unit	Winter	Summer	Monsoon	Post-Monsoon	Avg. Results
Physical Parameters							
1.	pH (30 gm in 75 ml water)	---	7.7	7.0	6.8	6.3	7.0
2.	E. Conductivity (1: 5 ratio)	μ mho/cm	74	400	518	109	275.3
3.	Moisture Content	% by mass	7	7.6	8.6	7.4	7.7
4.	Texture	---	Silty sand	Silty sand	Sandy Silt	Silty Sand	Silty Sand

5.	Particle Sizes Sand Silt Clay	% by mass	 45 49 6	 43 52 05	 51 48 01	 58 41 01	 49.3 47.5 3.2
6.	Water Holding Capacity	% by mass	58.8	54.6	49.6	46	52.3
Chemical Characteristics							
1.	Alkalinity as $CaCO_3$	% by mass	Nil	Nil	Nil	Nil	Nil
2.	Organic Carbon	% by mass	0.17	0.24	0.14	0.63	0.3
3.	Chlorides as Cl	% by mass	0.17	0.13	0.08	0.03	0.16
4.	Sulphates as SO_4	% by mass	<0.01	<0.01	<0.01	<0.01	<0.01
5.	Available Nitrogen as N	mg/kg	87.4	279	202	200	192.1
6.	Available Potassium as K	mg/kg	47.8	84	59	61	63
7.	Available Phosphorus as P	mg/kg	24.3	8.6	7.6	9.0	12.4
8.	Sodium as Na_2O	% by mass	0.4	0.9	0.8	0.9	0.8
9.	Copper as Cu	mg/kg	2.8	52	14	14	20.7
10.	Zinc as Zn	mg/kg	57.5	149	87	110	100.9
11.	Lead as Pb	mg/kg	10	45	42	176	68.3
12.	Iron as Fe_2O_3	% by mass	6.2	2.5	2.6	3.1	3.6
13.	Cadmium as Cd	mg/kg	0.66	1.8	0.5	0.05	0.8
14.	Chromium as Cr	mg/kg	64.1	54	26	51	48.8
15.	Sodium absorption ratio (SAR)		1.3	4.5	4.7	5.1	3.9

Soil Quality

Soil analysis study was taken because the fall out of heavy metals and other pollutants present in the smoke and dust emitted from vehicles and other sources may get accumulated in the soil and ultimately affects the trace metal concentration. The migration of pollutants released in an environment in the land seeps through the ground & when interacts with the water table can pollute the ground water making it unsuitable for domestic and agricultural use. Studies were carried out in the study area for estimation of physico-chemical characteristics of the soil. Soil samples were collected from 6 locations in the study area. Sampling locations were chosen to represent the soil quality of the study area. Details of the soil sampling locations are given in Table 6.5 (1). In the study area of 5-km radius, two different types of soils have observed, and classified according to texture as sandy silt and silty sand. The texture of soil samples collected from project site was observed sandy silt with 58% sand and 43% silt, 8.8% average moisture content and 48% water holding capacity. pH of all the soil samples lies in the range of 4.5-7.1. Results of analysis indicate that the soil is slightly acidic and alkalinity was found nil. Electrical conductivity was in the range of 78-918 mmho/cm. Organic carbon content was around 0.1-0.66% by mass. All the parameters were found to be in low concentration. Heavy metals (like Pb, Cd, Cu, Cr, Zn) were found to be present in different quantity i.e. Cu 24.7 mg/kg, Zn 74.3 mg/kg, Pb 136.7 mg/kg, Cd 1.3 mg/kg and Cr 44.7 mg/kg. Sulphate concentration in all the samples is Below Detection Limit. Average available N, P and K were found 184.5, 14.0 and 85.3 mg/kg. Average Sodium absorption Ratio (SAR) was found 6.1 during the study period at this site.

The texture of soil samples collected from Menchu was observed sandy silt with 7.2% average moisture content and 49.8% water holding capacity. pH of all the soil samples lies in the range of 4.9-6.3. Results of analysis indicate that the soil is slightly acidic and alkalinity was found nil. Electrical conductivity was in the range of 62-353 mmho/cm. Organic carbon content was around 0.21-0.64% by mass. All the parameters were found to be in low concentration. Heavy metals (like Pb, Cd, Cu, Cr, Zn) were found to be present in different quantity i.e. Cu 21.2 mg/kg, Zn 83.7 mg/kg, Pb 127.0 mg/kg, Cd 0.8 mg/kg and Cr 66.3 mg/kg. Sulphate concentration in all the samples is Below Detection Limit. Average available N, P and K were found 208.5, 71.9 and 142.9 mg/kg. Average Sodium absorption Ratio (SAR) was found 3.8 during the study period at this site.

The texture of soil samples collected from Nganglam was observed sandy silt with 6.8% average moisture content and 51.0% water holding capacity. pH of all the soil samples lies in the range of 3.8-7.1. Results of analysis indicate that the soil is slightly acidic and alkalinity was found nil. Electrical conductivity was in the range of 60-280 mmho/cm. Organic carbon content was around 0.14-0.60% by mass. All the parameters were found to be in low concentration. Heavy metals (like Pb, Cd, Cu, Cr, Zn) were found to be present in different quantity i.e. Cu 24.8 mg/kg, Zn 121.3 mg/kg, Pb 110.8 mg/kg, Cd 0.8 mg/kg and Cr 52.3 mg/kg. Sulphate concentration in all the samples are

Below Detection Limit. Average available N, P and K were found 206.8, 27.9 and 51.9 mg/kg. Average Sodium absorption Ratio (SAR) was found 3.7 during the study period at this site. The texture of soil samples collected from Gacheri was observed sandy silt with 7.7% average moisture content and 50.5% water holding capacity. pH of all the soil samples lies in the range of 5.0-5.7. Results of analysis indicate that the soil is slightly acidic and alkalinity was found nil. Electrical conductivity was in the range of 53-296 mmho/cm. Organic carbon content was around 0.17-0.63% by mass. All the parameters were found to be in low concentration. Heavy metals (like Pb, Cd, Cu, Cr, Zn) were found to be present in different quantity i.e. Cu 16.0 mg/kg, Zn 63.8 mg/kg, Pb 91.7 mg/kg, Cd 1.0 mg/kg and Cr 78.4 mg/kg. Sulphate concentration in all the samples are Below Detection Limit. Average available N, P and K were found 187.9, 35.0 and 134.8 mg/kg. Average Sodium absorption Ratio (SAR) was found 4.2 during the study period at this site.

The texture of soil samples collected from Kangrizhe Mines were observed silty sand with 6.9% average moisture content and 51.9% water holding capacity. pH of all the soil samples lies in the range of 4.5-6.6. Results of analysis indicate that the soil is slightly acidic and alkalinity was found nil. Electrical conductivity was in the range of 58-356 mmho/cm. Organic carbon content was around 0.22-0.69 % by mass. All the parameters were found to be in low concentration. Heavy metals (like Pb, Cd, Cu, Cr, Zn) were found to be present in different quantity i.e. Cu 18.9 mg/kg, Zn 64.2 mg/kg, Pb 92.6 mg/kg, Cd 0.9 mg/kg and Cr 34.5 mg/kg. Sulphate concentration in all the samples are Below Detection Limit. Average available N, P and K were found 201.4, 24.0 and 67.2 mg/kg. Average Sodium absorption Ratio (SAR) was found 2.5 during the study period at this site.

The texture of soil samples collected from Marung Ri Mines were observed silty sand with 7.7% average moisture content and 52.3% water holding capacity. pH of all the soil samples lies in the range of 6.3-7.7. Results of analysis indicate that the soil is very slightly acidic or neutral and alkalinity was found nil. Electrical conductivity was in the range of 74-518 mmho/cm. Organic carbon content was around 0.14-0.63% by mass. All the parameters were found to be in low concentration. Heavy metals (like Pb, Cd, Cu, Cr, Zn) were found to be present in different quantity i.e. Cu 20.7 mg/kg, Zn 100.9 mg/kg, Pb 68.3 mg/kg, Cd 0.8 mg/kg and Cr 48.8 mg/kg. Sulphate concentration in all the samples are Below Detection Limit. Average available N, P and K were found 192.1, 12.4 and 63.0 mg/kg. Average Sodium absorption Ratio (SAR) was found 3.9 during the study period at this site.

REFERENCES

Bharti, Pawan K., Singh, V. and Kumar, P. (2013): Post Irrigation Impact of Textile Industrial Effluent on the Composition of Soil System at Panipat (Haryana), India. International Journal of Higher Education and Research, 2(1): 11-15.

Bharti, Pawan K. and Singh, V. (2013): Heavy Metals Distribution in Sediment and Water of Phrinkaruh River in East Khasi Hills, Meghalaya. International Journal of Higher Education and Research, 2(1): 55-63.

Bharti, P. K., Kumar, P. and Singh, V. (2013): Impact of Industrial Effluents on Ground Water and Soil Quality in the Vicinity of Industrial Area of Panipat City, India. J. of Applied and Natural Sciences, 5(1): 132-136. (Print ISSN: 0974-9411 I Online ISSN: 2231-5209. NAAS RATING 5.08)

Bharti, P.K., Singh, V. and Tyagi, P.K. (2017b): Heavy Metals in Ichchamati River Ecosystem in East Khasi Hills, Meghalaya, India. Octa Journal of Environmental Research, 5(4): 221-227 (ISSN: 2321-3655).

Bharti, P. K. (2013): Soil Quality Assessment in the Vicinity of an Industrial Area, In: Soil Quality and Contamination (Eds.-Bharti, P.K.; Chauhan, A.), Discovery Pub. House, Delhi, pp: 1-31 (ISBN: 9350563614).

Bharti, P. K. (2013): Assessment of Heavy Metals in Agricultural Soil, In: Soil Quality and Contamination (Eds.- Bharti, P.K. and Chauhan, A.), Discovery Publishing House, Delhi, pp: 87-125 (ISBN: 93-5056-361-4).

Bharti, Pawan K. (2013): Soil and Sediment Quality Assessment Larsemann Hills, Antarctica, In: Soil Quality and Contamination (Eds.- Bharti, P.K. and Chauhan, A.), Discovery Publishing House, Delhi, pp: 134-140 (ISBN: 93-5056-361-4).

Bharti, P.K. and Chauhan, A. (2017): Land Reclamation, Soil Quality and Agriculture, Discovery Publishing House, Delhi, pp: 193 (ISBN: 978-93-5056-882-8).

Bharti, P. K. and Chauhan, Avnish (2013): Soil Quality and Contamination, Discovery Publishing House, Delhi, pp: 186 (ISBN: 978-93-5056-361-8).

Bharti, P.K. (2007): Effect of Textile Industrial Effluents on Ground Water and Soil Quality in Panipat Region (Haryana), PhD Thesis Submitted to Gurukula Kangri University, Haridwar, pp: 197

Chauhan, A. and Bharti, P. K. (2015): Soil Characteristics and Agro-ecology, Discovery Publishing House, Delhi, pp: 177 (ISBN: 978-93-5056-758-6).

Ezeaku, P.I. and Bharti, P. K. (2015): Soil Contamination and Conservation, Discovery Publishing House, Delhi, pp: 200 (ISBN: 978-93-5056-737-1).

Malik, D. S. and Bharti, P.K. (2007c): Soil Quality of Irrigated Agricultural Fields in Textile Industrial Area of Panipat City, Asian J. Exp. Sciences, 21 (2): 445-451. (ISSN: 0971-5444)

Malik, D. S.; Bharti, P.K.; Yadav, R. and Deepmala (2008): Distribution of Heavy Metals in Pond Sediment in Textile Industrial Area at Panipat (Haryana), Journal of Ecology and Fisheries, 1(1): 39-44.

Malik, D. S.; Bharti, P.K. and Yadav, R.; Kumar, P. and Chauhan, P. (2008): Dispersion of Heavy Metals in Textile Effluent and Pond Environment in Panipat Industrial Area, Env. Cons. J. 9 (3): 77-81.

Soil Ecosystem and Lithosphere **Pages 36-50**
Edited by: Dr. Abhishek Swami, Dr. Prasann Kumar and Dr. Pawan Kumar 'Bharti'
ISBN: 978-93-88854-50-4
Edition: 2020
Published by: Discovery Publishing House Pvt. Ltd., New Delhi (India)

4 Phytoremediation of Heavy Metal Contaminated Soil

Prasann Kumar[1,2*] & Shipa Rani Dey[1]

GRAPHICAL ABSTRACT

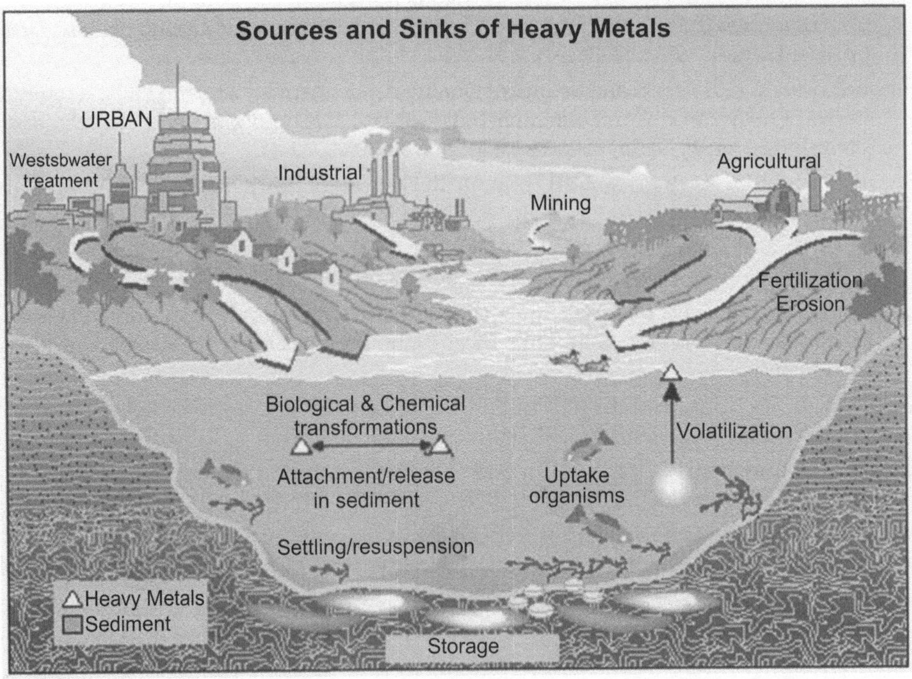

Keywords: *Agriculture, Biological, Chemical, Density, Fertilizers*

Introduction

- The term heavy metals refers to any metallic chemical element that has a relatively high density and is toxic or poisonous at low concentrations.

[1] Department of Agronomy, School of Agriculture, Lovely Professional University, Jalandhar, Punjab, India, 144411
[2] Divison of Research and Development, Lovely Professional University, Jalandhar, Punjab, India, 144411

- Heavy metals are conventionally defined as elements with metallic properties and an atomic number >20.
- The most common heavy metal contaminants are Cd, Cr, Cu, Hg, Pb, and Zn.

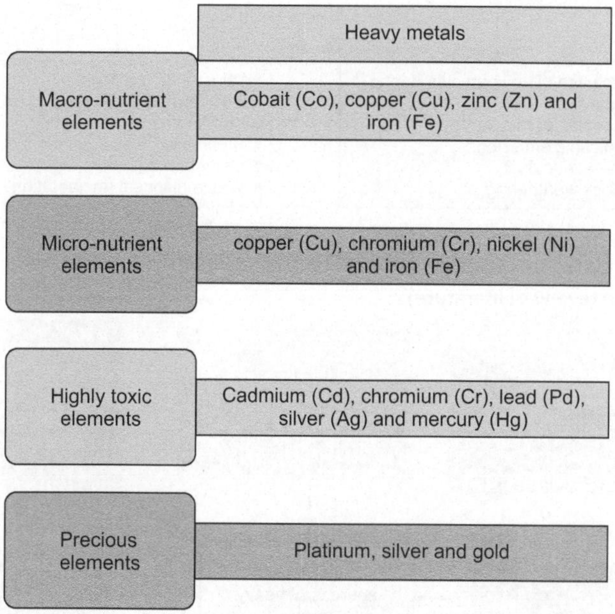

Fig. 4.1: Heavy metals

(**Source:** Based on review of literature)

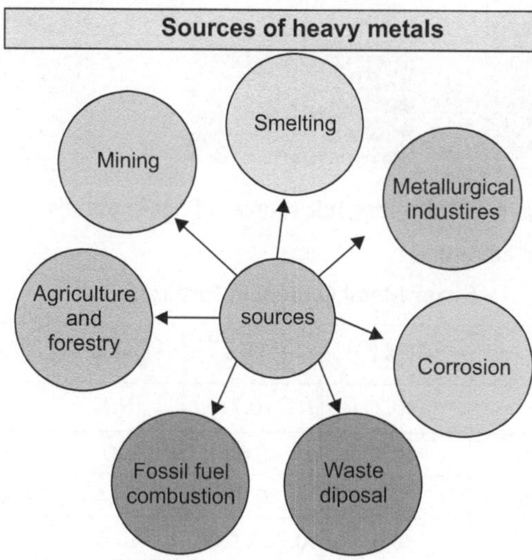

Fig. 4.2: Sources of heavy metals

(**Source:** Based on review of literature)

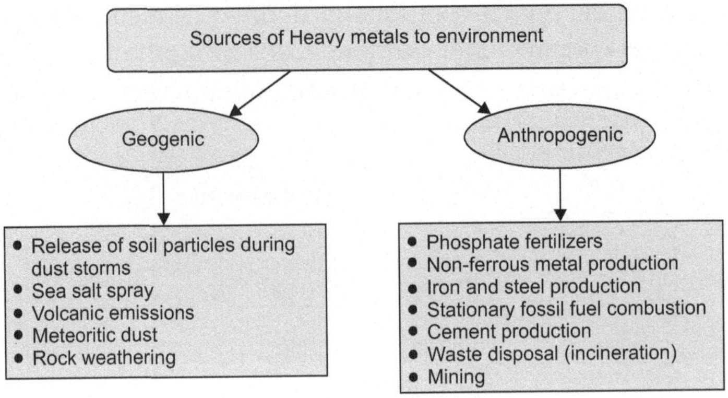

Fig. 4.3: Metals in environment

(**Source:** Based on review of literature)

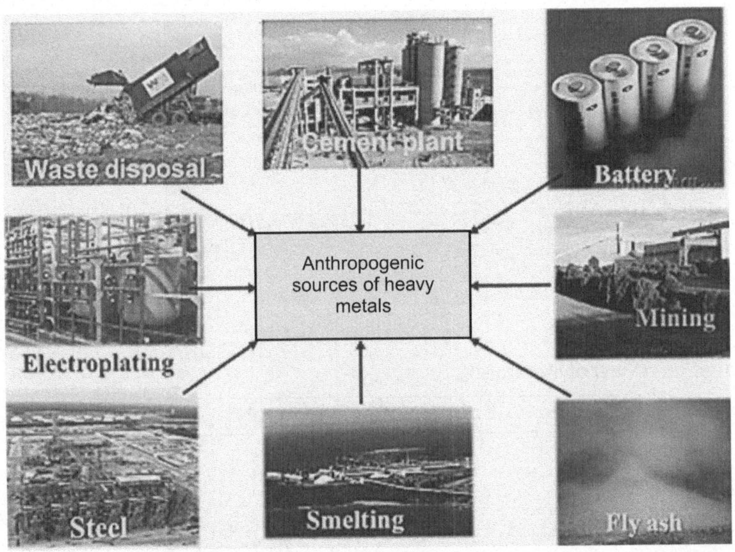

Fig. 4.4: Anthropogenic sources of heavy metals

(**Source:** Based on review of literature)

Heavy Metal Content in Fertilizers

S.No.	Sample	Cdmg g^{-1}	Comg g^{-1}	Crmg g^{-1}	Nimg g^{-1}	Pbmg g^{-1}
1.	Urea	<0.2	<0.7	ND	<0.2	<0.4
2.	Ammonium nitrate	<0.2	<0.07	ND	<0.2	<0.4
3.	Ammonium sulfate	<0.3	<0.07	2.14	<0.2	<0.4
4.	MAP	<0.3	0.78 ± 0.62	16.9	0.6 ± 0.4	<0.2
5.	DAP	4.6	3.24 ± 0.30	ND	22.2	2.9
6.	Triple Super PO_4	5.0	6.61 ± 0.49	88.9 ± 4.8	25.2	11.1

7.	Kcl	<0.2	< 0.07	< 1.05	<0.2	<0.4
8.	North Corolina	RP 48.8	< 0.08	140 ± 7	16.8	4.6
9.	Tilemsi RP	1.3	19.6	33.2 ± 3.2	50.4	29.2
10.	Calcite	0.7	< 0.08	ND	1.4	1.1
11.	Dolomite	<0.2	0.03 ± 0.09	32.3 ± 1.8	3.3	0.7
12.	Manures	0.7	2.23 ± 0.54	ND	ND	0.7
13.	Compost 1	0.5	3.57 ± 0.69	14.4 ± 1.3	14.4	7.5

Fig. 4.5: Heavy metals content in fertilizers

(**Source:** Based on review of literature)

Sources	As	Cd	Cr	Cu	Hg	Ni	Pb	Zn
Agricul-ture and food waste	0–0.6	0–0.3	4.5–90	3-38	0-1.5	6-45	1.5-27	12-150
Fannyard manure	1.2-4.4	0.2-1.2	10.60	14.80	0.02	3-36	3.2-20	150-320
Logging and timber industry wastes	0-3.3	0-2.2	2.2-18	3.3-52	0-2.2	2.2-23	6.6-8.2	13.65
Municipal wastes	0.09-0.7	0.88-7.5	6.6-33	13-40	0-0.26	2.2-10	18-62	22-97
Municipal studge	0.01-0.24	0.02-0.34	1.4-11	4.9-21	0.01-0.8	5.0-22	2.8-9.7	18.57
Organic wastes	0-0.25	0-0.01	0.1-0.48	0.04-0.61	–	0.17-3.2	0.02-1.6	0.13-2.1
Metal process-ing solid wastes	0.01-0.21	0.-0.08	0.65-2.4	0.95-7.6	0.-0.08	0.84-2.5	4.1-11	1.7-19
Coalash	6.7-37	1.5-13	149-446	93-335	0.37-4.8	56-279	45-242	112-484
Fertilizer	0.-0.02	0.03-0.25	0.03-0.38	0.05-0.58	-	0.20-3.5	0.42-2.3	0.25-1.1
Marl	0.04-0.5	0.011	0.04-0.19	0.15-2.0	0-0.02	0.22-3.5	0.45-2.6	0.15-3.5
Commod-ity impu-rities	36-41	0.78-1.6	305-610	395-790	0.55-0.82	6.5-32	195-390	310-620

Atmosh-peric deposi-tion	8.4-18	2.2-8.4	5.1-38	14-36	0.63-4.3	11-37	202-263	49-135
Total	52-112	5.6-38	484-1309	541-1367	1.6-15	106-544	479-1113	689-2054

Fig. 4.6: Metal contamination in the soil of world

(**Source:** Based on review of literature)

City/ Country	Cu	Cu	Pb	Zu	NI	Cd	Hg	As
Beijing	75.74	28.05	18.48	81.10	-	.18	-	-
Guangz-bou	64.65	24.00	58.00	16.60	-	20.28	0.73	10.-90
Spain	63.48	107.65	213.93	427.80	34.75	1.42	-	-
America	-	95.00	23.00	-	57.00	0.78	-	-
Korea	-	2.98	5.25	4.78	-	0.12	0.05	0.78
Stovakia	-	65.00	139.00	140.00	29.00	-	-	-
USA	48.5	4855		88.5	29	13.5	-	-
India	2.19	1.20	0.95	2.24	4.35	0.82	-	-
India	1.23	2.62	2.82	4.65	0.14	0.05	-	-
Iran	10.36	9.62	5.17	11.56	11.28	0.34	-	-
Iran	11.15	-	-	-	-	-	-	-
Range	1.23-75.74	1.20-107.65	0.95-213.93	4.65-427.8	0.14-57.00	0.05-13.50	0.05-0.73	0.78-10.90

Fig. 4.7: Metals in the Agricultural soils

(**Source:** Based on review of literature)

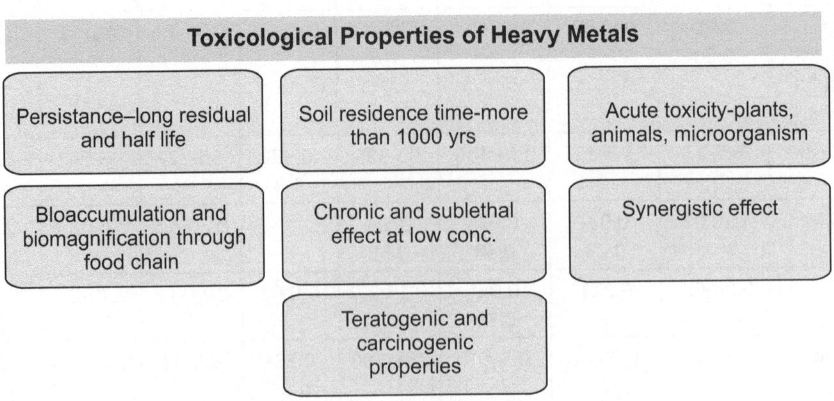

Fig. 4.8: Toxicological properties of heavy metals

(**Source:** Based on review of literature)

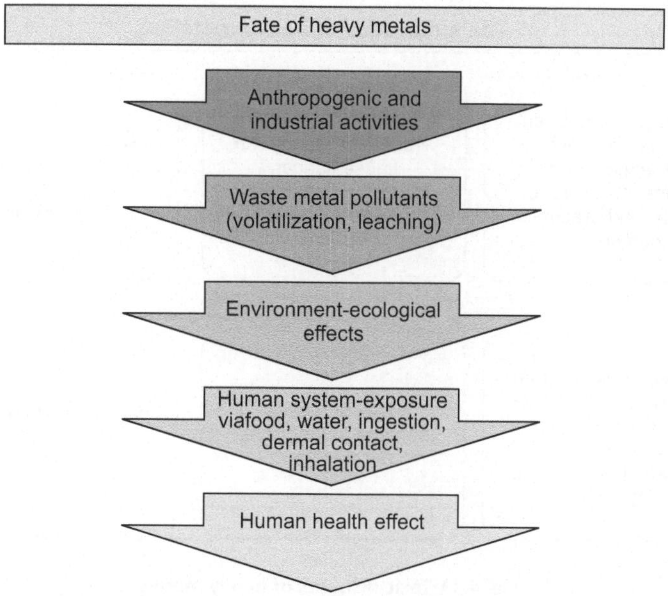

Fig. 4.9: Fate of heavy metals

(**Source:** Based on review of literature)

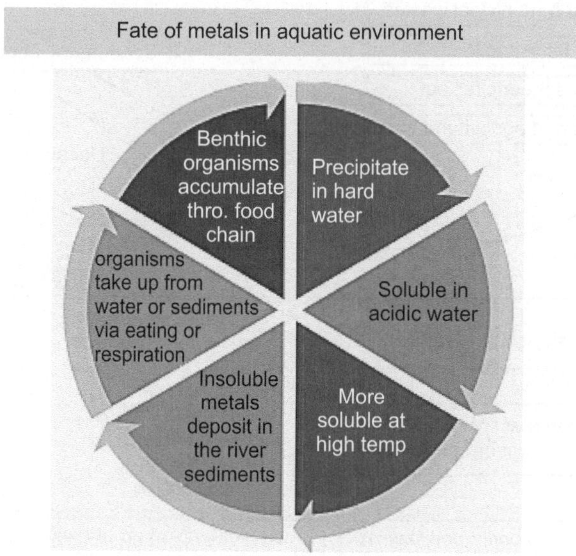

Fig. 4.10: Fate of metals in aquatic environment

(**Source:** Based on review of literature)

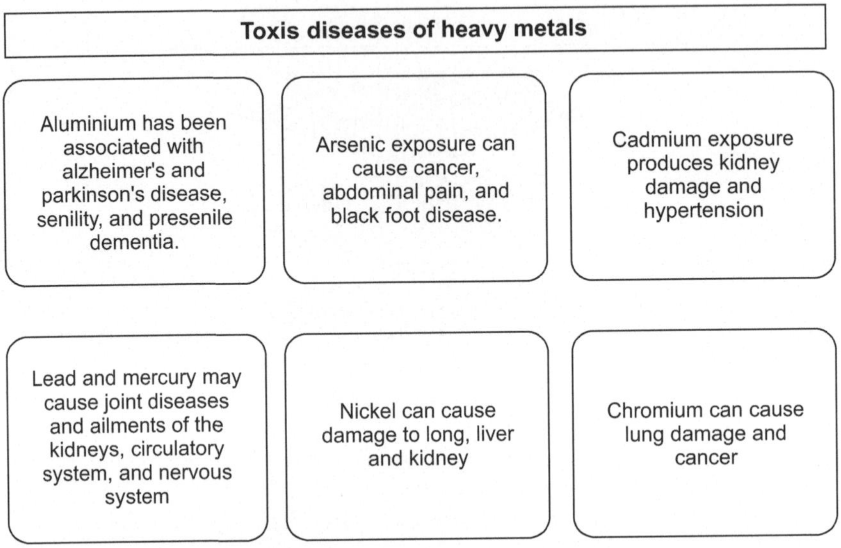

Fig. 4.11:Toxic diseases of heavy metals

(**Source:** Based on review of literature)

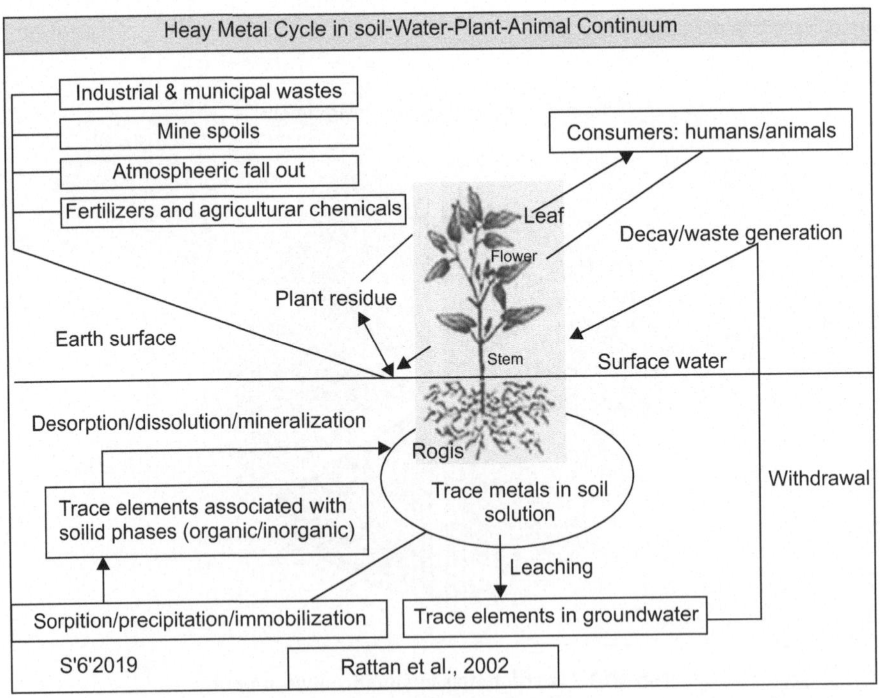

Fig. 4.12: Metal Cycle in SPAC

(**Source:** Based on review of literature)

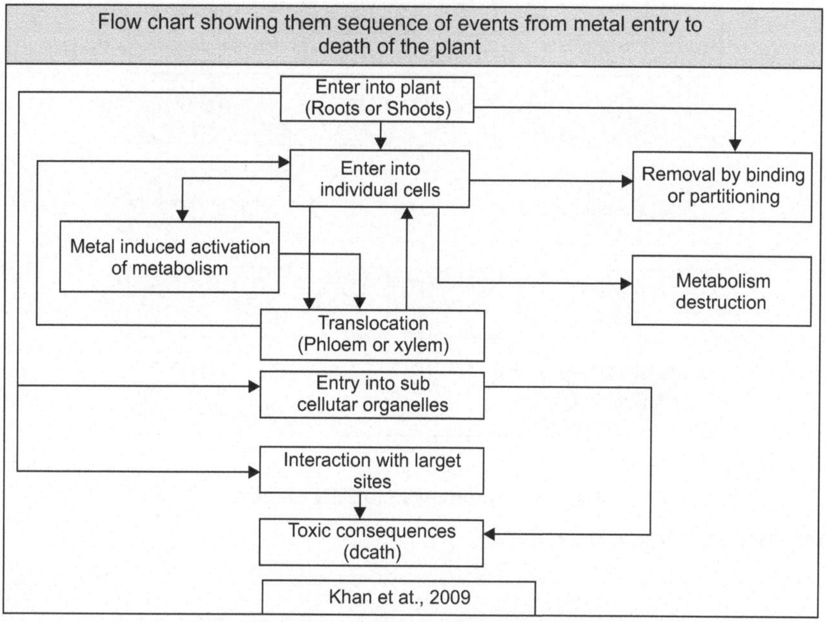

Fig. 4.13: Metal entry to death of the plant

(**Source:** Based on review of literature)

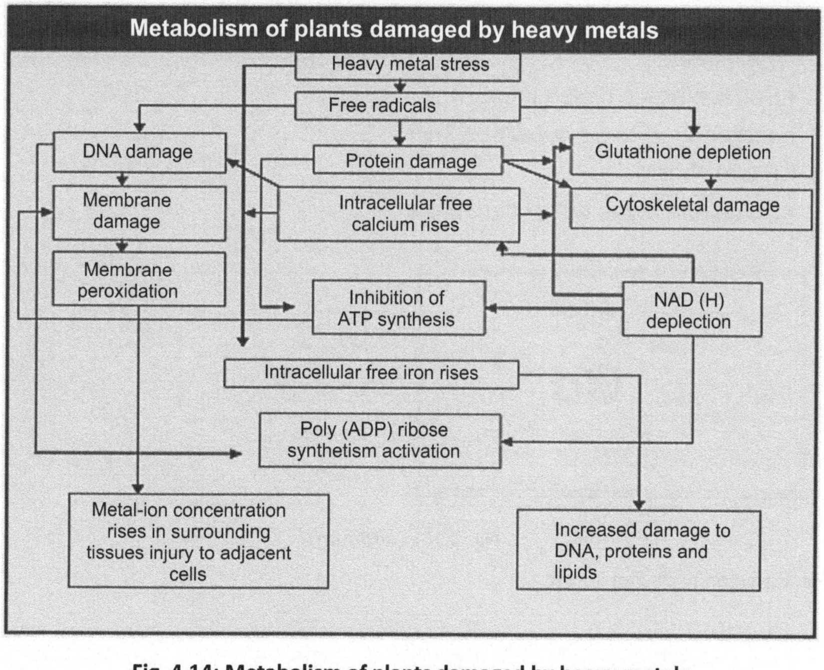

Fig. 4.14: Metabolism of plants damaged by heavy metals

(**Source:** Based on review of literature)

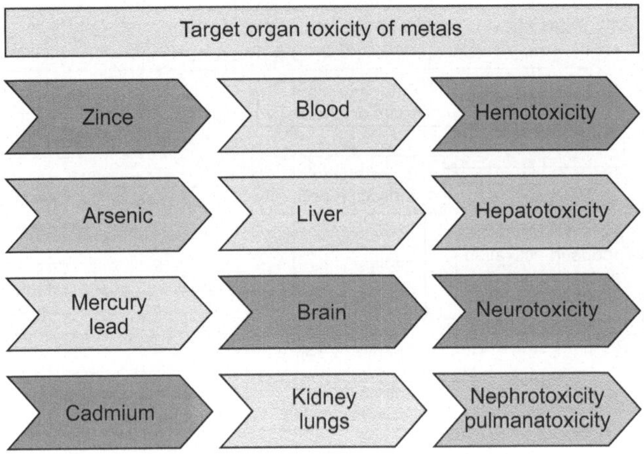

Fig. 4.15: Target organ toxicity of metals

(**Source:** Based on review of literature)

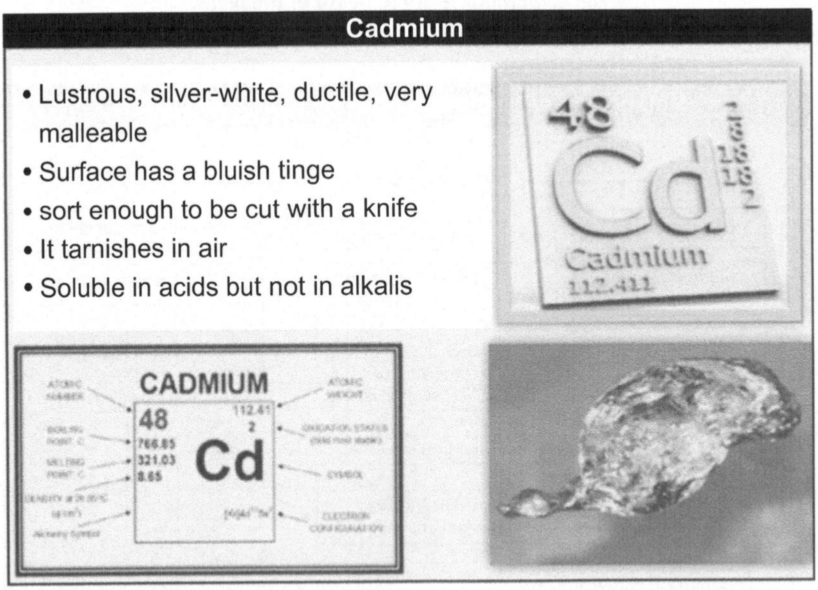

Fig. 4.16: Cadmium

(**Source:** Based on review of literature)

Cd Toxicity (200 mg kg^{-1} wt)

Metal-binding protein found in liver and kidney

Has very high affinity for Cd and Zn

Cd disrupts the normal functions of Zn and Ca

White-tailed ptarmigan

itai-itail disease is a multi-system disorder characterized by:

Severe osteoporosis and bone fragility
Disruption of calcium metabolism (increased excretion)
Nutritional definciencies (Vit. D, Ca)

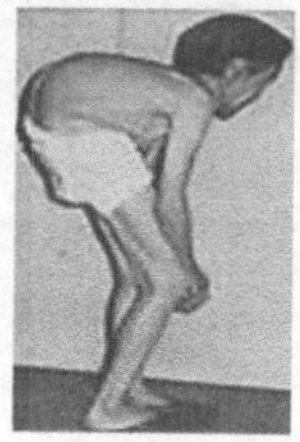

Fig. 4.17: Cd Toxicity

(**Source:** Based on review of literature)

Hg occurs In organic & Inorganic forms

- Inorganic forms most often or when Hg is combined with chlorine, sulfur or oxygen.
- Organic forms occur when mercury combines with carbon.
- The uptake of Hg: decreases growth induces disorientation of roots and shoots, plant tissue, and finally the cell wall.

Hg Sources

- Metallic forms of Hg are not absorbed by plants, but are converted by microorganisms to organic forms such as methyl mercury, which arc taken up by plants.
- Environmental sources Include pesticide-metallurgy, and vapours from burning coal am other fuels.
- Fish.

Fig. 4.18: Mercury

(**Source:** Based on review of literature)

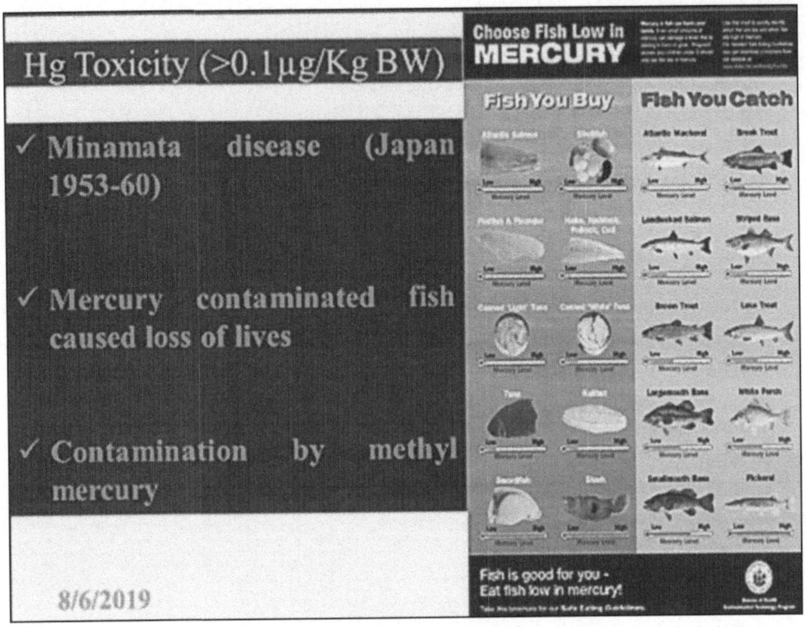

Fig. 4.19: Hg toxicity

(**Source:** Based on review of literature)

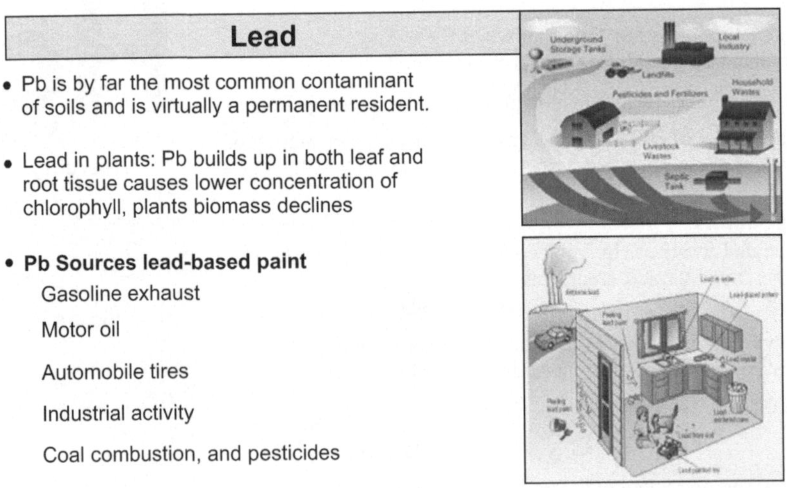

Fig. 4.20: Lead

(**Source:** Based on review of literature)

SYMPTOMS FROM LEAD TOXICITY ARE RARE!

Symptoms at a Glance

Below 45 μg/dL (2.17 μmol/L) in children and 60 μg/dL (2.90 μmol/L) in adults, lead exposure is usually asymptomatic. (See page 23 for who should be tested)

Moderate	Severe	Medical Emergency
Children > 25 μg.dL (1.2 μmol/L) Adults > 60 μg/dL	Children 55 to 70 μg/dL (2.64 to 3.38 μmol/L)	Children > 70 μg/dL+ (3.38 + μmol/L) Adults > 80 μg/dL+
Muscle pains Paresthesia Mild fatigue Aggressivenass Irritability Lethargy Abdominal discomfort	Arthralgia General fatigue Poor concentration Tremor Heaache Diffuse abdominal pain Constipation Weight loss	Paresis or paralysis Paralysis Brain oedema Stupor or coma Fits and vomiting Gingival lead line Colic Death

Fig. 4.21: Symptoms from lead toxicity

(**Source:** Based on review of literature)

- Arsenic is very common in most geological environments, igneous, metamorphic and sedimentary, causing a high background in many pails of north America.
- Chalcophile, oxyanionic or metalloid element often associated with sulphide ores.
- Crustal abundance: 1.8 ppm, ranging from 0.1 to several hundred ppm.
- Major source of anthropogenic arsenic mobilization is weathering of mine waste rock and tailings as gold is often associated with arsenopyrite especially in Canada
- Also common in reduced environment of coal deposits

Fig. 4.22: Arsenic

(**Source:** Based on review of literature)

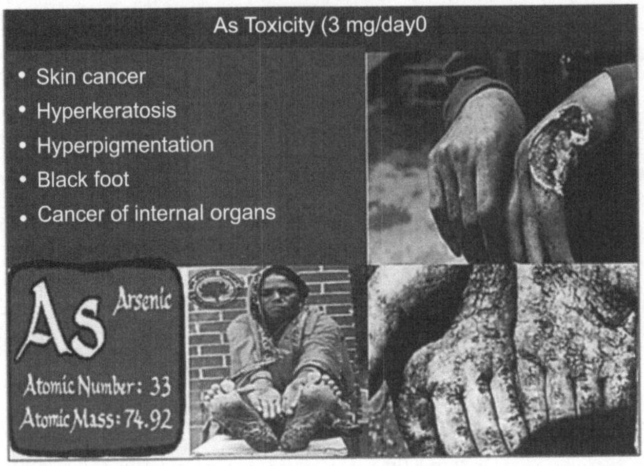

Fig. 4.23: As toxicity

(**Source:** Based on review of literature)

Chromium

- It is one of the less common elements and does not occur naturally in elemental form, but only in compounds.
- Chromium is mined as a primary ore product in the form of the mineral chromite, $FeCr_2O_4$.

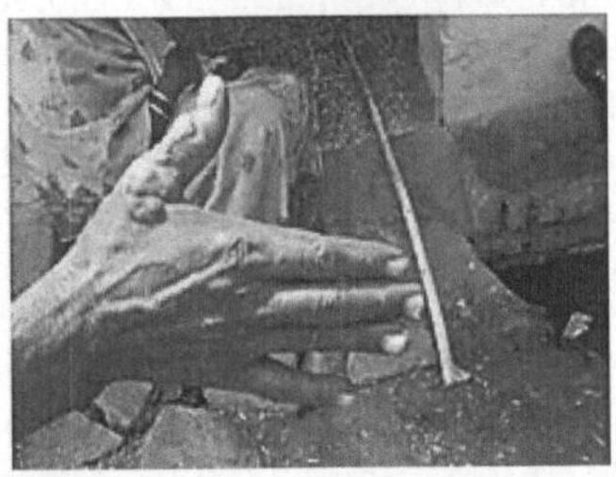

Source of Cr

- Electroplating processes disposal of Cr containing wastes

Fig. 4.24: Chromium

(**Source:** Based on review of literature)

Toxic effects of chromium in plants

crops are not affected by low Cr concentration (3.8 × 10–4 μM), Cr is toxic to higher plants at 100 μM kg^{-1} dry weight.

EFFECTS OF CHROMIUM ON PLANT PHYSIOLOGY

Process	Crop/Plant	Effects
Photosynthesis	Wheat, peas, rice, maize, beams, sunflower	Electrons transport inhibition.
		Calvin in cycle enzyme inactivation, reduced CO_2 fixation chloroplast disorganization.

Water relations	Bush beams, sunflowr, mung beam	Decreased water potential, increased transpiration rate, reduced diffusive resistance, wilting, reduction in trachcary vessel diameter
Mineral nutrition	Soybeam, tomato, bush beam, sunflower, maize	Uptake of N, P, K, Fe, Mg, Ma, Mo, Zn, Cu, Ca, B affected
Enzymes and other compounds	Nymphaca aiba and various cereals and legunes	Inhibition of assimilatory enzymes, increase activity of ROS sevavenging enzymes, changes in glutathione pool, no production of phytochelatins (Shanker et al., 2005)

Fig. 4.25: Toxic effect of chromium in plants

(**Source:** Based on review of literature)

REMEDIATION

- To develop the suitable techniques for waste disposal and management and treatment
- Control use of fertilizer having a high cadmium content
- They may use the alternative raw material so to reduce the chances of contamination of soil, air and water bodies
- Consideration of site selection, crop, fertilizer management, soil Ph, liming and irrigation water quality should be there
- To identify the way out to make the environment safe phytoremediation is the best approach and the tolerant and sensitive plant genotype....

Fig. 4.26: Remediation

(**Source:** Based on review of literature)

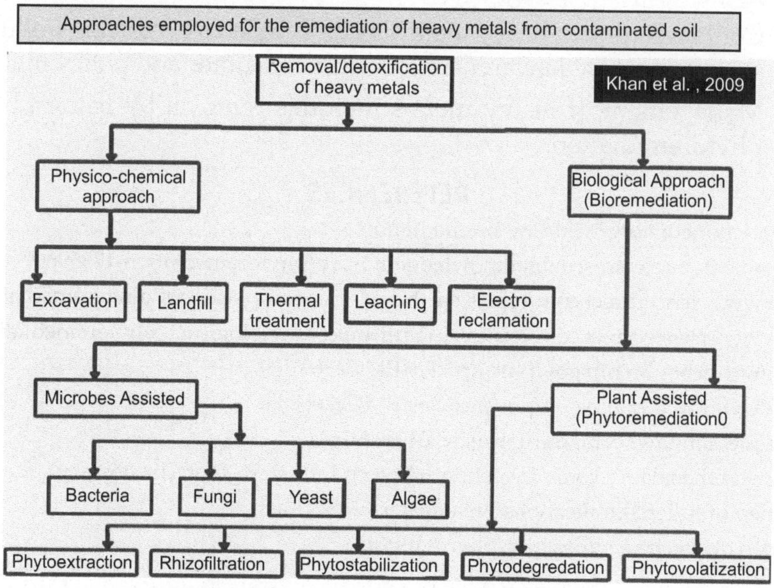

Fig. 4.27: Approaches for remediation

(**Source:** Based on review of literature)

Different approaches of phytoremediation

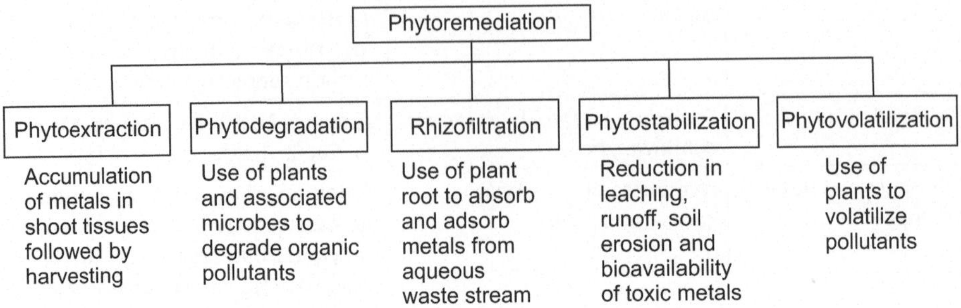

Fig. 4.28: Approaches for phytoremediation

(**Source:** Based on review of literature)

Conclusion

- Heavy metals of greatest concern are lead, mercury, arsenic, and cadmium.
- Essential nutrient becomes toxic to plant, animal and human being when present in higher amount.
- Heavy metals have more effect on quality concern of crop rather than yield of crop.
- Toxicity of arsenic, cadmium, lead, mercury and other heavy metal becoming more popular in peri urban areas.
- Irrigation with sewage water should be avoided.
- Contamination of heavy metal can be avoided by reducing pollution at source, increased awareness amongst consumer and policy makers.
- Management of heavy metals includes removal by using plants as phytoremidiation.

REFERENCES

https://en.wikipedia.org/wiki/Phytoremediation

https://www.nature.com/scitable/knowledge/library/phytoremediation-17359669

https://www.sciencedirect.com/topics/earth-and-planetary-sciences/phytoremediation

https://www.sciencedirect.com/topics/agricultural-and-biological.../phytoremediation

https://www.ncbi.nlm.nih.gov/pmc/articles/PMC1369103/

https://www.ncbi.nlm.nih.gov/pmc/articles/PMC2266886/

https://www.hindawi.com/journals/ijce/2011/939161/

https://www.thebalance.com › Investing › Biotech Industry › Biotech Glossary

www.unep.or.jp/Ietc/Publications/Freshwater/FMS2/1.asp

www.cpeo.org/techtree/ttdescript/phytrem.htm

Soil Ecosystem and Lithosphere Pages 51-60
Edited by: Dr. Abhishek Swami, Dr. Prasann Kumar and Dr. Pawan Kumar 'Bharti'
ISBN: 978-93-88854-50-4
Edition: 2020
Published by: Discovery Publishing House Pvt. Ltd., New Delhi (India)

5 Characteristics of Various Soil Amendments

Dr. Ashok K. Rathoure

Introduction

The primary role of soil amendments is to provide nutrients for crop growth or to provide materials for soil improvement. Misuse of soil amendments can result not only in damage to crops but can also cause negative impacts on the receiving soil, water, air or habitat environment. A soil amendment is any material added to a soil to improve its physical properties, such as water retention, permeability, water infiltration, drainage, aeration and structure. The goal is to provide a better environment for roots. To do its work, an amendment must be thoroughly mixed into the soil. If it is merely buried, its effectiveness is reduced, and it will interfere with water and air movement and root growth. Amending a soil is not the same thing as mulching, although many types of mulch also are used as amendments. Mulch is left on the soil surface. Its purpose is to reduce evaporation and runoff, inhibit weed growth, and create an attractive appearance. Mulches also moderate soil temperature. Organic mulches may be incorporated into the soil as amendments after they have decomposed to the point that they no longer serve their purpose. Common sources of micronutrients and metals are manure and chemical fertilizer. Some metals are plant micronutrients while some can become contaminants (toxic to soil microorganisms or plants). The availability of these elements varies, depending on soil type and soil pH. The major micronutrients and metals found in manure are iron, manganese, boron, chlorine, zinc, copper and molybdenum. Under both neutral soil pH and average organic matter conditions, most micronutrients in manure are available to the crop.

Amendments in Soil

Organic vs. Inorganic Amendments

There are two broad categories of soil amendments: organic and inorganic. Organic amendments come from something that was alive. Inorganic amendments, on the other hand, are either mined or man-made. Organic

Biohm Consultare Pvt. Ltd., Surat Gujarat, India

amendments include sphagnum peat, wood chips, grass clippings, straw, compost, manure, bio-solids, sawdust and wood ash. Inorganic amendments include vermiculite, perlite, tire chunks, pea gravel and sand. Wood ash, an organic amendment, is high in both pH and salt. It can magnify common soil problems and should not be used as a soil amendment. Organic amendments increase soil organic matter content and offer many benefits. The organic matter improves soil aeration, water infiltration, and both water- and nutrient-holding capacity. Many organic amendments contain plant nutrients and act as organic fertilizers. Organic matter also is an important energy source for bacteria, fungi and earthworms that live in the soil. The landscape and garden soils are improved to 4-5% organic matter. At this level, the mineralization (release) of nitrogen from the organic matter will be adequate for most plants without additional fertilizers. Many cities now require that the landscape soils be brought up to this level in new developments as a water conservation technique. With the improved aeration and deeper rooting, plants are more efficient in capturing rain events. Where the soil amendments may be high in salts, the rate is limited due to the salt problem. Salt burn of roots and death of landscape and garden plants is common from over application of salty soil amendments.

Wood Products

Wood products can tie up nitrogen in the soil and cause nitrogen deficiency in plants. Microorganisms in the soil use nitrogen to break down the wood. Over several months to years, as microorganisms complete the rapid decomposition process, the nitrogen is released and again becomes available to plants. This hazard is greatest with sawdust, because it has a greater surface area than wood chips. Compost wood products, before using them as soil amendments. For these products to decompose rapidly, add a nitrogen source to the compost pile. This could be plant residues high in nitrogen (such as grass clippings or manure), or a nitrogen fertilizer. The un-composted wood products or sawdust as a soil amendment should not be used. It is slow to break down, ties up nitrogen, interferes with seedbed preparation, and interferes with soil and water movement through the soil profile.

Sphagnum Peat vs. Mountain Peat

Sphagnum peat is an excellent soil amendment, especially for sandy soils, which will retain more water after sphagnum peat application. Sphagnum peat is generally acid (i.e., low pH) and can help gardeners grow plants that require a more acidic soil. The bogs can be re-vegetated after harvest in this moist environment. However, the harvest rate greatly exceeds the vegetation rate of the peat bogs, so it is considered a semi-renewal resource. The mountain peat is not a good soil amendment. It often is too fine in texture and generally has a higher pH. Mountain peat is mined from highaltitude wetlands that will take hundreds of years to rejuvenate, if ever. This mining is extremely disruptive to hydrologic cycles and mountain ecosystems.

Biosolids

Biosolids are byproducts of sewage treatment. They may be found alone or composted with leaves or other organic materials. The primary concerns about bio-solids are heavy metal content, pathogen levels and salts. Class A bio-solidshave been treated to reduce the bacterial content. Class A bio-solids are approved for use in production agriculture. However, it is advisable to avoid application to vegetable gardens due to the potential for heavy metals (such as cadmium and lead). Application of bio-solids is a cost-effective method to boost soil quality and plant growth and for the disposal of treated sludge. Although, bio-solids are a valuable source of nutrients, they contain lower N, P, and K contents compared to commercial fertilizers. Besides, sewage sludge also contains undesirable HMs, organic chemicals, and pathogens. Sewage sludge-amended soils irrigated with high rates of water causes leaching of nutrients and their further transport through the soil column to potential shallow aquifers. The nutrients and HMs through runoff and sediments enter water bodies and promote growth of algae and cause a wide array of water quality problems. HMs from soil, in diluted form and adhering to clay and organic matter colloidal particles, are transported to surface water bodies through runoff and sediments.

Manure

Fresh manure can harm plants due to elevated ammonia levels. To avoid this problem, use only aged or composted manure. Human pathogens, including E. coli, are another potential problem with fresh manure, especially on vegetable gardens. For vegetables with direct contact with the soil, fresh manure must be applied at least four months prior to harvest. For other fruits and vegetables, fresh manure must be applied at least three month prior to harvest. Aged manure refers to manure that has been piled for at least six months. Excessive ammonia will have escaped. Salt levels may be higher as the salts concentrate in the decomposing material, or may be leach out with high rainfall. Weed seeds will be viable. Composted manure technically refers to manure that has been through multiple active heating cycles and turned in between. If heated above 145 degrees F, it will kill pathogens and weed seeds. In composted manure, the organic matter is stabilized (through the rapid decomposition process) making it an ideal soil amendment. Salt level may be concentrated or may be leach out with high rainfall. As a point of clarification, composts and manures are not regulated. Many commercially available products are labeled as composted. However, this does not mean that it has been through the active decomposition process.

The use of animal manures as soil amendments must be done in a comprehensive manner to maximize their agricultural value and minimize their potential impacts on environmental quality and human health. There is no doubt that animal manures are valuable natural resources, particularly in countries where the availability of inorganic fertilizers is limited. When managed properly, manures provide plant nutrients, build soil organic matter, and improve soil physical properties, all of which are vitally important for soil quality and crop production. At the same time, the growing global trend toward intensification of animal production is gradually concentrating manure generation on smaller amounts of land. Transportation costs and the lack of an organized, efficient manure processing and distribution infrastructure are the major limitations to relocation of manures from areas where they are in surplus to areas where they are badly needed. When an adequate land base is not available to recycle manure nutrients in a balanced manner, over-application of nutrients such as N and P, which can negatively affect air, soil, and water quality, becomes a potential problem. Regional- and/or national-scale planning is required to develop and implement programs that can sustain modern animal production and use animal manures in an environmentally sound manner.

Compost

Compost refers to decomposed organic matter. It is not regulated, so there is no standard about the state of decomposition. In commercially available products the term compost is often used generically, and does not infer that the product has been through the actively heating, decomposition process. The combination of plant-based compost, manure-based composts, bio-solids, and other agriculture by-products (such as chicken feathers) are widely available. Compost made solely from plant-based products (such as wood chips and yard wastes) are low in salts. These are preferred over manure based composts which are often higher in salts.

Fertilizers

These are defined as any organic material such as manure or inorganic material of natural or synthetic origin such as granular ammonium nitrate that is added to a soil to significantly supply one or more nutrients essential for plant growth. The primary goal of fertilizer application is to provide sufficient nutrients in a balance suitable for crop use. Fertilizers counteract imbalances in the soil and replace nutrients removed by crop harvest. Organic materials that are classified as fertilizers have a carbon to nitrogen ratio of less than 30 to 1.

Soil amendments can have a profound effect on the physiological condition of a crop plant. Consequences of these changes for pest management depend on soil variability; the growth, developmental, and biochemical responses of the plant; the direct effects of these changes on herbivores; and the secondary impact on natural enemies. A considerable amount of work has been done on herbivore response to fertilizers that increase nitrogen (N) levels in plants. Mattson (1980) suggests that foliage N level is a major regulator of herbivory rate. Although increased plant quality (higher N) commonly leads to improved performance by individual insects (e.g., growth rates, survival, and fecundity), general statements on the direct responses of herbivores to N fertilizer are not possible due to the array of responses by different species. Other experiments on links between soil amendments and pest management concern effects on the pest via their response to resistant and susceptible varieties under conditions of different sources or levels of calcium, magnesium, nitrogen, phosphorus (P), potassium (K), or sulfur. The environment of a natural enemy is affected by soil amendments through changes in plant quality, as well as by concomitant changes in the herbivores.

Direct effects of fertilizer on biological control are not well documented. Many herbivores exhibit marked increases in population growth on nitrogen-enriched hosts. Concern emerges for the ability of natural enemies to track their prey/hosts under these conditions, but biological control of mites was maintained among apple treated with three levels of nitrogen fertilizer. Although the fecundity of the herbivore Panonychusulmi (Koch) increased with N level up to a fourfold increase when Amblyseiuspotentillae (Garman) predators were not present, the predators were able to compensate for most of the increase in prey reproduction. In contrast, fertilized (NPK) cotton plots exhibited higher levels of Heliothiszea than did control plots despite significantly higher population densities of Hippodamiaconvergens Guérin-Méneville, Coleomegillamaculatalangi Timberlake, and Oriusinsidiosus (Say) in fertilized cotton. Chiang (1970) demonstrated that fertilized midwestern corn fields (at 50 tons of manure per acre) had significantly fewer (half) corn rootworms than did unfertilized control plots. Although ground beetles and spiders were not affected, the populations of predaceous and herbivorous mites were three times higher in manure treatment plots. Through three seasons of field and laboratory experiments, Chiang concluded that predation by mites accounted for a 20% control of corn rootworm under natural field conditions and a 63% control when manure was applied.

Other effects of fertilizers on natural enemies may be predicted based on the combined information of related studies. For example, the parasitoid Diaretiellarapae (McIntosh) attacks the green peach aphid Myzuspersicae (Sulzer) more readily when the aphid is associated with Brassica spp. The mustard oils in crucifers serve as attractants for the wasp. It has also been shown-demonstrated that some glucosinolates are inversely related to N fertilizer level. Therefore, soil fertility may have dramatic effects on pest control by constraining the production of semiochemicals that play an important role in mediating interactions between plants, herbivores, and natural enemies.

Soil Conditioners

These are defined as any material(s) that contain limited amounts of nutrients, but are managed primarily for their beneficial impact on the biological, physical or chemical nature of the soil. They can also be used as a plant growth medium. Soil conditioners can be organic such as compost or wood waste or inorganic such as lime or perlite. Organic soil conditioners typically have high levels of organic matter but are not an immediate or significant source of plant nutrients and have a carbon to nitrogen ratio greater than 30 to 1. Addition of soil amendments with a high C:N ratio may result in crop available nitrogen being tied up (immobilized). Nutrients will be temporarily tied up in the soil, unavailable for plant use unless nitrogen is added to the soil to decrease the C:N ratio.

Most soil amendments are added to improve the structure of the soil, to increase the organic content so that the soil is more capable of holding nutrients and moisture. When these organic materials are added to the soil, they also act in varying degrees as fertilizers, providing a mix of nutrients to plant roots.

Table 5.1: Soil Amendments

S.No.	Name	Description
1.	Alfalfa Meal	Primarily a plant source of nitrogen, Alfalfa Pellets also contains trace minerals and triacontanol, a plant growth promoter.
2.	Azomite	A natural source of minerals and trace elements! Azomite is used in gardens as a re-mineralizer for soils and an anti-caking agent in animal feeds.
3.	Blood Meal	A strong, slow release source of nitrogen, Blood Meal (13-1-0) is also chock-full of trace minerals.
4.	Bone Meal	Granulated for easy application and quick uptake by plants, Bone Meal contains 20% phosphate and up to 23% calcium.
5.	Chicken Manure	Composted Chicken Manure (3-2-2) provides a well-balanced supply of nutrients and is excellent for mulching and moisture retention.
6.	Coconut Coir	Made from compressed coconut fiber, coir is an eco-friendly peat alternative! Works anywhere you would normally use peat moss, rockwool, vermiculite, perlite or pumice.
7.	Compost	No amount of organic fertilizer can make up for poor soil. Compost provides a microbially active source of organic matter and other important soil builders required by plants.
8.	Greensand	Contains about 7% total potash, along with iron, magnesium, silica and as many as 30 other trace minerals. May also be used to loosen heavy, clay soils.
9.	Gypsum	Used to loosen heavy clay soils, Agricultural Gypsum contains about 23% available calcium and 18% sulfur.

10.	Kelp Meal	A great source of micronutrients and beneficial plant growth promoters. Kelp Meal also encourages tolerance to stresses such as pests, disease, frost and drought.
11.	Dolomite Lime	Sweetens soil (raises pH in acidic soils) and is a quality source of calcium (Ca) and magnesium (Mg). Promotes healthy plant growth.
12.	Rock Dust	Improves soil vitality and plant health. Rock Dust contains a broad range of trace minerals, many of which have been lost through the ages, by erosion, leaching and farming.
13.	Rock Phosphate	Provides up to a 10 year reserve of phosphorous! Contains 27% total phosphate, 33% elemental calcium and many other trace minerals. Great for flowering plants.
14.	Shellfish Meal	A source of calcium (23%), nitrogen, phosphorus and trace minerals. Contains chitin, which stimulates the growth of soil microbes that inhibit root-knot nematodes.
15.	Sulfur	Lowers pH in alkaline soils. Elemental Sulfur contains 90% sulfur with 10% bentonite as a binder. Great around acid loving plants such as blueberry, azalea and rhododendron.
16.	Sul-Po-Mag	Also known as sulfate of potash-magnesia, Sul-Po-Mag is a quick release source of potassium and contains 22% soluble potash, 22% sulfur and 11% magnesium.
17.	Worm Castings	Gardeners know Worm Castings to be the most nutrient dense organic compost available. In soil, they retain water and release nutrients in a form that is easily used by plants.

Common Soil Amendments

Common soil amendments used to maintain high permeability in sodic soils include gypsum that provides electrolytes to prevent clay dispersion and organic polymers that stabilize soil aggregates. Phosphogypsum (PG) and flue gas desulfurization gypsum (FGDG), which are by-products of the phosphate and power generation industries, are readily available and therefore frequently used. Spreading powdered PG at rates of 5 Mg ha^{-1} on the soil surface can be effective in slowing down the rate of IR decline and maintaining a higher final IR compared with the control, even in soils of ESP < 2.5 (Figure 5.5), indicating that some chemical dispersion takes place even at very low ESP values, and possibly even in Ca-saturated soils. The use of PG is also very effective in maintaining high IR in soils with high ESP. The favorable effect of PG on IR should be attributed not only to its effect on the EC of the percolating water but also to: (*i*) the physical interference with the continuity of the seal; and (*ii*) the partial mulching of the soil surface which protects the soil from the beating action of the raindrops.

Organic polymers used for improving aggregate stability, maintaining high IR, and reducing seal formation are mainly polysaccharides (PSD) and polyacrylamides (PAM). The addition of small amounts of these polymers (10–20 kg ha^{-1}), either sprayed directly on to the soil surface or added to the applied water, was noted to be effective in stabilizing and cementing aggregates together at the soil surface, and hence maintaining high IR values in soils with ESP < 5. On the other hand, when added to soils with high ESP (>20), polymers were ineffective in controlling seal formation and maintaining high IR values; in soils with moderate ESP (10–15) the effects of polymers were inconsistent and depended on water quality and the amount of polymer added. The efficacy of anionic polymers in preventing seal formation is enhanced when the soil clay is maintained in a flocculated state and the resulting final IR could be 10 times higher than the control. It is therefore recommended that in soils exposed to rain, polymer application should be accompanied by spreading a source of electrolytes (e.g., gypsum) at the soil surface. Of the polymers currently available and under study, anionic polyacrylamide with high molecular weight (>10^6 Da) has been found to be the most effective in controlling seal formation and maintaining high IR.

Organic Fertilizers and Water Quality

Organic fertilizers are extensively used as a soil amendment and fulfill the nutrient requirement of crops (Brady, 1974). In addition to providing nutrients, organic fertilizers maintain soil aeration, moisture, and nurture the growth of soil microorganisms. On the other hand, organic manure contains fecal coliforms, HMs, nutrients that enter water bodies and degrade water quality and pose serious threats to the environment and public health (Jenkins *et.al.*, 1998; 2002). Most of the organic agricultural systems use compost or manures as N source and the rates of manure application are based on crop N requirements. Therefore, a farmland with successive years of manure or compost application will generally accumulate excess P. In contrast, other studies show a decrease in P concentration in organic production systems. Generally, N and P present in the manure, accumulate in the soil and may contribute to increased NO_3^- levels in groundwater and eutrophication of surface waters. Therefore, agriculture fields, supplemented with manures, also act as potential nonpoint source of water pollution.

Successive applications of high rates of dairy manure or sewage sludge can increase the risk of surface and groundwater pollution (Mohammadi *et.al.*, 2009; Rees *et.al.*, 2011). Various studies have been conducted to test the harmful effects of various types of manure on water quality parameters. Investigators observed that application of organic manure did not increase N recovery by crops; organic manure reduced NO_3^--N accumulation in the soil profile, but the total NO_3^- leaching was larger. Researcher analyzed groundwater samples collected near a pig farming operation; they contained about tenfold higher NO_3^--N and NH_4^+-N concentrations than the permissible limits. They also observed that river water showed a significant degradation in water purity. Hill *et.al.* (2005) studied the effect of animal waste application on biological and physicochemical characteristics of runoff water using simulated rainfall events. They observed a significant increase in bacterial and nutrient concentrations after the simulated rainfall events which could contribute to water pollution. Mishra *et.al.* (2006) observed that the application of manure causes significant edge-of-field nutrient losses, if rainfall occurs soon after application. Poultry manure is considered to be one of the sources that enhances SOM and improves soil fertility. On the other hand, poultry manure may act as a serious contaminant and pose potential risks to surface water quality. Mohammadi *et.al.* (2009) reported that organic fertilizer increased the water extractable and bioavailable P content of soil. Rees *et.al.* (2011) studied the effects of time of poultry manure application on soil erosion and runoff water quality. They applied manure in late fall, pre-planting, and pre-hilling on 11% and 8% slope plots. Their results showed that fresh poultry manure applications at the rate of 4 Mg ha^{-1} had no effect on annual runoff, but significantly reduced the May to October runoff when manure was applied in PH stage on 11% slope compared to the F stage on 8% slope. Fall manure applications significantly increased flow-weighted yearly runoff concentrations of nutrients, whereas, PH treatment lowered nutrient losses, runoff, and soil loss. They also reported increased concentrations of Escherichia coli in runoff after manure application. Rainfall events play a significant role in transporting human pathogens through water runoff from bio-solids-applied fields to surface water supplies and shallow groundwater (Sinton *et.al.*, 1999).

Salt Content and pH of the Amendment

High salt content and high pH are common problems in the soils. Therefore, avoid amendments that are high in salts or that have a high pH. Amendments frequently high in salts and/or pH include wood ash, the mountain peat and manures, and manurebased compost, bio-solids, and bio-solidbased compost. An amendment with up to 10 mmhos/ cm total salts is acceptable if mixed well into low-salt soils (less than 1 mmhos/cm). Amendments with a salt content greater than 10 mmhos/ cm are questionable. A low-salt amendment for soils testing high in salts should be chosen. Sphagnum peat and compost made from purely plant sources are low in salts and are good choices for amending the soils.

Conclusion

Soil amendment includes all inorganic and organic substances mixed into the soil for achieving a better soil constitution regarding plant productivity. Soil amendment does not include mulching, which includes substances lying on top of the soil. There are different substances for different soils and plants to optimize the soil conditions. A very common amendment is the addition of organic matter like compost, due to its low production costs.Soil amendments improve the physical properties resulting in better conditions for water storage, root development and soil ecosystems. Soil amendments can be produced locally, especially organic amendments, which are cheap to produce. The incorporation of the soil amendment (especially of organic amendments) can be time consuming. If too many nutrients or organic matter are put into the soil, they can be released and cause an outflow of nutrients into the groundwater and sur-rounding rivers and lakes, which can result in water pollution. Soil amendments can be applied almost everywhere by almost anybody.

REFERENCES

Brady, N.C. 1974. Nature and Properties of Soils, 8thed. p. 118, 133-4,413-417. Mcmillan Publ. Co. NY.

Chiang H.C. (1970). Effect of Manure Application and Mite Predation on Corn Rootworm Population in Minnesosa. Journal of Economic Entmology, 63: 934-936.

Hill Dagne D., William E. Owens and Paul B. Tchounwou (2005). Impact of Animal Waste Application on Runoff Water Quality in Field Experimental Plots. Int. J. Environ. Res. Public Health 2005, 2(2), 314–321.

Jenkins, M. B., Bowman, D. D. & Ghiorse, W. C. (1998). Inactivation of Cryptosporidium Parvumoocysts by Ammonia. Appl. Environ. Microbiol. 64, 784–788.

Jenkins, M. B., Bowman, D. D., Fogarty, E. A. & Ghiorse, W. C. (2002). Cryptosporidium Parvumoocyst Inactivation in Three Soil Types at Various Temperatures and Water Potentials. Soil Biol. Biochem. 34, 1101–1109.

Mishra A., Benham B.L., Mostaghini S. (2006). Bacterial Transport from Agricultural Lands Fertilized with Animal Manure (2006). Water Air and Soil Pollution 189(1):127-134

Mohammadi S., M. Kalbasi, and H. Shariatmadari (2009). Cumulative and Residual Effects of Organic Fertilizer Application on Selected Soil Properties, Water Soluble P, Olsen-p and P Sorption Index.J. Agr. Sci. Tech.11: 487-497

Rees, H. W., Chow, T. L., Zebarth, B. J., Xing, Z., Toner, P., Lavoie, J. and Daigle, J.-L. 2011. Effects of Supplemental Poultry Manure Applications on Soil Erosion and Runoff Water Quality from a Loam Soil Under Potato Production in Northwestern New Brunswick. Can. J. Soil Sci. 91: 595-613

Sinton LW, Finlay RK, Lynch PA. (1999). Sunlight Inactivation of Fecal Bacteriophages and Bacteria in Sewage-polluted Seawater. Appl Environ Microb. 4(8): 3605–3613

Soil Ecosystem and Lithosphere **Pages 61-69**
Edited by: Dr. Abhishek Swami, Dr. Prasann Kumar and Dr. Pawan Kumar 'Bharti'
ISBN: 978-93-88854-50-4
Edition: 2020
Published by: Discovery Publishing House Pvt. Ltd., New Delhi (India)

6 Metal Extraction from Soil by Microorganism-Assisted Plant

Prasann Kumar[1,2]*, Shipa Rani Dey[1]

GRAPHICAL ABSTRACT

Arbuscular mycorrhizal symbiosis

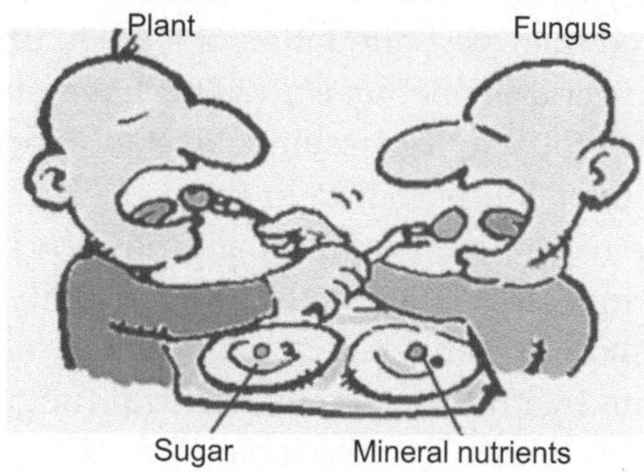

Keywords: *Arbuscular, Biotic, Crop, Mycorrhiza, Symbiosis*

Introduction

Some microorganism reduce the metal toxicity for plants by [1] Decreasing their accumulation into the plants while some others increase the amount of metal extracted by plants or [2] By increasing either the biomass of plants (diluting effects) or the concentration of metals accumulated in plants. Microorganisms just minimize the stress produced due to accumulation of excess metal in the plants.

$$+ \text{Increase in Biomass of plant} = \frac{1}{\text{Concentration of metals per unit biomass}}$$

*[**Source:** Drawn by the authors, unpublished, 2016]*

1 Department of Agronomy, School of Agriculture, Lovely Professional University, Jalandhar, Punjab, India, 144411
2 Divison of Research and Development, Lovely Professional University, Jalandhar, Punjab, India, 144411

Enhancement of Metal Accumulation by Plants

A. Bioavailability of metals

Low availability of the metals in the soil solution is the one of the major significant factor for the lower amount of metals extracted by plants from the soil. In general, scientist reported that, they oftenaccount for less than 1% of the total metal in soil (Whiting *et.al.*, 2001; Braud *et.al.*, 2006b) and the rate of availability is influenced by the several soil physical and chemical characteristics such as pH, CEC and organic matter (Kayser *et.al.*, 2001). Scientist reported that, the positive effects will be observed if we apply soil-bioaugmentation. It is happens due to more fraction of metal present in the soil solution. Braud *et.al.*, 2006b have shown that, if we take Pseudomonasaeruginosa and Pseudomonasfluorescens for remediation purpose of heavy metal especially lead, then it increases the available lead concentration in the soil solution by the 11.3%. So naturally it remediation will enhanced due to bio-augmentation of plants. It is observed that, the boundation of lead occurs with Fe-Mn oxides and organic matter. Abou-Shanab *et.al.*, (2006) have shown an increase of extractable Ni with Microbacteriumarabinogalactanolyticum by a factor up to 15 with respect to the Ni concentration in the soil. The availability of metals also affected with the nature of metal itself and physio-chemical properties of the soil. The pH has inverse relation with the availability of metals in the soil whereas the acidity shows positive relation with the availability of the metals. In a soil bio-augmented with the ecotomycorrhizal fungus Paxillusinvolutus, the concentration in NH_4NO_3-extractable Cd, Cu, Pb and Zn were, respectively, up to 1.22, 1.11, 1.33 and 1.33 fold higher than those recorded in the non-bioaugmented soil depending on the soil composition (Baum *et.al.*, 2006). Microbial performances cannot be compared with each other because the methods used to estimate the bioavailable fractions of metals vary from one experiment to other experiment. Indeed several extractants are used such as water (Chen *et.al.*, 2005; Di Gregorio *et.al.*, 2006; Wu Q.T. *et.al.*, 2006; Wu S.C. *et.al.*, 2006b), $MgCl_2$ (Braud *et.al.*, 2006b), NH_4NO_3 (Baum *et.al.*, 2006), DTPA (Chen *et.al.*, 2004a; Di Gregorio *et.al.*, 2006b), KNO_3 (Di Gregorio *et.al.*, 2006) and HCl (Wang *et.al.*, 2007b). Bioavailability of metals is even divided into three different pools (Cao *et.al.*, 2007): immediately soluble metals (with water), exchangeable metal forms (with KNO_3) and complexes or adsorbed metal form (with EDTA).

Microbial siderophores, manly localized in the rhizosphere (Bossier *et.al.*, 1988), enhance the Fe (III) mobility and also various other cations (Hofte *et.al.*, 1993; Diels *et.al.*, 2002) (Figure 6.1). Principle component analysis (PCA) shows close positive relationships between the microorganisms that produce siderophores and the amount of Cr and Pb in the exchangeable fraction (Braud *et.al.*, 2006b). Bacteria such as Azotobacterchroococcum (N-fixing bacteria), Bacillusmegaterium (P-solubilizer) and Bacillusmunilaginosus (K-solubilizer) (Wu Q.T. *et.al.*, 2006; Wu S.C. *et.al.*, 2006b) and Bacillus sp. RJ 16 (Sheng and Xia 2006) can decrease the pH value, probably by excreting low molecular weight organic acids, enhancing the bioavailability of Cd, Pb and Zn (Chen *et.al.*, 2005). The metal concentrations in the majority simply extractable fractions have been showing to amplify in the bio-augmentation (Braud *et.al.*, 2000b; Sheng and Xia 2006). Subsequent to six months, the concentrations of accessible metals are still elevated within the bio-augmented soil compared on the way to the non-bioaugmented ones (Baum *et.al.*, 2006) signifying with the intention of inoculated microorganisms does stay alive and be metabolically active. A number of other studies have made known, nevertheless, the opposing, i.e., bio-augmentation has refusal consequence on metal speciation. Meant for instance, Glomuscaledonium (Chen *et.al.*, 2004a) and Glomusmosseae (Citterio *et.al.*, 2005) have no effect on the speciation of Cd and Zn, Cr and Ni, respectively (Figure 6.1). No effect of bio-augmentation by these microorganisms on the rate of phytoextraction has been observed to confirm these results.

B. Metal extraction by plants

The metal concentration in plants has been shown to be higher or lower compared to the control (non-bioaugmented soil), depending on the metal (Bi *et.al.*, 2003a; Baum *et.al.*, 2006) and/or its concentration in the soil (Chen *et.al.*, 2003). Nevertheless bio-augmentation almost always increases the rate of metal extracted by plants. With the figure 6.1, we are giving the root morphology, which acts an important role in the bioaugmentation of contaminated soil of hazardous waste site. Most often metal concentration in microorganisms-assisted plant is higher than the control (non-bioaugmented soil). Bacteria, mainly PGPR and fungi, mainly AMF are used as pure cultures or as co-cultures. Whether the soil is bioaugmented or not, metal concentration in roots are generally higher than in shoots, by a factor exceeding 10 for most experiments. When the concentration of metals accumulated by plants increase with bioaugmentation, this increase most of the time is proportionally higher in roots than in shoots. Some experiments have, however, show the contrary with bacteria (de Souza *et.al.*, 1996b) and fungi (Liao *et.al.*, 2003; Malcova *et.al.*, 2003; Leung *et.al.*, 2006). PGPR such as Agrobacterium, Alcaligenes, Arthrobacter, Azospirillum, Azotobacter, Bacillus, Burkholderia, Serratia, Pseudomonas and Rhizobium (O'Sullivn and O'Gara 1992; Hoflich etal., 1994; Carlot *et.al.*, 2002; Glick 2003) are particularly interesting for metal extraction by plants since they increase both the rate of metals accumulated by plants and the plant biomass. Pseudomonads are well-known producers of siderophores involved in the modification of metal speciation in soils. Siderophores synthesized by P. fluorescens improve Fe uptake by tomatoes (Duss *et.al.*, 1986), carnations and oats (Dujiff *et.al.*, 1991), vine and maize (Sharma and Johri 2003a, b) with the disappearance of the chlorosis phenomena in peanut (Jurkevitch *et.al.*, 1988). Few hydroxamate siderophores, such as desferrioxamine B, can complex with Pb (Dubbin and Louise Ander 2003) and potentially helping Pb uptake by plants. However, complexation of Cd, Cu and Zn is much higher with nitrilotria-complexation of Cd, Cu and Zn is much higher with nitrilotriacetate compared to desferrioxamine B (Neubauer *et.al.*, 2000). PGPR lowers the metal toxicity by reducing ethylene produced by plant in response to heavy metals. Conversely the most common auxin, indole-3-acetic acid (IAA) synthesized by rhizobacteria has been shown to be involved in the metal uptake. IAA produced by Bacillussubtilis SJ-101 increases Ni concentration in B. juncea by a factor of 1.5 (Zaidi *et.al.*, 2006). In hydroponic conditions, simultaneous addition of EDTA and IAA synthesized by rhizobacteria increase Pb extraction by plant by a factor of 28 against 6 with EDTA (Lopez *et.al.*, 2005). AMF can also enhance metal extraction by plants, e.g., Cd in bean and maize (Guo *et.al.*, 1996), alfalfa (El- Kherbawy *et.al.*, 1989), clover (Joner and Leyval 1997) and soyabean (Heggo *et.al.*, 1990) depending on the soil characteristic and pH of the give soil. Soil bioaugmentation with Glomus intraradices has been shown to act upon Pb accumulation and translocation in plants but the effect varies according to plant species and metal localization in plants. For example,

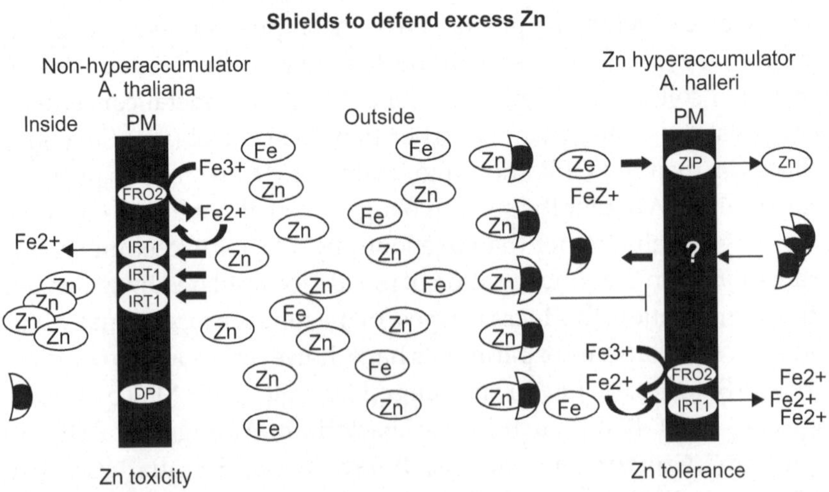

Fig. 6.1: Shields to defend excess Zn with reference to hyperaccumulator and Non-hyperaccumulator plants

(**Source:** http://en.wikipedia.org/wiki/Image.jpg)

mycorrhization reduces Pb concentration in roots and leaves of Zea mays but the concentration of Pb increase in roots of Agrostiscapillaries (Malcova *et.al.*, 2003) (Figure 6.4). Where; (*a*) Plant-associated microbes improve plant metal uptake by producing metal mobilizing chelators. Plant associated microbes reduce plant metal uptake and/or translocation through; (*b*) producing metal immobilization metabolites; (*c*) metal reduction and/or; (*d*) metal biosorption.

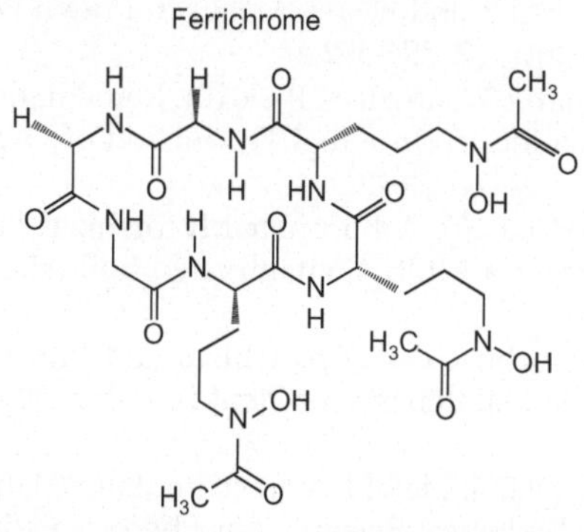

Fig. 6.2

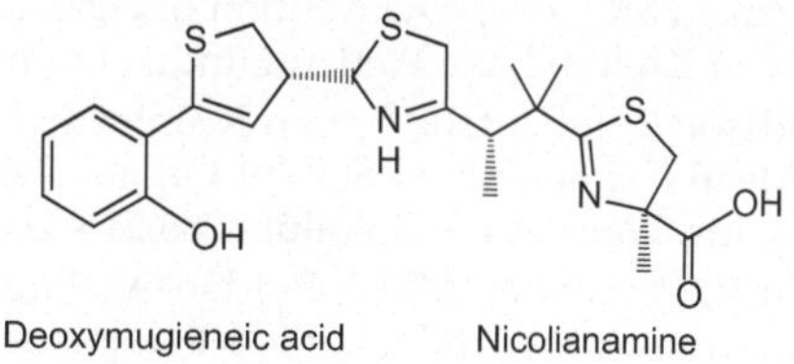

Fig. 6.3

(**Source** of Fig. 6.2 & 6.3: http://en.wikipedia.org/wiki/Image.jpg)

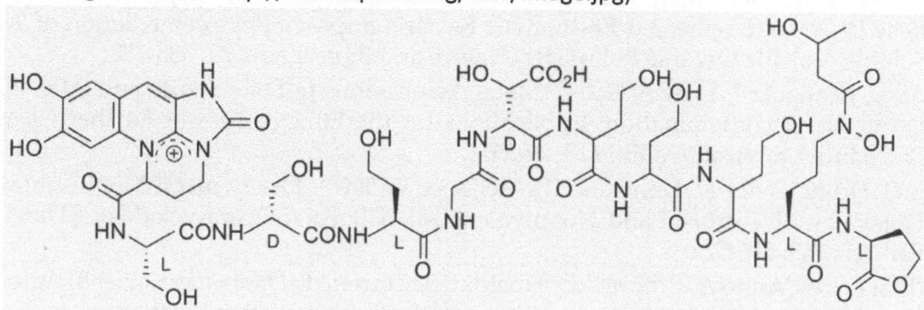

Fig. 6.4

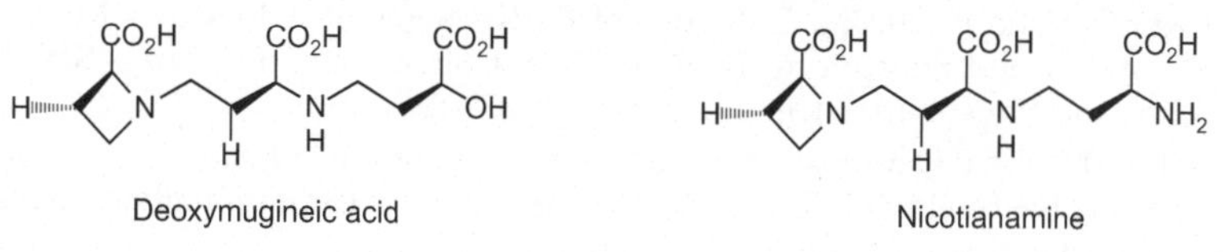

Fig. 6.5

(**Source** of Fig. 6.4 and 6.5: http://en.wikipedia.org/wiki/Image.jpg)

where;

Fig. 6.2 = Ferrichrome, a hydroxamate siderophore

Fig. 6.3 = Yersiniabactin, a mixed-ligand siderophore

Fig. 6.4 = Azotobactin

Fig. 6.5 = Deoxymugineic acid and nicotianamine

REFERENCES

Aafi NE, Brhada F, Dary M, Maltouf AF, Pajuelo E (2012). Rhizostabilization of Metals in Soils Using Lupinus Luteus Inoculated with the Metal Resistant Rhizobacterium Serratia sp. MSMC 541. Intl. J Phytoreme., 14:261–74.

Abou-Shanab RAI., Angle JS., Chaney RL (2006). Bacterial Inoculants Affecting Nickel Uptake by Alyssum murale from Low, Moderate and High Ni Soils. Soil Biol. Biochem., 38: 2882-2889

Amaraneni SR (2006). Distribution of Pesticides, PAHs and Heavy Metals in Prawn Ponds Near Kolleru Lake Wetland, India. Environ. Intl., 32: 294-302.

Arwidsson Z, Johansson E, von Kronhelm T, Allard B, van Hees P (2010). Remediation of Metal Contaminated Soil by Organic Metabolites from Fungi Production of Organic Acids. Water Air Soil Pollut., 205:215–26.

Azcón R, Perálvarez MDC, Roldán A, Barea JM (2010). Arbuscular Mycorrhizal Fungi, Bacilluscereus, and Candida Parapsilosis from a Multi Contaminated Soil Alleviate Metal Toxicity in Plants. Microb. Ecol., 59:668–77.

Babu AG, Reddy S (2011). Dual Inoculation of Arbuscular Mycorrhizal and Phosphate solubilizing Fungi Contributes in Sustainable Maintenance of Plant Health in Fly Ash Ponds. Water Air Soil Pollut., 219:3-10.

Baker AJM, McGrath SP, Reeves RD, Smith JAC (2000). Metal hyperaccumulator Plants: A Review of the Ecology and Physiology of a Biological Resource for Phytoremediation of Metal-polluted Soils. Lewis Publisher, Boca Raton, FL.

Barac T, Taghavi S, Borremans B, Provoost A, Oeyen L, Colpaert JV, Vangronsveld J, van der Lelie D (2004). Engineered Endophytic Bacteria Improve Phytoremediation of Water-Soluble, Volatile Organic Pollutants. Nature and Biotechnol., 22: 583-588.

Barona A, Aranguiz I, Elias A (2001). Metal Associations in Soils Before and After EDTA Extractive Decontamination: Implications for the Effectiveness of Further Clean-up Procedures. Environ. Pollu., 113: 79-85.

Baum C, Hrynkiewicz K, Leinweber P, Meissner R (2006). Heavy-metal Mobilization and Uptake by Mycorrhizal and Nonmycorrhizal Willows (Salixdasyclados). J Plant Nut. Soil Sci., 169: 516-522.

Beolchini F, Dell'Anno A, Propris LD, Ubaldini S, Cerrone F, Danovaro R (2009). Auto- and Heterotrophic Acidophilic Bacteria Enhance the Bioremediation Efficiency of Sediments Contaminated by Heavy metals. Chemosphere, 74: 1321–6.

Bi YL, Li XL, Christie P (2003a). Influence of Early Stages of Arbuscular Mycorrhiza on Uptake of Zinc and Phosphorus by Red Clover from a Low Phosphorus Soil Amended with Zinc and Phosphorus. Chemosphere, 50: 831-837.

Blaylock MJ (2000). Field Demonstrations of Phytoremediation of Lead Contaminated Soils. In: Terry, N., Ba~nuelos, G. (Eds.), Phytoremediation of Contaminated Soil and Water. Lewis Publishers, Boca Raton, FL, pp. 1-12.

Bossier P, Hofte M, Verstraete W (1988). Ecological Significance of Siderophores in Soil. Adv. Microbiol. Ecol., 10: 385-414.

Bouwman LA, Bloem J, Romkens PFAM, Japenga J (2005). EDGA Amendment of Slightly Heavy Metal Loaded Soil Affects Heavy Metal Solubility, Crop Growth and Microbivorous Nematodes but not Bacteria and Herbivorous Nematodes. Soil Biol. Biochem., 37: 271-278.

Braud A, Jézéquel K, Bazot S, Lebeau T (2009b). Enhanced Phytoextraction of an Agricultural Cr, Hg and Pb-contaminated Soil by Bioaugmentation with Siderophore Producing Bacteria. Chemosphere, 74: 280–6.

Braud A, Jezequel K, Vieille E, Tritter A, Lebeau T (2006b). Changes in Extractability of Cr and Pb in a Polycontaminated Soil After Bioaugmentation with Microbial Producers of

Biosurfactants, Organic Acids and Siderophores. Water, Air and Soil Pollu., 6: 261-279.

Bubb JM, Rudd T, Lester JN (1991). Distribution of Heavy Metals in the River Yare and Its Associated Broads II. Copper and Cadmium. Sci. Tot. Environ., 102: 169-188.

Cao A, Carucci A, Lai T, La Colla P, Tamburini E (2007). Effect of Biodegradable Chelating Agents on Heavy Metals Phytoextraction with Mirabilis Jalapa and on Its Associated Bacteria. Europ. J Soil Biol., 43: 200-206.

Carlot M, Giacomini A, Casella S (2002). Aspects of Plant Microbe Interactions in Heavy Metal Polluted Soil. Acta Biotechno., 22: 13-20.

Chatterjee S, Sau GB, Mukherjee SK (2009). Plant Growth Promotion by a Hexavalent Chromium Reducing Bacterial Strain, Cellulosimicrobium Cellulans KUCr3. World J Microbiol. Biotechnol., 25:1829–36.

Chen SY, Lin JG (2001). Effect of Substrate Concentration on Bioleaching of Metal-Contaminated Sediment. J Hazard Mater, 82:77–89.

Chen B, Shen H, Li X, Feng G, Christie P (2004a). Effects of EDTA Application and Arbuscular Mycorrhizal Colonization on Growth and Zinc Uptake by Maize (Zea mays L.) in Soil Experimentally Contaminated with Zinc. Plant and Soil, 261: 219-229.

Chen BD, Li X., Tao HQ, Christie P, Wong MH (2003). The Role of Arbuscular Mycorrhiza in Zinc Uptake by Red Clover Growing in a Calcareous Soil Spiked with Various Quantities of Zinc. Chemosphere, 50: 839-846.

Chen YX, Wang YP, Lin Q, Luo YM (2005). Effect of Copper-tolerant Rhizosphere Bacteria on Mobility of Copper in Soil and Copper Accumulation by Elsholtzia Splendens. Environ. Intl., 31: 861-866.

Citterio S, Prato N, Fumagalli P, Aina R, Massa N, Santagostino A, Sgorbati S, Berta G (2005). The arbuscular mycorrhizal fungus Glomus mosseae induces growth and metal accumulation changes in Cannabissativa L. Chemosphere, 59: 21-29.

Di Gregorio S, Lampis S, Vallini G (2011). Selenite Precipitation by a Rhizospheric Strain of Stenotrophomonas sp Isolated from the Root System of Astragalusbisulcatus: a Biotechnological and Microbial Community Changes in Rice Rhizospheres Affected by Sulfur. Molecules, 16:1409–17.

Di Gregorio S, Barbafieri M, Lampis S, Sanangelantoni AM, Tassi E, Vallini G (2006). Combined Application of Triton X-100 and Sinorhizobium sp. Pb002 Inoculum for the Improvement of Lead Phytoextraction by Brassica Juncea in EDTA Amended Soil. Chemosphere, 63: 293-299.

Di Simine CD, Sayer JA, Gadd GM (1998). Solubilization of Zinc Phosphate by a Strain of Pseudomonas Fluorescens Isolated from a Forest Soil. Biology and Fertility of Soils, 28: 87-94.

Dickinson NM, Pulford ID (2005). Cadmium Phytoextraction Using Short Rotation Coppice Salix: The Evidence Trail. Environ. Intl., 31: 609-613.

Diels L, De Smet M, Hooyberghs L, Corbisier P (1999). Heavy Metals Bioremediation of Soil. Mole. Biotechnol., 12: 154-158.

Diels L, van der Lelie N, Bastiaens L (2002). New Developments in Treatment of Heavy Metal Contaminated Soils. Rev. Environ. Sci. Biotechnol., 1: 75-82.

Dimkpa CO, Merten D, Svatoš A, Büchel G, Kothe E (2009b). Metal-induced Oxidative Stress Impacting Plant Growth in Contaminated Soil is Alleviated by Microbial Siderophores. Soil Biol Biochem., 41:154–62.

Dimkpa CO, Merten D, Svatoš A, Buchel G, Kothe E (2009a). Siderophores Mediate Reduced and Increased Uptake of Cadmium by Streptomyces Tendae F4 and Sunflower (Helianthus annuus), Respectively. J Appl. Microbiol., 107: 1687–96.

Dimkpa CO, Svatos A, Merten D, Buchel G, Kothe E (2008). Hydroxamate Siderophores Produced by Streptomyces Acidiscabies E13 bind Nickel and Promote Growth in Cowpea (Vignaunguiculata L.) Under Nickel Stress. Can. J Microbiol., 54:163–72.

Dubbin WE, Louise Ander E (2003). Influence of Microbial Hydroxamate Siderophores on Pb(II) Desorption from a-FeOOH. Appl. Geochem., 18: 1751-1756.

Duijff BJ, Bakker PAHM, Schippers B (1991). Influence of Pseudobactin- 358 on the Iron Nutrition of Plants. In: Sixth International Fe Symposium.

Duss F, Mozafar A, Oertli JJ, Jaeggi W (1986). Effect of Bacteria on the Iron Uptake by Axenically-Cultured Roots of Fe-efficient and Fe-inefficient tomatoes (Lycopersiconesculentum Mill.). J Plant Nut., 9: 587-598.

El-Kherbawy M, Angle JS, Heggo A, Chaney RL (1989). Soil pH, Rhizobia, and Vesicular-Arbuscular Mycorrhizae Inoculation Effects on Growth and Heavy Metal Uptake of alfalfa (Medicago sativa L.). Biol. Fert. Soils, 8: 61-65.

Fasim F, Ahmed N, Parsons R, Gadd GM (2002). Solubilization of Zinc Salts by a Bacterium Isolated from the Air Environment of a Tannery. FEMS Microbiol. Lett., 213:1–6.

Fomina MA, Alexander IJ, Hillier S, Gadd GM (2004). Zinc Phosphate and Pyromorphite Solubilization by Soil Plant-symbiotic Fungi. Geomicrobiol. J., 21:351–66.

Femsre.oxfordjournals.org

Gadd GM (2004). Bioremedial Potential of Microbial Mechanisms of Metal Mobilization and Immobilization. Curr. Opin. Biotechnol., 11: 271–9.

Glick BR (2003). Phytoremediation: Synergistic Use of Plants and Bacteria to Clean up the Environment. Biotechnol. Adv., 21: 383-393.

Gohre V, Paszkowski U (2006). Contribution of the Arbuscular Mycorrhizal Symbiosis to Heavy Metal Phytoremediation. Planta, 223:1115–22.

Gonzalez-Chavez MC, Carrillo-Gonzalez R, Wright SF, Nichols KA (2004). The Role of Glomalin, a Protein Produced by Arbuscular Mycorrhizal Fungi, in Sequestering Potentially Toxic Elements. Environ. Pollut., 130:317–23.

Guo Y, George E, Marschner H (1996). Contribution of an Arbuscular Mycorrhizal Fungus to the Uptake of Cadmium and Nickel in Bean and Maize Plants. Plant and Soil, 184: 195-205.

Heggo A, Angle JS, Chaney RL (1990). Effects of Vesicular Arbuscular Mycorrhizal Fungi on Heavy Metal Uptake by Soybean. Soil Biol. Biochem., 22: 856-869.

Herman D, Artiola J, Miller R (1995). Removal of Cadmium, Lead and Zinc from Soil by a Rhamno Lipid Biosurfactant. Environ. Sci. Technol., 29: 2280-2285.

Hoflich G, Wiehe W, Kuhn G (1994). Plant Growth Stimulation by Inoculation with Symbiotic and Association Rhizosphere Microorganisms. Experientia 50.

Hofte M, Buysens S, Koedam N, Cornelis P (1993). Zinc Affects Siderophore-mediated High Affinity Iron Uptake Systems in the Rhizosphere Pseudomonas Aeruginosa 7NSK2. BioMetals 6: 85-91.

Hoberg E, Marschner P, Lieberei R (2005). Organic Acid Exudation and pH Changes by Gordonia sp. and Pseudomonas Fluorescens Grown with P Adsorbed to Goethite. Microbiol. Res., 160:177–87.

Hrynkiewicz K, Dabrowska G, Baum C, Niedojadlo K, Leinweber P (2012). Interactive and Single Effects of Ectomycorrhiza Formation and Bacillus Cereus on Metallothionein mt1 Expression and Phytoextraction of Cd and Zn by willows. Water Air Soil Pollut., 223:957–68.

http://en.wikipedia.org/wiki/Image.jpg

Idris R, Trifonova R, Puschenreiter M, Wenzel WW, Sessitsch A (2004). Bacterial Communities Associated with Flowering Plants of the Ni Hyperaccumulator Thlaspi Goesingense. App. Environ. Microbiol., 70: 2667-2677.

Joner EJ, Leyval C (1997). Uptake of 109Cd by Roots and Hyphae of a Glomusmosseae/Trifoliumsubterraneum Mycorrhiza from Soil Amended with High and Low Concentrations. New Phytologist., 135: 353-360.

Joshi PM, Juwarkar AA (2009). In vivo Studies to Elucidate the Role of Extracellular Polymeric Substances from Azotobacter in Immobilization of Heavy Metals. Environ. Sci. Technol., 43:5884–9.

Jurkevitch E, Hadar Y, Chen Y (1988). Involvement of Bacterial Siderophores in the Remedy of Lime-induced Chlorosis in Peanut. Soil Sci. Soc. Amer. J., 52: 1032-1037.

Juwarkar AA, Nair A, Dubey KV, Singh SK, Devotta S (2007). Biosurfactant Technology for Remediation of Cadmium And Lead Contaminated Soils. Chemosphere, 10: 1996–2002.

Kayser G, Korckritz T, Markert B (2001). Bioleaching for the Decontamination of Heavy Metals. Wasser and Boden., 53: 54-58.

Khan MS, Zaidi A, Wani PA, Oves M (2009). Role of Plant Growth Promoting Rhizobacteria in the Remediation of Metal Contaminated Soils. Environ. Chem., Lett., 7: 1-19.

Khan AG (2006). Mycorrhizremediation an Enhanced form of Phytoremediation. J. Zhejiang University e Science B., 7: 503-514.

Khan AG, Kuek C, Chaudhry TM, Khoo CS, Hayes WJ (2000). Role of Plants, Mycorrhizae and Phytochelators in Heavy Metal Contaminated Land Remediation. Chemosphere, 41: 197-207.

Kidd P, Barcelo J, Bernal MP, Navari-Izzo F, Poschenrieder C, Shilev S *et.al.* (2009). Trace Element Behaviour at the Root–soil Interface: Implications in Phytoremediation. Environ. Exp. Bot., 67:243–59.

Krupa P, Kozdrój J (2007). Ectomycorrhizal Fungi and Associated Bacteria Provide Protection Against Heavy Metals in Inoculated Pine (Pinus sylvestris L.) Seedlings. Water Air Soil Pollut., 182:83–90.

Kuiper I, Lagendijk EL, Bloemberg GV, Lugtenberg BJJ (2004). Rhizoremediation: A Beneficial Plant Microbe Interaction. Mol. Pla. Micr. Inter., 17: 6-15.

Lasat MM (2002). Phytoextraction of Toxic Metals: A Review of Biological Mechanisms. J. Environ. Qual., 31: 109-120.

Leung HM, Ye ZH, Wong MH. (2006). Interactions of Mycorrhizal Fungi with Pteris Vittata (As hyperaccumulator) in As-contaminated soils. Environ. Poll., 139: 1-8.

Li WC, Ye ZH, Wong MH (2010). Metal Mobilization and Production of Short-chain Organic Acids by Rhizosphere Bacteria Associated with a Cd/Zn Hyperaccumulating Plant. Sedum Alfredii. Plant Soil, 326:453–67.

Liao JP, Lin XG, Cao ZH, Shi YQ, Wong MH (2003). Interactions between Arbuscular Mycorrhizae and Heavy Metals Under Sand Culture Experiment. Chemosphere, 50: 847-853.

Lombi E, Zhao FJ, Dunham SJ, Mcgrath SP (2001). Phytoremediation of Heavy Metal-contaminated Soils: Natural Hyperaccumulation versus Chemically Enhanced Phytoextraction. J. Environ. Qual., 30: 1916-1926.

Lopez ML, Peralta-Videa JR, Benitez T, Gardea-Torresdey JL (2005). Enhancement of Lead Uptake by Alfalfa (Medicagosativa) Using EDTA and a Plant Growth Promoter. Chemosphere, 61: 595-98.

Ma Y, Prasad MNV, Rajkumar M, Freitas H (2011a). Plant Growth Promoting Rhizobacteria and Endophytes Accelerate Phytoremediation of Metalliferous Soils. Biotechnol., Adv., 29:248–58.

Madhaiyan M, Poonguzhali S, Sa T (2000). Metal Tolerating Methylotrophic Bacteria Reduces Nickel and Cadmium Toxicity and Promotes Plant Growth of Tomato (Lycopersicon esculentum L.). Chemosphere, 69: 220–8.

Majewska M, Kurek E (2005). Effect of Microbial Activity on Cd Sorption/desorption Processes in Soil Polluted with Various Cd Sources. Geo. Res. Abs. 7: 04332.

Malcova R, Vosatka M, Gryndler M (2003). Effects of Inoculation with Glomus Intraradices on Lead Uptake by Zea Mays L. and Agrostiscapillaris L. Appl. Soil Ecol., 23: 55-67.

Soil Ecosystem and Lithosphere **Pages 70-77**
Edited by: Dr. Abhishek Swami, Dr. Prasann Kumar and Dr. Pawan Kumar 'Bharti'
ISBN: 978-93-88854-50-4
Edition: 2020
Published by: Discovery Publishing House Pvt. Ltd., New Delhi (India)

7 Assessment of Soil Environmental Quality of Vineyards Under Intensive System of Cultivation

Davamani, V*., E. Parameswari, P. Kalaiselvi and M. Kavitha[1]

Introduction

Grapes (*Vitisvinifera*) are one of the most important commercial crops of India which contributes to the maximum share of the export from India to other parts of the world. Area under grape in India is 79.6 thousand hectares with an annual production of 1878.3 thousand metric tonnes (MT). Most of the area of grape cultivation is in Maharashtra, Andhra Pradesh, Kamataka and Tamil Nadu. It is being cultivated in North Indian states as temperate crop. Punjab occupies an area of 777 hectares with annual production of 22,088 MT. Out of total production, 87% is consumed as table grapes while 10% is dried and produced for raisin, 2% for juice and 1% for wine.

Soil conservation plays major role on the sustainable development and preservation of ecosystems and biodiversity. Soil contamination by heavy metals, exposes a risk to the productive capacity and balance of the ecosystems. The soil is exposed to contamination by several anthropic activities, mainly by agriculture. The soil has a diverse heavy metal concentration that is dependent on the parent material on which it is formed, formation processes, composition, proportion of components of the solid phase. This concentration may be affected by several anthropic activities such as: irrigation, fertilizer, chemical applications, and industrial or urban sewage incorporation. The soil type, topography, geology and the erosive processes influence the concentration and distribution of heavy metals in the environment, including their bioavailability.

Need for the Study of Soil Health

Soil is a dynamic living system. The overdose of chemical pesticides retains the residue in soil. Pesticides may reach the soil through direct application (or) incorporation to soil. Excessive use of chemicals has put forth question mark on sustainability of Agriculture by contaminating the soil, there by

Dept. of Environmental Sciences, Tamil Nadu Agricultural University, Coimbatore, India
1 Horticultural College &Research institute,Tamil Nadu Agricultural University, Coimbatore, India

declining food quality (Van *et.al.,* 2007). About 60-70% of total production of seed less grapes are produced in Nasik district. Out of 10-12 metric tons of grapes produced every year, the export rate tunes only to 1% due to excess application of pesticides, which declines quality of grapes. However, heavy metal accumulation in agriculture soil is a major environmental problem that can affect plant productivity, food quality and human health.

Fungicide Usage in Vine Yard

Most of the vine yard farmers are using various types of pesticides viz. Copper Oxy Chloride (COC), Bordeaux mixture, Prophenofos, Methomil, Penthoate, Alphamethrin, Imidachlorpid, Acephate, Pyraclostrobin, Azoxystrobin, Mancozeb, Hexaconzole, Terpeuconayole and Tetraconayole to the vineyards. These pesticides contain Arsenic, Copper, Zinc, Manganese, Lead and Mercury which readily persists long in the soil. They may be leached out by water, wind, erosion.

There are currently 47 different fungicides (active ingredients) registered for use in vineyards, representing 40% of the total number of the fungicide registered for use in viticulture. Most of the fungicides registered for use in viticulture are used to control downy mildew and powdery mildew (AWRI, 2010). The chemicals used are inorganic copper compounds, $Cuso_4$, COC, Copper hydroxide, Copper ammonium acetate, Copper oxide), Triazole groups (Fluslazole, Hexaconazole, Muclobutanil, Perconayole, Ttebuconayole, Tetraconazole, Triadomefone, Triademenol) Dithiocarbonate (Mancozeb, Metriam, Propineb, Thiram, Zineb, Ziram), Carboximide, Pyrimidine (Cyprodinl, Fenarimol, Pyrimetanil), Amide, Quinone/ Quinoline (Dithianon, Qunoxyfen), Benzamidayole (Carbendazim), Chloronitrile (Chlorothalonil), Hydrazide (Oxadixyl), Morphine (Dimetomorph), Phenylpyrole and Phtalamide (Captan).

Thus preventative fungicide application was widely considered to offer the best insurance in protection against fungal infection. In grapevine, this tends to involve applying around 4-6 preventative fungicide applications during foliage growth. Copper based compounds to control downy mildew and sulphur to control powdery mildew have been in use since the mid to late 1800's and still widely used. Historically, Cu was applied as a mixture of copper sulphate and lime (Bordeaux mixture). Cu and sulphur are contact fungicide with multisite activity and applied at a high rate up to 50 kg/ha/yr. For instance, a recent survey of vineyards in 10 different regions of Australia was found that mean Cu usage was 5-13 kg/ha/yr. (AWRI, 2010).

During the 1970's, systemic fungicide with greater activity and more specific modes of action were introduced and these are able to stop fungal development. Recently different natural fungicide products are available. e.g. Beneficial micro-organisms, biosurfactant, phosphoric acid, clay preparation, cow's milk. In most cases, their effectiveness has not been fully demonstrated. In 2001, agrochemical usage data was collected in a major dairy and horticultural production region in Northern Victoria, Australia. Analysing the available data, it was found that sulphur accounted for over 90%, Cu (54%), Mancozeb (70%).

Accumulation of Fungicide in Soil

The two most commonly used inorganic fungicides, Cu, S are elements and thus do not breakdown in the environment. It is generally considered that microbial degradation is the most significant degradation mechanism.

Organic fungicide persists for varying lengths of time in the environment which is often expressed in terms of their expected half-life. Both inorganic and organic fungicide compound can be strongly bound within soil. Cu being a divalent cation, binds strongly to inorganic and organic material in the soil and known to accumulate in soils.

The environmental availability of fungicides in soil is related to the extend and type of the adsorption and desorption process. Copper binds strongly to negatively charged sites on inorganic mineral constituents in soil with specific adsorption to Fe, Al, Mn oxides. Specifically, adsorbed Cu is easily released and is considered to be inert and not biologically available. Soil organisms release organically bound Cu as they utilize organic matter for nutrition and also modify the chemistry of the surrounding soil. For example, by changing pH ionic strength, macronutrient, cation concentration and excreting organic ligands.

Chemicals that are adsorbed in soil are likely to persist for longer periods of time due to their decreased availability for microbial degradation. Chemicals with half-life less than 30 days are considered tohave low persistence in soil, half-life between 30-100 days have moderately persistence and >100 days have high persistence in soils.

Impact of Used Agrochemicals on Soil Quality

Soil degradation refers to the process that cause a reduction in its capacity to produce goods (eg: crop fodder for livestock production) and services. It results in land becoming less useful and productive. Estimate indicate that 38% of the land cultivated in the world has been damaged to some degree by post agricultural practices. Soil can be degraded by salting, water logging, compaction, pesticide contamination, decline in soil structure quality, loss of fertility and erosion.

Agrochemicals are used in agriculture setting in an effort to ensure an abundant food supply. These are largely associated with increased yields of plants and animal crops and less spoilage during storage. Extensive application of external agriculture inputs to agriculture production systems leads to soil quality degradation. Organic pollutants (carbon based) that impact soil quality include pesticides. Pesticides which are persistent insoil, slowly break down and result in source of contamination.

There are many ways in which a insecticides reaches the soils and are more risky in the soils as a result of their residues. Therefore, continues and heavy application of these agrochemicals and other soil amendments can potentially exacerbate the accumulation of heavy metals in agricultural soils.

Need for the Study of Trace Metals in Soil

Currently extensive use of inorganic fertilizers and indiscriminate use of pesticides are adopted for increased fruit production to meet the higher demands for human consumption. Large quantities of fertilizers are regularly added to soils in intensive farming system to provide adequate N,P, K which increases the mineral contents of soil and plant tissues. The chemical compounds contain trace amounts of heavy metals (eg. Cd & Pb) as impurities some heavy metals are needed in trace amounts as Zn, Cu, Mn and Fe for plants.

Soil is an important compartments of the environment in which anthropogenic loading of trace metals puts ecosystems and their inhabitants at a health risk. Accumulation of trace metals in soils has potential to restrain the soil functions, cause toxicity to plants and enter the food chain. Cultivation may cause soil contamination by heavy metals, specifically copper in vineyard areas. High concentration of these metals in the agriculture ecosystem may lead to an excessive accumulation of metals which may be toxic to plants and cause possible health problems to animals and human.

Copper Contamination in Soil

Copper is one of the major toxic metals and a highly reactive one elevated levels of Cu in agriculture soils result from the use of Cu containing compounds to control blast disease. The application may lead to Cu toxicity. Copper based preparation has been used for over 200 years. Their use becomes widespread after the accidental discovery of a Bordeaux mixture in 1880.

Copper occurs in the earth crust at concentrations between 25-75 mg kg^{-1}. In soils, it is present as organic matter, oxides and minerals that readily release copper ions under acidic conditions.In soil solution, copper can occur ionic or non-ionic form and exchangeable form. Long term use of fungicides increases copper level even in the lower soil layers. Cu^{2+} is the dominant form of copper in a soil solution with a pH value below 6.9. Copper concentration in calcareous soils are low. Copper accumulates in the upper soil layers and bound to clay particles (Van Zwieten *et.al.,* 2007).

Copper positively influences micro and macro nutrient content and it intake. Increased N & P levels negatively affect Cu availability in soils. The resulting Cu deficiency hinder Ca transports to upper plant parts excessive Cu amounts negatively affect Fe reception & Fe deficiency can lead to Cu toxicity in plants.

In Tamil Nadu, the soil available nitrogen status is low. The increase in available nitrogen content of the soil under poplar based agroforestry systems was attributed to addition of organic matter in soil in the form of litter fall and fine root biomass and the mineralization of organic matter released nutrient into the soil.

Available phosphorus was high under kapok plantation and was very low in the nearby agricultural lands and might be due to addition of litter components and decomposition led to increase in available phosphorus content in the soil under plantation. The present investigation was in conformity with Basavaraja *et.al.* (2007) who observed the available phosphorus status of soil in ten years old plantation of Prosopisjulifloraas compared with barren land in which available phosphorus increased from 20.0 kg ha^{-1} to 26.3 kg ha^{-1}.

The soil fertility rating classes calculated based on nutrient index value, which indicates the organic carbon status. It was adequate in surface soil and marginal in subsurface soil. This might be due to continuous accumulation of litter and decomposition of organic matter. Low and very low fertility rating was noticed for available nitrogen status in surface and subsurface soil respectively. With regard to available phosphorus, the results showed very high status at both the depths which might be due to neutral pH which might have favoured the availability. Very high available potassium status in surface soil and marginal in subsurface soil might be attributed to the fact that the soil would have contained higher percentage of illitic clay and also due to genesis of soil

It was determined that Cu concentration are always greatest at the surface due to retention on the soil sorption complex and their concentration decreases with increasing depth, confirm the anthropogenic orgin of Cu in vineyard soil. In temperate climate, copper does not penetrate below the first 20-30 cm of the vineyard soil profile. Higher levels of 26-199 mg Cu Kg^{-1} found in calcareous in China were attributed to irrigation with mine waste water and smelting operations. The average global concentration of soil Cu is 30mgKg^{-1} and this should never exceed the limits of 50 mg kg^{-1}.

Fractionation and Bioavailability of Copper in Soils

The concepts of "Bio-availability" and "Bio-accessibility" were introduced to express whether the actual concentration of a toxic element would have effects on organisms. Trace element mobility and bioavailability is determined by their transfer between the soil solid phase and the potentially toxic liable fraction. Water soluble and exchangeable copper fractions are considered to be bio available Cu complexed with oxide, carbonate and organic matter are potentially bioavailable fractions and mineral fraction is non available.

Metal speciation is one of the most important properties that determine the behaviour and toxicity of the metals in environment. Chemical specification of an element refers to its specific form characterized by a different isotopic composition, molecular structure and electronic or oxidation state.

Copper availability in soil depends on soil pH, redox potential, cation exchange capacity, amount and nature of organic matter and soil minerals. Soil pH determines aqueous metal specification, affecting metal sorption and desorption of the solid phase. Plants may directly decrease copper bioavailability near roots by recreation of metal binding compounds that can complex the free cupric ions.

Copper Toxicity

The higher concentration of Cu is usually found in root tissues approximately, 70% of the total leaf Cu content is located in chloroplast. Prior to being used as fungicide and micronutrients copper was used as herbicide. Copper ions are toxic to all plant cells and used in specific dosage to avoid tissue damage of the plants.

Copper toxicity inhibits plant growth and to interfere with important cellular process such as photosynthesis and respiration,therefore plants grown in excessive levels of Cu shows reduced biomass and symptoms of chlorosis. Copper toxicity is seen in acidic soils where Cu is not tightly bound to soil particles and thus more available to plants. Excess of Cu alter nitrogen metabolism in grapevines and enzyme activity reduced. Cu accumulation in soil have a phytotoxic effect on grapevines. Symptoms of phytotoxicity appears, when average plant-copper concentration of 15 to 25 mg g^{-1} dry weight exceeded.

Heavy Metal Accumulation in Soil

Since 90's heavy metals pollution turns out to be a problem in some major viticulture regions. Comparative studies were done in region of brestnik-plodiv (Sd, Cr, Pb, Zn) into the soil. The heavy metals could accumulate in the soil and contaminate agriculture products with the food chain, the heavy metal pollutants gets into the human body. It results in the body chronic poisoning and damage to human health potentially. So that it is very important to strengthen the monitoring on the environment quality at the production bases of agricultural products from heavy metal pollution.

In China,the administration has issued a series of national and divisions standards for nuisance free and green agricultural products to provide criteria on testing the environmental quality of producing area. The contents of soil heavy metals in the agricultural land are the important indicators.

The copper sulphate actually used for Bordeaux mixture preparation in Brazil vineyards studies plot contain Zn-1309 mg kg-1, Pb-95 mg kg^{-1}, Cr-19 mg kg^{-1}, Ni -10 mg kg^{-1} , Cd-1.4 mg kg^{-1}. Municipal solid waste or any other compost which could contributes to vineyards metal contamination.

The heavy metal pollution studied in the Breastavineyard, should that among there heavy metals, Cd and Cr are highly toxic, while Pb is moderately toxic and Zn, Mn, Cu are essential elements and micronutrients. The ranking order of occurence of the heavy metals in vineyard soil was Mn>Zn>Cr>Pb>Co >Cd, indicating that Mn followed by Zn was in maximum concentration ad Cd minimum concentration.The soil profile from Breastavineyards, on the depth of 0-29 cm depth,for a soil pH of 6.04, the highest values are observed for Cu-66.5 ppm, Zn-72.5 ppm, Ni-7.5 ppm, Mn-261ppm, Cr-57.5 ppm, Cd-0.701 ppm. Humus has the highest value of 3.44 %. On the depth of 62-83 cm, 83-110 cm, 110-150 cm, the pH increase from 6.23 to 8.3, amount of Cu decrease from 17.5 ppm to 15.3 ppm, Mn from 217.5 to 164.5 ppm, Cd-0.654 -0.35 ppm.Also noticed that decrease in Zn content. Zinc mobility decrease with increasing pH and P contents due to the formation of Zn_3 $(Po_4)_2$ insoluble.

Regarding the content of Zn, Pb, Co, Ni, Cr values decrease from 29-40 cm to 40-62 cm depth and for 62-83 cm contents of these elements are higher , except Co which records the lowest values for Zn, Pb, Co, Mn, Cd, it is observed that the content of these metals are higher on the depth of 110-115 cm compared with the previous depth. The analysed result of the soil samples from the plain of Alasehir, Turkey shows that Cd was more concentration in upper soil layers and its mobility was more than that of Pb & Cu.

Cobalt pollution was determined as 23.1% of soils in 0-30 cm and 53.8% of the soils in 30-60 cm were contaminated. Additional to agricultural and industrial practices, that may cause pollution in the soils, the distance between agricultural areas and the highways are linked to the soil pollution in terms of Cd, Pb, Ni concentration.The source of Pb pollution can the use of phosphorus fertilizers, pb containing fuel and transmitted with air movements.

Heavy Metals in the Irrigation Water

The irrigation water samples analysed at a Ningbo vineyard, China shows that Hg could be that first potential heavy metal pollutants with a 73% of sharing rate. The concentration of Hg ($8.5 \times 10^{5)}$ dominated the index level of irrigation water. The concentration of heavy metals in the irrigation water are Cr-$1.1 \times 10^{-}3$, As-2.6×10^{-6}, Pb-5.9×10^{4}.

Environmental Fate

Whilst a farmers objective is to apply fungicides to the agricultural crops/ plant, inevitably a proportion of the chemical spray will miss its target. Much of the lost chemical will enter the soil surface where it will persist for a period of time and potentially migrate off-site due to leaching and / or runoff. In addition, some of the agrochemicals applied on farm will migrate offsite due to aerial drift. Once agrochemicals have migrate off–site they can potentially enter nearby waterways and ground water resource where they can cause adverse effects to aquatic organisms.

The fate and behaviour of agrochemicals including fungicides in the environment is influenced by the properties of the chemicals e.g.; ability to bind to soil, susceptibility to degradation and environmental factors (eg) : Soil type, rainfall, topography, agricultural management practices.

Impact on Soil Beneficial Organisms

Soil microorganisms play a key role in soil. They are essential for maintenance of soil structure, transformation and mineralization of organic matter, making nutrients available for plants. External agricultural inputs such as mineral fertilizers, organic amendments, microbial inoculants and pesticides are applied with the ultimate goal of maximizing productivity and economic returns, while side effects on soil organisms are often neglected.

The microorganisms of soil are more spoiled by soil disturbance by application of chemicals than any other parameters. The communities of beneficial microorganisms in soil have declined due to overuse of pesticides, which has a negative impact on the available nitrogen, phosphorus and potassium (NPK) from soil, there by degrading the soil quality. Fungicides generally had even greater effects on soil organisms than herbicides (or) insecticides. As these chemicals are applied to control fungal disease. Copper based fungicides were found to have very significant negative effect, which caused long term reductions of earthworm population in soil. Organophosphate insecticides had a range of soil enzymes as well as reduction in collembolan density and earthworm reproduction.

Conclusion

Long term application of P fertilizers and pesticides are likely sources of heavy metals in agricultural soils. Development and adoption of plan/policy is needed to check and reduce the metal concentration, their contamination in vineyard soils and transfer to crop plants which could defend our environment from pollution and thus peril to health of human can be minimized.

REFERENCES

AWRI, (Australian Wine Research Institute), 2010. E- news.

Basavaraja, P.K., S.D. Sharma, M.S. Badrinath, S. Sridhara and G.R. Hareesh. (2007). Prosopisjuliflora – An Efficient Tree Species for Reclamation of Salt Affected Soils. Karnataka Journal ofAgricultural Sciences 20(4): 727 731.

Valladares, G.S., O.A.D.Camargo; J.R.P.D. Carvalho; A.M.C. Silva. 2009. Assessment of Heavy Metals in Soils of a Vineyard Region with the Use of Principal Component Analysis. Sci. Agric. 66 (3) p.361-367.

Van Zwieten, M. Stovold, G. and Van Zwieten, L. (2007). Literature Review and Inventory of Alternatives to Copper: for Disease Control in the Australian Organic Industry (Publication no. 07/110). Rural Industries Research and Development Corporation (RIRDC). ISBN 1 74151 507 6. Kingston, ACT, Australia.

Soil Ecosystem and Lithosphere **Pages 78-95**
Edited by: Dr. Abhishek Swami, Dr. Prasann Kumar and Dr. Pawan Kumar 'Bharti'
ISBN: 978-93-88854-50-4
Edition: 2020
Published by: Discovery Publishing House Pvt. Ltd., New Delhi (India)

8

Forecasting Productivity Losses Cost by Sheet and Rill Erosion

A Case Study of Nigeria

[1]Ezeaku, P. I. and [2]Ofem, K. I

ABSTRACT

The future of the environment and particularly, agriculture for food security is bleak without proper erosion control measures. Increased degradation and declining fertility of soils in the sub Saharan Africa and more specifically, Nigeria contributes to food insecurity and poverty. However, the recognition of the role of economics in soil productivity at farm, national and global levels have not been given the recognition they deserve while attending to food insecurity, perhaps due to the difficulty in data collection as well as the economics of soil losses. Soil productivity losses however, goes beyond the scope of 'soil volume loss through erosion' and is not limited to the contribution of soil nutrients alone. It includes soil structure, water holding capacity, nutrient exchange capacity, acidity and more. Though not easily noticed at farm level, sheet and rill erosions are the primary enemies of farmers. They go on 'un-noticed', causing latent damages to crops and indirectly depriving farmers of the benefits they deserve at the end of a farming season. Forecasting productivity losses likely to result from sheet and rill erosions at the planning stage of farm budgeting and putting up measures to limit such losses is the way forward, if food security issues must be tackled. This may be achieved by quantification and estimation of soil and nutrient losses by sheet and rill erosions, as well as estimating the cost of productivity loss of crops due to erosion. This way, the farmers may put up soil management or conservative measures to curb the forecasted losses.

Introduction

Local geology and its interaction with climate variables determine the nature and type of soil that occurin an area. The geological characteristics of principal importance in this respect are mineralogical composition of the bed rock which determines its chemical stability under different climate regimes. The structure of the rock mass, such as the distribution of discontinuities; bedding

1 Department of Soil Science and Land Resources Management, University of Nigeria, Nsukka, Nigeria
2 Department of Soil Science, University of Calabar, Nigeria

planes, joints and faults determines the ease by which weathering agents can gain access to the rock mass to initiate the weathering process. In a study on the assessment of soil vulnerability to erosion in Cross River State, NEWMAP (2018) identified geology as the major link to extent and severity of erosion development, with sandstone derived soils topping the chat in the central part of the state. Unfortunately, this rock type dominates the geology of Cross River State thus affecting food security and sustainable land management of Sub-Saharan Africa at large and indeed the tropical humid areas and facilitating the resource loss leadingto degradation of the ecosystem.

The increased degradation and declining fertility of these soils contributes to food insecurity and poverty. However, the recognition of the role of economics in soil productivity at farm, national and global levels have not been given the recognition they deserve while attending to food insecurity, perhaps due to the difficulty in data collection as well as the economics of soil losses. The concept of soil productivity losses goes beyond the scope of 'soil volume loss through erosion' and is not limited to the contribution of soil nutrients alone. It includes soil structure, water holding capacity, nutrient exchange capacity and acidity. Conventional economic analyses of soil productivity begins with the interaction between components of the agro ecosystem and soil fertility (FAO, 2001).

Initial erosion prediction technology began with the ideas and concepts described by Cook (1936) in the 1930's. Zingg (1940) was among the first to propose an erosion equation for use in conservation planning. His equation related soil loss by sheet and rill erosion to slope length and steepness. Sooner, Smith and Whitt (1947) added other factors reflecting the effect of cover, management, and supporting practices to Zingg's basic equation. The USLE was developed by Wischmeier and his associates from an empirical analysis of a large mass of data collected from erosion plots at over 40 locations across eastern US (Wischmeier and Smith, 1978). Erosion prediction technology proceeds along two fronts; current empirically based erosion prediction technology, like the WEQ for erosion by wind and the USLE for sheet and rill erosion by water (Hagen and Foster, 1990). However, soil erosion in the European Union was estimated using the latest state-of-the-art soil erosion model, RUSLE 2015 (Panagos *et.al.*, 2015) which is based on the principle of RUSLE model.

Rill and sheet erosion are most prominent forms of soil erosion in the tropics (Yaro *et.al.*, 2015). Sheet erosion is gradual and affects only the upper part of the soil profile but covers larger areas (Alfsen *et.al.*, 1996). Loss of the nutrient rich surface layer has a direct detrimental impact on site and crop productivity (Lemma *et.al.*, 2017) and on off-site sedimentation and nutrient inputs (Soil Survey Division Staff, 2017). Water erosion has been described as a critical environmental problem (Ma *et.al.*, 2014, Schonbrod-stitt *et.al.*, 2013

& Wei *et.al.*, 2007) that results from the removal of soil material by flowing water, including the detachment of soil material by the impact of raindrops. Four kinds of accelerated water erosion are commonly recognized; sheet, rill, gully and tunnel (SSDS, 2017). However, it occurs mainly in the form of sheet, rill and gully erosion (Morgan, 2005, Le Roux *et.al.*, 2008). Sheet erosion is the removal of soil from an area without the development of conspicuous water channels. The channels are tiny, numerous, and unstable. It is less apparent in its early stages and can be a problem for soils that have slope gradient of 1-2% and worsens as slope gradient increases. On the other hand, rill erosion involves the removal of soil as concentrated run off cuts creating many small but conspicuous channels (Haile & Fetene, 2012). It is intermediate in degree between sheet and gully erosion. The channels are shallow enough to be obliterated by tillage.

Soil loss through sheet and rill erosion is difficult to assess because of variability in soil loss within an area and the problem of measuring something that is not there. Sheet and rill erosion greatly reduces productivity (Aldrick *et.al.*, 1988). The most fertile top soil is stripped off by the forces of erosion, reducing nutrients availability; especially organic matter and subsequently productivity. Soil erosion caused by rainfall and runoff is recognized as a major environmental problem in Sub-Saharan Africa (Lu *et.al.*, 2001). Suspended sediment concentrations in streams affect water use and ecosystem health. High concentrations of sediment reduce stream clarity, inhibit respiration and feeding of stream biota, diminish light needed for plant photosynthesis, and require treatment for human water use. To minimize the decline of soil productivity and water quality, spatially distributed patterns of the hazard sources and associated soil loss rate, it is essential to identify crucial areas appropriate for more detailed investigations, such as forecasting productivity losses cost due to sheet and rill erosion; hence the present study.

Need for the Forecast and Assessment of Productivity Losses Cost in Nigeria

Soil properties are strongly influenced by soil management systems and changes in land use pattern, and may in turn affect the level of agricultural land productivity and the rate of loss of soil materials. Nigeriais known for its rich agricultural potential and cultural heritage, and farmers practice agriculture at various scales from which food crops like Yam, Rice, Cassava, Millet, Maize etc; and cash crops like Oil palm, Rubber, Cocoa and Gmelina are successfully grown. However, not so much priority has been given to the soils on which its inhabitants and neighboring countries depend for food. The continuous cultivation of the soils without appropriate management measures has exposed it to fertility as well as physical degradation resulting in low nutrient fertility and multiple nutrient deficiencies which accompany high sediment loss in the area (Iwara, 2014; Ofem, 2014). Furthermore, the population of Nigeria and indeed Sub Saharan Africa increases geometrically, making it difficult for the food produced to sustain the populace. This has caused the farmers to practice continuous cropping to ensure food security or meet up with the increasing demand. This has brought about the mining and exhaustion of soil nutrients in the high rainfall region. It is therefore imperative to evaluate the cost of productivity losses due to sheet and rill erosion in the area.

Economic Effects of Soil Erosion in Africa

A comparative national economic effects of soil erosion in Africa is presented in Table 8.1. It uses gross annual immediate loss, which considers only the economic value of production lost in the same year in which degradation takes place; gross discounted future loss, which includes the future stream of economic losses due to a given year's degradation; and gross discounted cumulative loss, which measures the full economic losses over time stemming from accumulating soil degradation (FAO, 2001). National economic losses are substantial and warrant an address of the problem. The problem is acute in some countries (E.g. Ethiopia) and has led to damage in a significant proportion of agricultural GDP.

Table 8.1: Comparative National Economic Effects of Soil Erosion in Africa

Country	Gross annual immediate loss		Gross discounted future loss		Gross discounted cumulative loss	
	US$ million	% Ag. GDP	US$ million	% Ag. GDP	US$ million	% Ag. GDP
Ethiopia	130	4	22	<1	2431	36
Ghana	166.4	5				
Madagascar	4.9-7.6	<1				
Mali	2.9-11.6	<1	19.3-6.6	4		
South Africa	18	<1	173	4	503	<1
Zimbabwe	117	9				

Source: FAO, 2001

Methods of Forecasting Productivity Losses Cost Due to Sheet and Rill Erosion

Method 1

Quantification of soil lost by rill erosion: The perspective of Lemma *et.al.*, 2017

Eight rigidly selected transect walks, 200 m apart were made along a contour. The rigidly selected transects included cultivated lands from twelve land types.Rill erosion was identified with weekly field visits in the months of peak rainfall. Rill erosion dimensions within transects (length, width and depth) were measured to estimate the volume of soil lost. The length of a rill was measured from its starting point up to the point of sedimentation. Furthermore, the width and depth were also measured at three different points along the length of each rill (upslope, midslope and down slope) and then the average was taken. Finally, rill volume, rill density, rill texture, soil loss and actual area damaged were determined after Getachew (2009).

Volume of soil loss (m^3) = 1.57 × width × depth × length; 1.57 = Π/2

Mass of soil loss by rills (t/ha/yr) = vol. of rill (m^3) × Bulk density (t/m^3)

Field size (ha)

$$\text{Damage area of total field size } (m^2/\text{ha}) = \frac{\text{width of rill (m)} \times \text{length of rill (m)}}{\text{Field size (ha)}}$$

Estimation of Nutrient Lost by Rill Erosion

The nutrients lost by rill erosion were analyzed through soil samples from the rills' side at soil depth equal to rills' depth. To estimate soil nutrient lost through rill erosion, the main soil nutrients were analyzed from the measured rills in the sampled cultivated area. Accordingly, representative disturbed composite soil samples were collected from each land type at 0–20 cm depth. Analysis of the soil nutrients helped to determine the amount of nutrients available in thesoil lost due to rill erosion. Bulk density was used as a multiplier to determine weight of soil lost (*t*/ha/yr) from volume of soil lost (m^3/ha).

$$\text{Nutrient loss (kg)} = \frac{\text{Soil loss (kg/ha/yr)} \times \text{\% of nutrient content of the soil} \times \text{field size (ha)}}{\text{Content of nutrient in 100 kg of fertilizer (kg)}}$$

$$\text{Cost estimation (\$)} = \frac{\text{Nutrient loss (kg)} \times \text{current cost of fertilizer (\$)}}{\text{Content of nutrient in 100 kg of fertilizer (kg)}}$$

Method 2

A simplified version of the Revised Universal Soil Loss Equation (RUSLE) was selected. Application of the RUSLE affords the following advantages:

1. It requires a modest amount of parameters that can be derived;
2. Used in conjunction with raster-based GIS, the RUSLE predicts erosion potential on a cell by cell basis for mapping spatial patterns;
3. The factor-based nature of the RUSLE allows easy analysis of the role of individual factors in contributing to the estimated erosion rate.

A similar approach has been applied by Rosewell (1996). Furthermore, seasonal patterns of rainfall and cover factors have been incorporated by Rosewell (1997) who also suggested these parameters for more accurate distinction of the pattern of soil erosion while Lu *et.al.* (2001) presented a spatial modelling framework designed for the Australian continent hillslope for sheet and rill erosion prediction.

Data and materials used to generate the RUSLE variables include:

1. Advanced Very High Resolution Radiometer to derive Normalized Difference Vegetation Index data,
2. 30 years of daily rainfall data obtained from appropriate Meteorological Agency,
3. National soil attributes maps or its generation through the collection of samples and analyses,
4. 1 km or less resolution of the landuse map of the area under coverage or its generation by the use of GIS techniques,
5. Digital elevation model (DEM) of the area or locally available higher resolution DEMs.

Methodology

The RUSLE calculates mean annual soil loss (Y) (t $ha^{-1}yr^{-1}$) as a product of six factors: rainfall erosivity factor (R), soil erodibility factor (K), hillslope length factor (L), hillslope gradient factor (S), ground cover factor (C) and supporting practice factor (P):

$$Y = R\,K\,L\,S\,C\,P \qquad ...(1)$$

Some of the above factors, especially K, L and S are likely to vary across an area. Using available spatial information for each factor provides a means for estimating the spatial patterns of sheet and rill erosion while the supporting practice factor (P) is excludeddue to lack of spatial data of contour cultivation and bank systems (Lu *et.al.* 2001).

The precise form of each factor is based on soil loss measurements on hillslope plots. Limited plot scale measurements of erosion have been undertaken in other parts of the world (Edwards, 1987; McIvor *et.al.*, 1995; Scanlan *et.al.*, 1996) while Yusuf *et.al.* (2016) used a rainfall simulated setting in parts of Nigeria which used factors in USLE. The application of such simulation had earlier been mentioned by Morgan(1986) while limited plots studies were first established in 1915 by the Forest Service in Utah, United States (Moldenhauer and Foster, 1981) and have since then been extensively used.

Mean annual values for rainfall erosivity and the cover factor are often used in direct application of the equation below to calculate mean annual hillslope erosion. To adequately represent the erosive potential of rainfall for each temporally distinctive period, Lu *et.al.* (2001)recommends the RUSLE model on a monthly averaged basis by calculating appropriate erosivity and cover factors for each month. The modifications of the equation below discussed above yield monthly soil loss rate which can be calculated as:

$$Yj = R_jKLSC_j$$

Where, Cj = , R_j and SLR_j are cover management factor, rainfall erosivity and the soil loss ratio, respectively for month *j*.

Rainfall Erosivity (R)

Rainfall erosivity (R) is defined as the mean annual sum of individual storm erosion index values, EI_{30}, where E is the total storm kinetic energy and I_{30} is the maximum rainfall intensity in 30 minutes. To compute storm EI_{30}, continuous rainfall intensity data are needed. This may be obtained via rainfall simulation. Wischmeier and Smith (1978) recommended that at least 20 years of rainfall data be used to accommodate natural climatic variations.

Yu and Rosewell (1996), and Yu (1998) proposed a rainfall erosivity model in which storm $EI_{30}$for the month *j* is related to daily rainfall amount, R_d, in the form:

$$EI_{30}(j) = \alpha\{1 + \eta \cos(2\Pi f j\text{-}w)\}$$

where Rd is the daily rainfall amount, Ro is the threshold rainfall amount to generate runoff set to 12.7 mm (Wischmeier and Smith, 1978), and N is the number of days with rainfall amount in excess of Ro in the month. The first part of the equation is a sinusoidal function with a wavelength of twelve months ($f = 1/12$). It is used to describe the seasonal variation of rainfall erosivity for agiven amount of daily rainfall. The parameter w is set at $\Pi/6$, implying that for a given amount of daily rainfall the corresponding rainfall erosivity is the highest in January, when the temperature is the highest for most part of the continent. Regional relationships were derived for parameters: α, β and η:

$$\alpha = 0.395\,\{1 + 0.098 \exp(3.26\psi/M)\}$$

$$\beta = 1.49$$

$$\eta = 0.29$$

where M is the mean annual rainfall and ψ is the mean summer rainfall.

20 years of gridded daily rainfall may be used. For instance, from 1st of January, 1999 to 31st of December, 2019. The ratio ψ/M may be calculated using the same daily rainfall data. The resulting calculated rainfall erosivities are the mean annual R factor (averaged annual EI_{30}), and mean monthly R factors for the 20 year period.

For parts of the tropics, predicted monthly R factor distributions change gradually from summer dominance to uniform, which is comparable with rainfall intensity distribution of Africa (Bureau of Meteorology, 1989; Yu and Rosewell, 1996; Yu, 1998). Quantitative assessment of the monthly distribution of R factor is technically challenging as many previously existing R factors were calculated using short periods of rainfall data. This causes serious bias for monthly distribution of the R factor towards single large storms in the period.

Soil Erodibility (K)

Soil erodibility (K) is a measure of the susceptibility of the soil to erosion. In the RUSLE model, it is a quantitative value determined experimentally. For a particular soil, it is the rate of soil loss per erosion index unit as measured on a unit plot maintained under continuous bare fallow. For satisfactory direct measurement of soil erodibility, erosion from field plots needs to be studied for periods generally well in excess of 5 years (Loch *et.al.*, 1998). This is costly and time-consuming, and data from field studies of adequate duration are available for only a few soils (Loch *et.al.*, 1998). Therefore, considerable attention has been paid to estimate soil erodibility from soil attributes such as particle size distribution, organic matter content and density of eroded soil (Wischmeier *et.al.*, 1971; Loch and Rosewell, 1992).

A modified nomograph equation (Wishmeier *et.al.* 1971) was used to estimate K factor for Australian soils. The soil erodibility surface was been generated using the equation by Loch and Rosewell (1992):

$$K = 2.77\ (100\ P_{125})^{1.14}\ (10^{-7})\ (12 - 2\ O_c) + 3.29\ (10^{-3})\ (Pr - 3)$$

where P_{125} is the percentage of particles with diameter less than 0.125 mm, Oc is organic carbon in percentage, and Pr is the soil permeability rating (Northcote *et.al.* 1960-1968), and a digital polygon coverage of the soil landforms of an area.

It is found, nationally, that heavy clay soils (Vertisols) are highly erodible as they are structurally unstable while soils with high organic matter content are less erodible than those with low organic matter content.

Cover and Crop Management Factor (C)

The cover and crop management factor (C) measures the combined effect of all the interrelated cover and crop management variables. It is defined as the ratio of soil loss from land maintained under specified conditions to the corresponding loss from continuous tilled bare fallow. It is an estimate of the combined effects of prior land use, crop canopy cover, surface cover, surface roughness, and organic material below the soil surface. It is usually expressed as an annual value for a particular cover and crop management system but is calculated from the soil loss ratios for shorter periods of time within which cover and management effects are relatively uniform. The soil loss ratios are combined in proportion to the applicable percentages of erosivity (R) to derive annual C values. At continental scale, deriving the appropriate C values essentially requires accurate estimation of canopy cover and ground cover as they offer very different erosion control protection. The best way to assess cover patterns across a large area is by interpretation of remote sensing data because satellite remote sensing offers the only practical means of continuously and consistently monitoring vegetation cover on a large scale.

Slope Length Factor (L) and Slope Steepness Factor (S)

Slope length factor (L) is defined as the ratio of soil loss from the field slope length to that from a 22.13 meter length under otherwise identical conditions. It represents the increase in storm runoff volume with increasing hillslope length. For cropping land, L is evaluated by the equations used in RUSLE (McCool *et.al.*, 1989; Renard *et.al.*, 1997) with:

$L = (X_h/22.13)^m$, where X_h is the horizontal slope length in meters and m is a variable slope length exponent which is related to the ratio of rill erosion to interrill erosion by the following equation:

$$m = \varepsilon/1 + \varepsilon$$

ε is calculated for conditions when the soil is moderately susceptible to both rill and interrill erosion using the following equation:

where is the slope angle. The slope steepness factor (S) is defined as the ratio of soil loss from the field slope gradient to that from a 9% slope under identical conditions. As it has been shown that the original slope steepness factor of USLE overestimates the soil loss from slopes steeper than 9%, as recommended in SOILOSS, the RUSLE slope steepness equation is used in this study. The equations are:

$S = 10.8^*\ \text{Sin} + 0.03\ \sigma$ less than or equal to 9%

$S = 16.8^*\ \text{Sin} - 0.50\ \sigma$ greater than 9%

Where is the angle of slope and σ is slope gradient in percentage. Previous studies have been conducted and presented on Table 8.2 on the cost estimation of agricultural productivity losses due to erosion while more specific studies on the productivity losses due to water erosion have been conducted and presented on Table 8.3.

Table 8.2: Methodologies for Estimating Costs of Agricultural Productivity Loss Due to Soil Erosion

Methodology	Valuing costs	Studies relevant to estimate of soil erosion cost
Cost–benefit analysis	Cost of soil erosion control measures (conversion arable into forest/pasture, terracing, buffer strips, residue management, cover crops, and conservation tillage)	Posthumus *et.al.* (2015), and Bizoza and de Graaff (2012)
Market price of soil	Commercial price of soil	Robinson *et.al.* (2014) and Panagos *et.al.* (2015
Crop productivity loss	Decreased crop production due to soil erosion	Gunatilake and Vieth (2000), Evans (1996), Enters (1998), Möller and Ranke (2006), this study, and 16 studies in Table 8.2

Replacement cost	Cost of fertilizers (N and P) to replace nutrient loss due to soil erosion	Martínez-Casasnovas and Ramos (2006), Möller and Ranke (2006), Hein (2007), Graves *et.al.* (2015), Dixon *et.al.* (1994), Enters (1998), and Bojo (1996)
Macroeconomic models (computable general equilibrium)	Estimate the cost represented by soil erosion loss in the agricultural sector	Panagos *et.al.* 2016

Source: Panagos *et.al.* 2016

Table 8.3: Studies Estimating the Agricultural Productivity Loss Due to Soil Erosion by Water

Reference	Estimation of crop yield loss due to soil erosion	Comments on estimation method
Lyles, 1975	Productivity loss ~6% per 2.5 cm of soil loss	Experiments in the United States
Pierce *et.al.*, 1983	2–4% productivity loss in case of severe erosion (>25 t ha−1 year−1)	U.S. croplands; NRI survey
Battiston *et.al.* 1987	8% productivity loss due to soil erosion	Corn yield experiments in Ontario
Magrath and Arens, 1989	0–12% annual productivity loss in case of severe erosion	North Central United States experiments
Pimentel *et.al.* 1995	Severe soil erosion by water (rates of higher than 17 t ha−1 year−1) can cause a crop productivity loss of 8% annually.	Review article
Crosson, 1995	Productivity loss to only 0.4% per year (8% productivity loss after 20 years).	Review study based on Pimentel *et.al.* 1995
Lal, 1995	Yield reductions due to severe erosion may range from 2 to 40%, with a mean of 8.2% for the continent.	A review of available data in African plots
Oyedele and Aina (1998)	Maize yield reduction of 10–17% on severely eroded soils	Plot experiments in Africa
Van den Born *et.al.*, 2000	9 % productivity loss for maize and other grains under high erosion risk	Europian union 15 countriesbased on ICONA 1991
De La Rosa*et. al.*,2000	12% reduction on crop productivity will be reached in 2100 with erosion rates of 16 t ha−1 year−1.	Based on results in Andalusia region (Spain)
Bakker *et.al.* (2004)	2.7% yield decrease per decade according to findings in de-surfacing experiments; yield reductions due to soil erosion are around 4.3% per 10 cm of soil lost.	Based on data analysis (field data collection) in Europe

den Biggelaar *et.al.* 2001	Crop productivity based on past plot studies for different crops in all continents, showing negligible effects for erosion rates <2 t ha−1 year−1.	Analysis of soil erosion–productivity experiments
Bakker *et.al.*, 2007	4.9% yield loss in case of 10 cm soil erosion	Based on available water capacity analysis
Montgomery, 2007	Soil loss rates less than 12 t ha−1 year−1 as tolerable for maintain the crop productivity	Based on the U.S. Department of Agriculture values
Larney *et.al.* 2009	Grain yields may fall by 2.1% annually per cm of soil removal	Experiments in Alberta, Canada

Note: NRI = National Resources Inventory
Source: Panagos *et.al.* 2016

Rate of loss in land productivity as established by Panagos *et.al.* 2016 in member states of the European Union is given by:

$$LPLr = SEA_r * 0.08$$

$$TAA_r$$

LPLr = Land productivity loss per member state (%)

r = country's index

SEA = Severe erosion area per MS

TAA = Total agricultural areas per MS

This assumes that the productivity loss is equally distributed across all crop types within MSs and the vulnerability within them is due to different % of severe erosion and total agricultural area.

Once the land productivity loss has been computed using the above equation, crop productivity loss per crop and MS is calculated as

$$CPL_{i,r} = LPL_r * CA_{i,r} * CP_{i,r}$$

where CPL is the crop productivity loss per MS and crop (tonnes), LPL is the land productivity loss estimated using the previous equation, CA is the crop area (ha), and CP is the crop productivity (t/ha). The variables i and r represent the crop and the country indices, respectively.

Finally, the crop productivity loss is multiplied by the market price of each crop, to calculate the overall monetary loss. The results are aggregated per crop type and per MS.

Cost of Productivity Loss of Crops Due to Erosion

Several methods of calculating the economic cost of a given loss of soil have been proposed (World Resources Institute and Tropical Science Center, 1991; Magrath and Arens, 1989; Fox and Dickson, 1988, and Devarajan and Weiner, 1991). Some cost estimates are very narrow and rely on, the replacement cost of nutrients lost while others are based on Hicks' concept of income (Hicks, 1946). Not all loss of soil is necessarily considered at an economic cost under this approach. For instance, if technological development takes place in the economy, some degradation of soil can be allowed without undermining the future consumption level (Alfsen *et.al.*, 1996). In the so-called wealth approach, soil is considered as a form of wealth providing an income stream. The cost of soil erosion is then calculated as the present value of future income loss due to soil degradation.

Sheet and rill erosion are more detrimental toagriculture than gully erosion because of their constant and uniform action which goes on imperceptibly until they finally result in a complete removal of the arable part of the soil (ISDR, 2008). The loss of soil due to water erosion degrades the arable land and eventually renders it unproductive (Pimentel *et.al.*, 1995). It is a threat to soil fertility and productivity (Scherr, 2000) and leads to a drop in potential agricultural productivity (Graves *et.al.*, 2015 and Pimentel, 2006). Soil erosion is the most well-known form of soil degradation (Lal, 2001) and generates on-site costs through loss and decline in fertile land (Colombo & Calatrava-Requena, 2005); however, Garcia-Ruiz *et.al.* (2017) recognized that it is difficult to evaluate the cost due to erosion.

The costs of losses in productivity are presented per crop type in Table 8.4. More than 12 million hectares of agricultural land in the EU (about 7.2% of the total) are potentially severely eroded every year from 2010. Almost 3 million tonnes of wheat and 0.6 million tonnes of maize are estimated to be lost annually due to severe erosion (Table 8.4). The highest productivity loss is found for rice and wheat because they are the most dominant crops in the most erosive areas of Mediterranean countries (Italy, Spain, and Greece) (Panagos *et.al.* 2016). On the other hand, rye has the lowest loss in productivity (0.18%), as it is mostly cultivated in countries with relatively low erosion rates (Germany and Poland). From the foregoing, parts of Nigeria support the cultivation of paddy Rice and is likely to experience similar losses especially as some tropical rainforest areas are underlain by sandstone which is most susceptible to rill and sheet erosion (NEWMAP, 2018).

The total economic loss in agricultural productivity due to severe erosion in the EU was around €1,257 million in 2010, which is about 0.43% of the EU's total agriculture sector contribution to GDP (€292,320 million). In 2001, the European Commission's Directorate-General for Agriculture obtained similar results, estimating the mean on-site effects of soil erosion to be 0.42% of gross agricultural value in 13 countries (Görlach *et.al.*, 2004). Compared to the overall agricultural productivity loss of €1,257 million in EU, soil erosion by water has the highest impact in Italy, with a cost of around €619 million per annum.

Table 8.3: Estimated Annual Productivity Loss Per Crop Using Direct Cost Evaluation (year 2010)

Crop	Total area (1,000 ha)	Actual productivity (1000 t)	Area severely eroded (1000 t)	Crop productivity loss in affected areas (1,000 t)	% of tonnes lost	Price (€/t)	Crop productivity loss (million €)
Maize	15,703.0	111,586	1,124.0	594.4	0.53	220.8	131.222
Barley	24,975.6	110,072	1,152.1	307.6	0.28	221.7	68.199
Rape, turnip rape, and soya	22,786.0	135,877	789.3	380.1	0.28	479.2	182.154
Sun flower	4,285.9	6,956	313.7	37.2	0.53	449.1	16.712
Potatoes	1,797.5	55,271	78.0	143.2	0.26	299.1	42.841
Sugar beets	1,661.0	116,017	50.4	327.2	0.28	43.6	14.265
Rye	2,500.3	9,082	66.6	15.9	0.18	200.5	3.202
Rice	894.0	6,091	191.4	104.6	1.72	362.1	37.883
Pulses	2,036.1	5,243	152.7	29.6	0.57	734.9	21.779
Wheat (All types)	90,647.9	422,883	8,141.3	3,037.7	0.72	243.4	739.365
Total	167,287.3		12,059.6				1,257.622

Source: Panagos *et.al.* 2016

The Case of Ugep: A Communal Agrarian Area in South-South Nigeria

Erosion has been identified to have a significant effect on environmental degradation in Ugep(Yaro *et.al.* 2015). Famesco (1989) attributed high rate of erosion in the tropical rainforest zone of Nigeria to geology, climate and high population density while Chijioke (1992) reported that areas prone to erosion threat are the areas underlain by unconsolidated sediments of quaternary coastal plain sands and weakly consolidated sediments of Tertiary to Cretaceous liquate formations. These descriptions fit appropriately to the Ugep communal agrarian area of Central Cross River State.

Erosivity computations by NEWMAP (2018) showed that the power of rainfall to cause erosion (erosivity) was greatest in the southern zone (Calabar), moderate in the central zone (Ugep) and least in the northern (Ogoja) parts of Cross River State. The mean annual rainfall (MAR) amount in central zone of CRS was 2370 mm with erosivity value of 1299 MJ mm ha^{-1} yr^{-1}. In assessing erosion sites around the state, most devastating conditions were found in the southern zone of the State, with gullies having dimensions of 300 to 600 m long, 8 to 28 m deep and 45 to 50 m wide found mainly in Calabar south, Calabar Municipality and Odukpani LGAs of the State. Few and shallow gullies were found in central and northern zone of CRS and mainly in soils developed on sandstone parent material. Geology was the major factor linked to extent and severity of erosion and gullies development in the state (NEWMAP, 2018). The soil parent materials were Coastal Plain Sands (CPS), Sandstones, and Basement Complex Rocks (BCR) in the southern, central and northern zones, respectively. Findings have attributed variability in vulnerability of the soils to erosion to parent materials, rainfall and other human induced factors, such as unplanned clearing and tilling, building of roads and other infrastructure without recourse to preventing erosion and general deforestation.

Summary and conclusion

Prediction of erosionis a powerful tool that has been used by soil conservationists since 1940's. Most conservation farm planning is done using the empirical Wind Erosion Equation (WEQ) andUniversal Soil Loss Equation (USLE) for sheet and rill erosion. These equations can identify situations where erosion is considered to be excessive and guide the selection of practices that will adequately control erosion. These empirical erosion prediction technologies have important limitations when used to analyze the impact of soil erosion on productivity. New process-based erosion prediction technologies are emerging to replace these empirical technologies. Two efforts, the Wind Erosion Prediction Systems (WEPS) and Water Erosion Prediction project (WEPP), are developing process-based erosion prediction models for wind and water erosion, respectively. These technologies are expected to replace the WEQ and USLE in the future. The USLE has been revised and updated to RUSLE. This effort was led by the USDA-Agricultural Research Service. There is need to examine the economic consequences of the degradation of soil quality. Empirical evidence of the physical relationship between soil quality and crop or livestock productivity links activities detrimental or beneficial to soil quality with consequent changes in crop yields or livestock outputs. These changes can be valued in financial or economic terms.

REFERENCES

Alfsen, K. H., De Franco, M. A, Gloms, S. and Johnsen, T (1996). The cost of soil erosion in Nicaragua. Ecological Economics 16: 129-145.

Bureau of Meteorology (1989). Climate of Australia. AGPS Press, Canberra.

Bakker, M. M., Govers, G. and Rounsevell, M. D. A. (2004). The Crop Productivity–Erosion Relationship: An Analysis Based on Experimental Work. Catena, 57(1), 55–76.

Battiston, L. A., Miller, M. H & Shelton, I. J (1987). Soil Erosion and Corn Yield in Ontario. 1. Field Evaluation. Canadian Journal of Soil Science, 67: 731-745.

Bizoza, A. R. and de Graaff, J. (2012). Financial Cost–benefit Analysis of Bench Terraces in Rwanda. Land Degradation and Development, 23(2), 103–115.

Bojo, J. (1996). The Costs of Land Degradation in Sub-Saharan Africa. Ecological Economics, 16, 161–173.

Chijioke, E. O. (1992). Erosion, the Environment and Rural Development. In: PP. 85-87., Role of Forestry in Stabilizing Fragile Ecosystem, Proceedings of the 21th Annual Conference of the Forestry Association of Nigeria, Uyo, AKS, 7-12 April.

Colombo, S., Hanley, N. and Calatrava-Requena, J. (2005). Designing Policy for Reducing the Off-Farm Effects of Soil Erosion Using Choice Experiments. Journal of Agricultural Economics, 56(1), 81–95.

Crosson, P. (1995). Soil Erosion Estimates and Costs. Science, 269(5223), 461–465.

Den Biggelaar, C., Lal, R., Wiebe, K. and Breneman, V. (2001). The Global Impact of Soil Erosion on Productivity. I: Absolute and Relative Erosion-induced Yield Losses. Advances in Agronomy, 81,1 –48.

De La Rosa, D., Moreno, J. A., Mayol, F. and Bonsón, T. (2000). Assessment of Soil Erosion Vulnerability in Western Europe and Potential Impact on Crop Productivity Due to Loss of Soil Depth Using the Impe1ERO Model. Agriculture, Ecosystems and Environment, 81(3), 179–190.

Devarajan, S. and Weiner, R.J.(1991). Natural Resource Depletion and National Income Accounting. Unpublished Manuscript.

Dixon, J. A., Scura, L. F., Carpenter, R. A. and Sherman, P. B. (1994). Economic Analysis of the Environmental Impacts (2nd ed.). (pp. 224). London: Earthscan Publication Ltd.

Edwards, K. (1987). Runoff and Soil Loss Studies in New South Wales. Technical Handbook No. 10, Soil Conservation Service of NSW, Sydney, NSW.

Enters, T. (1998). Methods for the Economic Assessment of the on- and Offsite Impacts of Soil Erosion. Internat. Board for Soil Research and Management. Issues in Sustainable Land Management no. 2. Bangkok: IBSRAM.

Evans, R. (1996). Soil Erosion and Its Impact in England and Wales. London: Friends of the EarthTrust.

Famesco, T. F. (1989). The Status of Soil Menace in South Eastern Nigeria and Prospects for Control. Biennial Conference of the Ecological Society of Nigeria (ECOSON). Forestry Research Institute of Nigeria, Ibadan, 14-19th August, Pp. 13.

Food and Agriculture Organization (FAO) of the United Nations (2001). The Economics of Soil Productivity in Sub-Saharan Africa. Rome, Pp. 58

Fox, G. and Dickson, E. J.(1988). What's Economic About the Economic Cost of Soil Erosion to Canadian Farmers? Discussion Paper DP88/3, Department of Agricultural Economics and Business, University of Guelph, Guelph, Ontario.

García-Ruiz, J. M., Beguería, S., Lana-Renault, N., Nadal-Romero, E. and Cerdà, A. (2017). Ongoing and Emerging Questions in Water Erosion Studies. Land Degrad. Develop., 28, 5 –21.

Getachew, A. (2009) Soil Erosion Assessment in Agricultural Landscape: The Case of Rekame Catchment, Alaba Woreda, Southern Ethiopia. Thesis, Addis Ababa University.

Graves, A. R., Morris, J., Deeks, L. K., Rickson, R. J., Kibblewhite, M. G., Harris, J. A. and Truckle, I. (2015). The Total Costs of Soil Degradation in England and Wales. Ecological Economics, 119, 399–413.

Gunatilake, H. M and Vieth, G. R. (2000). Estimation of On-site Cost of Soil Erosion: A Comparison of Replacement and Productivity Change Methods. Journal of Soil and Water Conservation, 55(2), 197–204.

Hagen, L. J and Foster, G. R (1990). Soil Erosion Prediction Technology. Soil Erosion and Soil Productivity , 90-118A: 117-135.

Haile, G & Fetene, M. (2012) Assessment of Soil Erosion Hazard in Kilie Catchment, East Shoa, Ethiopia. Land Degrad Dev 23:293–306.

Hein, L. (2007). Assessing the Costs of Land Degradation: A Case Study for the Puentes Catchment, Southeast Spain. Land Degradation and Development, 18, 631–642.

Hicks, J.(1946). Value and Capital. An Inquiry into Some Fundamental Principles of Economic Theory, 2nd edn. Oxford at the Clarendon Press, Oxford.

International Strategy for Disaster Reduction (ISDR) (2008). Disaster Risk Reduction Strategies and Risk Management Practices: Critical Element for Adaptation to Climate Change. Submission to the UNFCCC Adhock Working Group on Long Term Co-operative Action. Accessed at www.unisdr.org/risk - reduction/climate change ISDR paper pdf.

Iwara, A. I. (2014). Evaluation of the Variability in Runoff and Sediment Loss in Successional Fallow Vegetation of Southern Nigeria. Soil & Water Res. 9:77–82.

Lal, R. (2001). Soil Degradation by Erosion. Land Degradation and Development, 12(6), 519–539.

Lemma, B., Kebede, F., Mesfin., S., Fitiwy, I., Abraha, Z and Norgrove, L. (2017). Quantifying Annual Soil and Nutrient Lost by Rill Erosion in Continuously Used Semiarid Farmlands, North Ethiopia. Environment and Earth Science; 76:190 DOI 10.1007/s12665-017-6506

Le Roux, J. J., Morgenthal, T. L, Malherbe J, Pretorius DJ, Sumner P. D. (2008). Water Erosion Prediction at a National Scale for South Africa. Water SA 34:305–314

Loch, R.J. and Rosewell, C.J. (1992). Laboratory Methods for Measurement of Soil Erodibility (K Factors) for the Universial Soil Loss Equation. Australian Journal of Soil Research, 30: 233-48.

Loch, R. J., B. K. Slater, B. K. and Devoil, C. (1998). Soil Erodibility (Km) Values for Some Australian Soils. Australian Journal of Soil Research, 36: 1045-55.

Lu, H., Gallant, J., Prosser, I.P., Moran, C., and Priestley, G. (2001). Prediction of Sheet and Rill Erosion Over the Australian Continent, Incorporating Monthly Soil Loss Distribution. Technical Report 13/01, CSIRO Land and Water, Canberra, Australia.

Lyles, L. (1975). Possible Effects of Wind Erosion on Soil Productivity. Journal of Soil and Water Conservation 30:279- 283.

Magrath, W. and Arens, P.(1989). The Cost of Soil Erosion on Java: A Natural Resource Accounting Approach. Environment Department Working Paper no. 18, The World Bank, Wash- ington D.C.

McCool, D.K., Foster, G.R., Mutchler, C.K., and Meyer, L.D. (1989). Revised Slope Length Factor in the Universal Soil Loss Equation. Transactions of the American Society of Agricultural Engineers, 32: 1571-1576.

McIvor, J.G., Williams, J. and Gardener, C.J. (1995). Pasture Management Influences Runoff and Soil Movement in the Semi-arid Tropics. Australian Journal of Experimental Agriculture, 35: 55-65.

Moldenhauer, W.C. and Foster, G.R. (1981). Empirical Studies of Soil Conservation Techniques and Design Procedures. In Morgan, R.P. C., (ed.), Soil Conservation: Problems and Prospects, Chichester: John Wiley, 13-29.

Morgan, R. P. C. (2005) Soil Erosion and Conservation. In: Predicting Soil Erosion by Water: A Guide to Conservation Planning with the Revised Universal Soil Loss Equation (RUSLE), USDA, Agricultural Handbook No 703. 3rd edn. Blackwell Publishing, Oxford, p. 304

NEWMAP (2018). Assessment of Soil Vulnerability to Erosion in Cross River State, Nigeria. Draft Report by A. U. Akpanidiok, I. C. Idiong, P. B. Okon-Inyang, M. O. Eyong, S. M. Afu and E. E. Aki

Northcote, K.H., Beckmann G.G, Bettenay E., Churchward H.M., van Dijk D.C., Dimmock G.M., Hubble G.D., Isbell R.F., McArthur W.M., Murtha G.G., Nicolls K.D., Paton T.R., Thompson C.H., Webb A. A. and Wright M. J. (1960-68). Atlas of Australian Soils, Sheets 1 to 10, with Explanatory Data. CSIRO and Melbourne University Press: Melbourne. 2017).

Oyedele, D. J., and Aina, P. O. (1998). A Study of Soil Factors in Relation to Erosion and Yield of Maize on a Nigerian Soil. Soil and Tillage Research, 48, 115–125.

Ofem, O. O. and Inyang, B. (2014). Livelihood and Conflict Dimension Among Crop Farmers and Fulani Herdsmen in Yakurr Region of Cross River State. Mediterranean Journal of Social Sciences Rome-Italy. 5(8).

Panagos P., Borrelli, P., Poesen, J., Ballabio, C., Lugato, E., Meusburger, K and Alewell, C (2015).

The New Assessment of Soil Loss by Water Erosion in Europe . Environmental Science and Policy, 54: 438-447.

Panagos P., Borrelli, P., Poesen, J., Meusburger, K., Ballabio, C., Lugato, E. and Alewell, C (2016). Reply to the Comment on 'The new Assessment of Soil Loss by Water Erosion in Europe' by Fiener & Auerswald. Environmental Scienceand Policy, 54: 438-447

Panagos, P., Standardi, G., Borrelli, P., Lugato, E., Montanarella, L. and Bosello, F. (2018). Cost of Agricultural Productivity Loss Due to Soil Erosion in the European Union: From Direct Cost Evaluation Approaches to the Use of Macroeconomic Models. Land Degrad Dev. 1–14. https://doi.org/10.1002/ldr.287914

Pierce, F. J., Larson, W. E., Dowdy, R. H & Graham, W.A.P (1983). Productivity of Soils: Assessing Long Term Changes Due to Erosion. Journal of Soil and Water conservation, 38 (1): 39-44.

Pimentel, D. (2006). Soil Erosion: A Food and Environmental Threat. Environment, Development and Sustainability, 8(1): 119-137.

Pimentel, D., Harvey, C., Resosudarmo, P., Sinclair, K., Kurz, D., McNair, M., Crist, S., Shpritz, L., Fitton, L., Saffouri, R. and Blair, R. (1995). Environmental and Economic Costs of Soil Erosion and Conservation Benefits. Science, 267: 1117-1123.

Posthumus, H., Deeks, L. K., Rickson, R. J. and Quinton, J. N. (2015). Costs and Benefits of Erosion Control Measures in the UK. Soil Use and Management, 31, 16 –33.

Renard, K.G., Foster, G.A., Weesies, D.K., McCool, D.K., and Yoder, D.C. (1997). Predicting Soil Erosion by Water: A Guide to Conservation Planning with the Revised Universal Soil Loss Equation. Agriculture Handbook 703, United States Department of Agriculture, Washington DC.

Robinson, D. A., Fraser, I., Dominati, E. J., Davísdóttir, B., Jónsson, J. O. G., Jones, L and Clothier, B. E. (2014). On the Value of Soil Resources in the Context of Natural Capital and Ecosystem Service Delivery. Soil Science Society of America Journal, 78(3), 685–700.

Rosewell, C.J. (1997). Potential Source of Sediments and Nutrients: Sheet and Rill Erosion and Phosphorus Sources. Australia: State of the Environment Technical Paper Series (Inland Waters), Department of the Environment, Sport and Territories, Canberra.

Scanlan, J.C., Pressland, A.J. and Myles, D.J. (1996). Run-off and Soil Movement on Mid-slopes in North-east Queensland Grazed Areas. Rangeland Journal, 18: 33-46.

Scherr, S. J. (2000). A Downward Spiral? Research Evidence on the Relationship Between Poverty and Natural Resource Degradation. Food Policy, 25(4), 479–498.

Schonbrodt-Stitt, S., Bosch, A., Behrens, T., Hartmann, H., Shi, X and Scholten, T. (2013). Approximation and Spatial Regionalization of Rainfall Erosivity Based on Sparse Data in a Mountainous Catchment of the Yangtze River in Central China. Environ Sci Pollut Res 20:6917–6933.

Soil Science Division Staff (SSDS) (2017). Soil Survey Manual. C. Ditzler, K. Scheffe and H. C. Monger (Eds.). USDA Handbook 18. Government Printing Office, Wasghington, D. C

Smith, D. D. and Whitt, S. M. (1947). Estimating Soil Losses Fiorn Field Areas of Claypan Soil. Soil Science Society of America Proceedings. 12:485-490.

Wischmeier W.H., Johnson, C. B. and Cross, B. V. (1971). A Soil Erodibility Nomograph for Farmland and Construction Sites. Journal of Soil and Water Conservation, 26: 189-183.

Van den Born, G. J., de Haan, B. J., Pearce, D. W., & Howarth, A. (2000). Technical report on Soildegradation in Europe: An Integrated Economic and Environmental Assessment. RIVM Report 481505018. Netherlands: National Institute of Public Health and Environment, RIVM.

Wei, W., Chen, L., Fu, B., Huang, Z., Wu, D. and Gui, L. (2007). The Effect of Land Uses and Rainfall Regimes on Runoff and Soil Erosion in the Semi-arid Loess Hilly Area China. J Hydrol 335:247–258

Wischmeier, W. H. and Smith, D. D. (1978). Predicting Rainfall Erosion Losses: A Guide to Conservation Planning. US Department of Agriculture. Agriculture Handbook No. 537. (US Government Printing Office: Washington, DC).

World Resources Institute and Tropical Science Center(1991). Accounts Overdue. Natural Resource Depreciation in Costa Rica. Washington, DC.

Yaro, M. A., Okon, A. E and Ukpali, E. O (2015). Effects of Environmental Degradation on Residence of Yakurr LGA, Cross River State – Nigeria. International Journal of Science, Environment and Technology, 4(2): 488-500

Yu, B. and Rosewell, C. J. (1996a). An Assessment of a Daily Rainfall Erosivity Model for New South Wales. Australian Journal of Soil Research, 34: 139-52.

Yu, B. and Rosewell, C. J. (1996b). A Robust Estimator of the R-factor for the Universal Soil Loss Equation. Transactions American Society of Agricultural Engineers, 39, 559-61.

Yu, B. (1998). Rainfall Erosivity and its Estimation for Australia's Tropics. Australian Journal of Soil Research, 36, 143-165.

Yusuf, K. O., Omokore, S., Oyebode, O. O. and Adebayo, K. R. (2016). Effect of Vegetative Cover

and Slope on Soil Loss by Erosion Using Rainfall Simulator, Journal of Research in Forestry, Wildlife and Environment Volume 8, No 1: 45-52

Zingg, A. W. (1940). Degree and Length of Slope as it Affects Soil Loss in Runoff. Agricultural Engineering 2 1 59-64.

Soil Ecosystem and Lithosphere **Pages 96-119**
Edited by: Dr. Abhishek Swami, Dr. Prasann Kumar and Dr. Pawan Kumar 'Bharti'
ISBN: 978-93-88854-50-4
Edition: 2020
Published by: Discovery Publishing House Pvt. Ltd., New Delhi (India)

9

Microorganisms in Bioremediation
A Potential Tool for Restoration of Contaminated Areas

M.R.A. Manimala

Introduction

Microorganisms are widely distributed on the biosphere because of their metabolic ability is very impressive and they can easily grow in a wide range of environmental conditions. The nutritional versatility of microorganisms can also be exploited for biodegradation of pollutants. This kind of process is termed as bioremediation. It is continued through based on the ability of certain microorganisms to convert, modify and utilize toxic pollutants to obtain energy and biomass production in the process (Tang *et.al.*, 2007). Instead of simply collecting the pollutant and storing it, bioremediation is a microbiological well organized procedural activity which is applied to break down or transform contaminates to less toxic or non-toxic elemental and compound forms. Bioremediators are biological agents used for bioremediation in order to clean up contaminated sites. Bacteria, archaea, and fungi are typical prime bioremediators (Strong *et.al.*, 2008). The application of bioremediation as a biotechnological process involving microorganisms for solving and removing dangers of many pollutants through biodegradation from the environment. Bioremediation and biodegradation terms are more interchangeable words. Microorganisms act as a significant pollutant removal tools in soil, water, and sediments; mostly due to their advantage over other remediation procedural protocols. Microorganisms are restoring the original natural surroundings and preventing further pollution. (Demnerova *et.al.*, 2005).

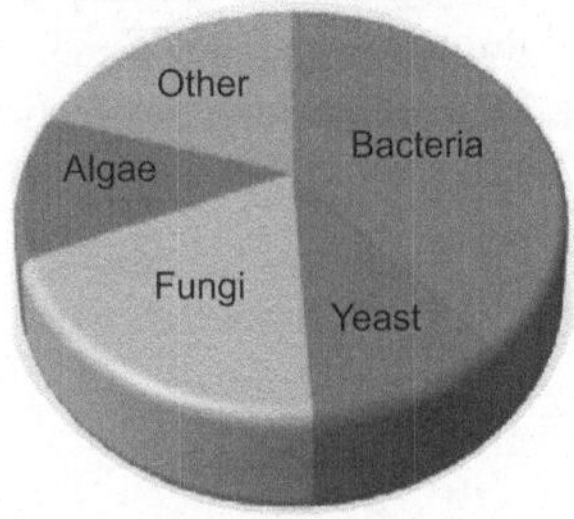

Fig. 9.1: Types of Microorganism used in bioremediation processes

Mother Terasa College of Agriculture (Affiliated to Tamil Nadu Agricultural University) Mettusalai, Illuppur, Pudukkottai – 622 102, TN, India

Bioremediation is a biological mechanism of recycling wastes in to another form that can use and reused by other organisms. Nowadays, the world is facing the problem of different environmental pollution. Microorganisms are essential for a key alternative solution to overcome challenges. Microorganisms are survive in all place on the biosphere because of their metabolic activity is astonishing; then come into existence in all over range of environmental conditions. The nutritional capacity of microorganisms is completely varied, so it is used as bioremidation of environmental pollutants. Bioremediation is highly involved in degradation, eradication, immobilization, or detoxification diverse chemical wastes and physical hazardous materials from the surrounding through the all-inclusive and action of microorganisms (Table 9.1). The main principle is degrading and transforming pollutants such as hydrocarbons, oil, heavy metal, pesticides, dye's and so on. That is carried out in enzymatic way through metabolizing, so it have great contribution role to solve many environmental problems. There are two types of factors these are biotic and abiotic conditions are determine rate of degradation. Currently, different methods and strategies are applied in the area in different part of the world. For example, biostimulation, bioaugementation, bioventing, biopiles and bioattenuation are common one. All bioremidation techniques it has its own advantage and disadvantage because it has its own specific application.

Table 9.1: Essential Factors for Microbial Bioremediation

S.No.	Factor	Desired Conditions
1.	Microbial population	Suitable kinds of organisms that can biodegrade all of the contaminants
2.	Oxygen	Enough to support aerobic biodegradation (about 2% oxygen in the gas phase or 0.4 mg/liter in the soil water)
3.	Water	Soil moisture should be from 50–70% of the water holding capacity of the soil
4.	Nutrients	Nitrogen, phosphorus, sulfur, and other nutrients to support good microbial growth
5.	Temperature	Appropriate temperatures for microbial growth (0–40°C)
6.	pH	Best range is from 6.5 to 7.5

Principle of Bioremediation

Bioremediation is defined as the process whereby organic wastes are biologically degraded under controlled conditions to an innocuous state, or to levels below concentration limits established by regulatory authorities. Microorganisms are suited to the task of contaminant destruction because they possess enzymes that allow them to use environmental contaminants as a food. The aim of bioremediation is encouraging them to work by supplying optimum levels of nutrients and other chemicals essential for their metabolism in order to degrade/detoxify substances which are hazardous to environment and living things. All metabolic reactions are mediated by enzymes. These belong to the groups of oxidoreductases, hydrolases, lyases, transferases, isomerases and ligases. Many enzymes have a remarkably wide degradation capacity due to their non-specific and specific substrate affinity. For bioremediation to be effective, microorganisms must enzymatically attack the pollutants and convert them to harmless products. As bioremediation can be effective only where environmental conditions permit microbial growth and activity, its application often involves the manipulation of environmental parameters to allow microbial growth and degradation to proceed at a faster rate (Kumar *et.al.*, 2011).

Bioremediation is occurred naturally and encouraged within addition of living things and fertilizers. Bioremediation technology is principally based on biodegradation. It refer to complete removal of organic toxic pollutants in to harmless or naturally occurring compounds like carbon dioxide, water, inorganic compounds which are safe for human, animal, plant and aquatic life (Jain *et.al.*, 2012). Numerous ways and pathways have been elucidated for the biodegradation of a wide variety of organic compounds; for instance, it is completed in the presence and absence oxygen.

Bioremediation of Soil

Soil is a major reservoir of microorganisms with each gram containing about one billion microbes. Microbes are used for bioremediation in situ of contaminated soil. Microorganisms that can remove contaminants from the environment are called bioremediators. Contaminations are most often caused by a mixture of pollutants and the best strategy for cleanup is to use a cocktail of different species since each one of them will be optimized for the degradation of a specific toxic compound. The microbe activity is usually monitored on such sites to ensure optimal conditions for bacterial growth and hence degradation. Decomposition of the toxic substances can be performed both in the presence (aerobically) and absence (anaerobically) of oxygen. The limiting factor for bioremediaton in soils is the bioavailability of the contaminant agents.

Bioremediation of Water

The treatment of sewage water is a critical process to assure the purification of wastewater that will prevent chemical and microbiological pollution of the environment, especially for the drinking water supplies. An important part of this process is the biological step which involves the activity of living organisms to clean the water from organic matter. This happens in the secondary step of sewage purification. Microorganisms substantially lessen the concentration of nutrients which if released in the environment can lead to undesirable overgrowth of microorganisms and algae. They also have the potential to clean the water from toxic components. The degradation is performed in the anaerobic,

aerobic, and composting steps. Anaerobic digestion by bacteria is allowed to proceed for almost two weeks to guarantee enough time to complete the process. During this time, the organic matter undergoes four different enzymatic transformations: hydrolysis, acidogenesis, acetogenesis and methanogenesis. The final products are water, carbon dioxide, and methane. In the aerobic step, oxygen is added into the system and the organic matter is converted to carbon dioxide. In the composting step, additional carbon sources are added to aid the final steps of degradation.

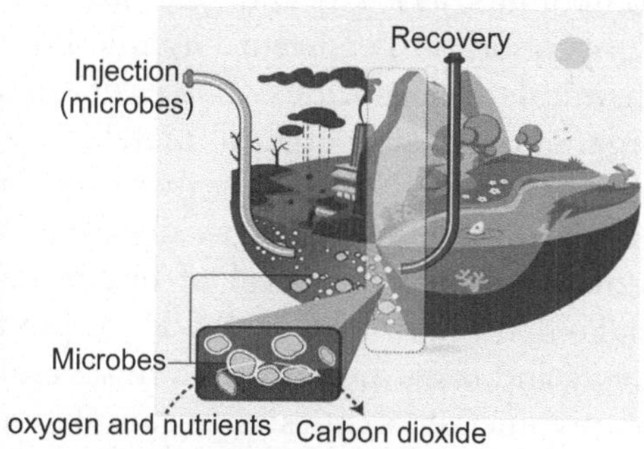

Fig. 9.2: Sewage Treatment Plant critical in lowering the levels of pollutants in the environment

In recent years, advances in genomics, proteomics, and bioinformatics studies of environmental microorganisms have revealed a tremendous potential in metabolic pathways. Such studies showed that Burkholderia xenovorans LB400 and Rhodococcus sp. strain RHA1, have evolved pathways to degrade aromatic compounds, which are some of the toughest contaminants to eliminate. The bacteria have genes coding for deoxygenases to open the aromatic ring structures of these chemicals. Hydrocarbons and their derivatives were long believed to be degraded only in the presence of oxygen. This would often lead to oxygen depletion in environments heavily polluted with oil. Studies in recent years have proven that there are numerous anaerobic bacteria species capable of decomposing this group of pollutants. A common feature among these bacteria is that they possess reductive dehalogenases. Bacterial species are assisted in the process of degradation by fungi (e.g., Aspergillus sp.), protozoa, and representatives of Archaea. The primary role of fungi is in secreting numerous extracellular enzymes that break down complex molecules into their components and make them readily available to the bacterial community.

Bioremediation of Petroleum Hydrocarbons

The organic pollutants introduced into the environment through industrial discharges, agricultural uses, or improper waste disposal practices. The persistence of these chemicals in the environment poses a chronic threat to the health and safety of human and wildlife. Chemical contaminants present in the aquatic ecosystem may be immobilized and accumulated in sediments or may be subject to transformation and activation processes. Depending on biogeochemical processes, many organic pollutants like hydrocarbons are involved in adsorption, desorption and transformation processes and can be made available to benthic organisms as well as organisms in the water column through the sediment-water interface. Hydrocarbons can become dangerous especially if they enter the food-chain, since several of the more persistent compounds, as PAHs and PCBs are carcinogenic. According to the Stockholm Convention on Persistent Organic Pollutants, 9 of the 21 persistent organic chemicals are pesticides. Classes of organic pesticides include organochlorine, organophosphate, organo metallic, pyrethroids, and carbamates among others. Relatively recently, there has been increasing interest on the use of bioremediation as the most desirable technology which uses plants (Phyto remediation) for removal of environmental pollutants or detoxification to make them harmless. Methods for phyto remediation of contaminated soils, rivers and lakes are described in several reviews (Brooks, 1998). Investigation on organic xenobiotics bioaccumulation/biodegradation in green algae is of great importance from environmental point of view because widespread distribution of these compounds in agricultural areas has become one of the major problems in aquatic ecosystem (Jin *et.al.* 2012). The algae proved to be effective in hyperaccumulation of heavy metals as well as degradation of xenobiotics (Suresh and Ravishankar 2004). (Table 9.2)

Table 9.2: Microorganisms and Hydrocarbon (Organic Compound) Interaction.

Microorganisms	Compound
Penicillium chrysogenum	Monocyclic aromatic hydro carbons, benzene, toluene, ethyl benzene and xylene, phenol compounds.
P. alcaligenes, P. mendocina and *P. putida, P. veronii, Achromobacter, Flavobacterium.*	Petrol and diesel polycyclic aromatic hydrocarbons toluene
Pseudomonas putida	Monocyclic aromatic hydrocarbons, e.g. benzene and xylene.
Phanerochaete chrysosporium	Biphenyl and triphenylmethane
A. niger, A. fumigatus, F. solani and *P. funiculosum*	Hydrocarbon
Coprinellus radians	PAHs, methylnaphthalenes, and dibenzofurans
Alcaligenes odorans, B. subtilis, Corynebacterium propinquum, Pseudomonas aeruginosa	Phenol

Tyromyces palustris, Gloeophyllum trabeum, Trametes versicolor	Hydrocarbons
Candida viswanathii	Phenanthrene, benzopyrene
Cyanobacteria, green algae and diatoms and *Bacillus licheniformis*	Naphtalene
Acinetobacter sp., *Pseudomonas* sp., *Ralstonia* sp. and *Microbacterium* sp.	Aromatic hydrocarbon
Gleophyllum striatum	Striatum, Pyrene, anthracene, Dibenzothiophene Lignin peroxidasse

Bioremediation of Heavy Metals

The presence of heavy metals in the environment is a major concern because of their toxicity to flora and fauna. Moreover, recovery of heavy metals from industrial waste streams is becoming increasingly important as society realises the necessity for recycling and conservation of essential metals. Industrial wastes, geo-chemical structure and mining of metals create a potential source of heavy metal pollution in the aquatic environment (Gumgum *et.al.* 1994). Heavy metals are major pollutants in marine, ground, industrial and even treated wastewaters. Rapid urbanization, industrialization, fertilizer and pesticide use has resulted in heavy metal pollution of land and water resources. The increasing load of heavy metals has caused imbalance in aquatic ecosystems and the biota growing under such habitats accumulate high amounts of heavy metals (Cu, Zn, Cd, Cr and Ni etc.) which in turn, are being assimilated and transferred within food chains by the process of magnification (Pergent *et.al.* 1999). The toxic metals can be broadly divided into two groups. The first group consists of metals that are essential as nutritional requirements at trace amount for many organisms but are toxic when present in greater amounts. This group includes As, Cr, Co, Cu, Ni, Se, Va and Zn. The second group includes Pb, Hg, Cd, Ur, Ag and Be, all of them are highly poisonous and are not known to have any nutritional value (Inthorn 2001). Heavy metals are not biodegradable and tend to accumulate in living organisms. Heavy metals showed to affect a wide range of micro algal cellular activities including cell viability and membrane structure and properties (Table 9.3).

Biosorption, which uses the ability of biological materials to remove and accumulate heavy metals from aqueous solutions, has received considerable attention in recent years because of few advantages compared to traditional methods. Microalgae, related eukaryotic photosynthetic organisms, and some fungi have preferentially developed the production of peptides capable to bind heavy metals. These molecules, as organometallic complexes, are further partitioned inside vacuoles to facilitate appropriate control of the cytoplasmic concentration of heavy metal ions, thus preventing or neutralizing their potential toxic effect (Cobbett and Goldsbrough 2002). In contrast to this mechanism used by eukaryotes, prokaryotic cells employ ATP consuming efflux of heavy metals or enzymatic change of speciation to achieve detoxification. Microalgae are superior in remediation processes as a wide range of toxic and other wastes can be treated with algae and they are non pathogenic. The risk of accidental release of pollutants into the atmosphere causing health safety and environmental problems are avoided when microalgae are employed for remediation. A microalga utilizes the wastes as nutritional sources and enzymatically degrades the pollutants. The xenobiotics and heavy metals are known to be detoxified/ transformed/or volatilized by microalgal metabolism. They have the ability to take up various kinds of nutrients like nitrogen and phosphorus (Ayse *et.al.*, 2005).

Table 9.3: Microorganisms Serve for Utilizing Heavy Metals.

Microorganisms	Compound
Saccharomyces cerevisiae	Heavy metals, lead, mercury and nickel
Cunninghamella elegans	Heavy metals
Pseudomonas fluorescens and *Pseudomonas aeruginosa*	Fe^{2+}, Zn^{2+}, Pb^{2+}, Mn^{2+} and Cu^{2+}
Lysinibacillus sphaericus CBAM5	Cobalt, copper, chromium and lead
Microbacterium profundi strain Shh49T	Fe
Aspergillus versicolor, A. fumigatus, Paecilomyces sp., *Paecilomyces* sp., *Trichoderma* sp., *Microsporum* sp., *Cladosporium* sp.	Cadmium
Geobacter spp.	Fe (III), U (VI)
Bacillus safensis (JX126862)	Cadmium
Pseudomonas aeruginosa, Aeromonas sp.	U, Cu, Ni, Cr
Aerococcus sp., *Rhodopseudomonas palustris*	Pb, Cr, Cd

Bioremediation of Oil

An oil spill is a release of a liquid petroleum hydrocarbon into the environment due to human activity, and is a form of pollution. It includes release of crude oil from tankers, offshore platforms, drilling rigs and wells, spills of refined petroleum products like gasoline, diesel and their by-products. It also includes heavier fuels used by large ships like bunker fuel, spill of any oily refuse or waste oil. Oil spill is a big environmental concern. Micro algal growth on the spills is to be monitored so as to check whether Microalgae has the potential to clean up the spill or not. Marine oil pollution has been receiving increasing attention since the middle of the 19th century with the intensification of tanker operations and oil use, marine tanker collisions, pollutant release from coastal refineries (Wake 2005) and continuous operative discharges from ships (Carpenter and MacGill 2001). Annually, 48% of the oil pollution in the oceans is due to fuels and 29% to crude oil.

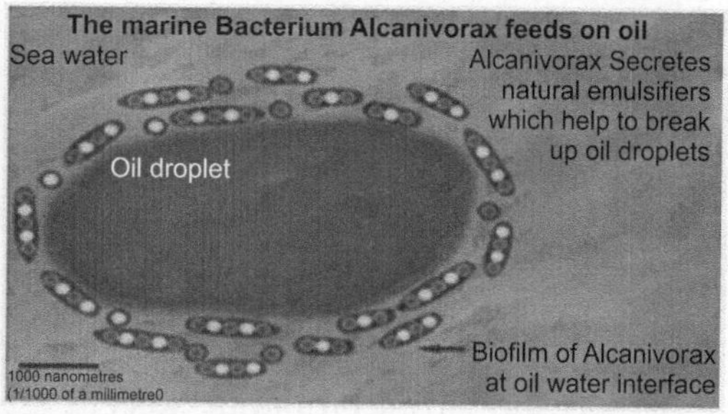

Fig. 9.3: Bacteria to clean up oil spills and bioremediation of oil spills using microbes.

Microalgae are potential biofuel feed stocks that can provide solutions to the twin challenges of energy security and environmental pollution. They have great potential for the removal of excess nitrogen and phosphorus from wastewater including the farm runoff. They can capture carbon dioxide from coal fired power plants thereby reducing greenhouse gas and also producing algal biomass, which can be converted into biofuel. Walker *et.al.* (1975) performed experiments with the microalgae which was found to degrade petroleum hydrocarbons found in crude and motor oils. Interestingly, in the crude oil, 38-60% of the saturated aliphatic hydrocarbons and 12-41% of the aromatic compounds were degraded, whereas in the motor oil, 10-23% of the saturated aliphatic hydrocarbons and 10-26% of the aromatic compounds were degraded. This suggested that the microalga were capable of degrading different oils to varying levels along with other microorganisms (Table 9.4).

Table 9.4: Groups of Microorganisms Important for Oil Bioremediation

Microorganisms	Compound
Fusarium sp.	Oil
Alcaligenes odorans, Bacillus subtilis, Corynebacterium propinquum, Pseudomonas aeruginosa	Oil
Bacillus cereus	Diesel oil
Aspergillus niger, Candida glabrata, Candida krusei and *Saccharomyces cerevisiae*	Crude oil
B. brevis, P. aeruginosa KH6, *B. licheniformis* and *B. sphaericus*	Crude oil
Pseudomonas aeruginosa, P. putida, Arthobacter sp and *Bacillus* sp.	Diesel oil
Pseudomonas cepacia, Bacillus cereus, Bacillus coagulans, Citrobacter koseri and *Serratia ficaria*	Diesel oil, Crude oil

Praepilas and Pakawadee (2011) investigated the potential of microalgae (Scenedesmus quadricauda and Chlorella sp.) for utilizing industrial wastewater as a cheap nutrient for their growth and oil accumulation. The cultures gave the highest lipid content at 18.58% and 42.86% in cases of S. quadricauda and S. obliquus. Many microalgae can accumulate lipids due to excess photosynthate and some species can accumulate amount of lipids under heterotrophy or environment stress, such as nutrient deficiency or salt stress (Takagi *et.al.*, 2006).

Bioremediation of Pesticides

A wide variety of organochlorine compounds are introduced into aquatic environments via domestic sewage, pesticide runoff from agricultural lands and industrial effluents. Recent studies have indicated that different microalgal species apparently have different sensitivity to pesticides (Solomon 1996).The response of pesticides vary widely depending upon concentrations used, duration of exposure, and algal species tested. Generally, there was a broad range of sensitivity among species and between divisions of algae tested. Biodegradation of pesticides is determined by two groups of factors, the first relates to microbial consortium and the optimum condition for their survival and activity while the second relates to the chemical structure of the pesticides. Factors related to microorganisms including the presence and number of appropriate microorganisms, the contact between microorganisms and the substrate (pesticide), pH, temperature, salinity, nutrients, light quality and intensity, available water, oxygen tension and redox potential, surface binding, presence of alternative carbon substrates and alternative electron acceptors. The second group of factors including chemical structure, molecular weight and functional groups of the applied pesticides, their concentration and toxicity and their solubility in water. Some information on the interactions between pesticides and algae was compiled by Kobayashi and Rittman (Kobayashi and Rittam 1982), showing that not only were microalgae capable of bioaccumulating pesticides, but they were also capable of bio transforming some of these environmental pollutants (Table 9.5).

Table 9.5: Potential Biological Agents for Pesticides

Microorganisms	Compound
Bacillus, Staphylococcus	Endosulfan
Enterobacter	Chlorpyrifos
Pseudomonas putida, Acinetobacter sp., *Arthrobacter* sp	Ridomil MZ 68 MG, Fitoraz WP 76, Decis 2.5 EC, malation
Acenetobactor sp., *Pseudomonas* sp., *Enterobacter* sp. and *Photobacterium* sp.	Chlorpyrifos and methyl parathion

Bioremediation of Toxins

Bioaccumulation of toxins is a separate issue to environmental toxicity, though there are likely to be direct relationships between toxin accumulation and the nature and strength of toxic effects. Bioaccumulation occurs where tissue-based concentrations exceed those available in the environment: the latter may include algal toxins available through drinking, dietary, and/or direct contact routes. Algae comprise the greatest abundance of plant biomass in aquatic environments and are a logical choice for aquatic toxicological studies, yet have been underutilized in this capacity. The lipid content of many algal species provides a point of entry for trophic transfer of lipophilic organic contaminants.

Bioremediation of Radioactive Compounds

Uranium is one of the most seriously threatening heavy metals because of its high toxicity and some radioactivity. Excessive amounts of uranium have found their ways into the environment through the activities associated with the nuclear industry. Uranium contamination posses a threat in some surface and ground waters (Laul 1992). There is a need for controlling the heavy metal especially uranium emissions into the environment. Conventional methods for removing heavy metals from industrial effluents (e.g. precipitation and sludge separation, chemical oxidation or reduction, ion exchange, reverse osmosis, membrane separation, electrochemical treatment and evaporation) are often ineffective and costly when applied to dilute and very dilute effluents (Aksu 1998). Marine algae are capable of biosorbing radionuclide such as radium, thorium and uranium has been known for a long time. The biosorption of uranium by Cystoseira indica, a brown algae biomass has been reported (Edgington *et.al.*, 1970).

Types of Organisms Used in Bioremediation

Typically, bioremediation is based on the cometabolism action of one organism or a consortium of microorganisms. In this process, the transformation of contaminants presents a little efficiency or no benefit to the cell, and therefore this process is described as non-beneficial biotransformation. Several studies have shown that many organisms (prokaryotes and eukaryotes) have a natural capacity to biosorb toxic heavy metal ions. Examples of microorganisms studied and strategically used in bioremediation treatments for heavy metals include the following:

1. **Bacteria:** Arthrobacter spp., Pseudomonas veronii, Burkholderia spp., Kocuria flava, Bacillus cereus, and Sporosarcina ginsengisoli;
2. **Fungi:** Penicillium canescens, Aspergillus versicolor, and Aspergillus fumigatus;
3. **Algae:** Cladophora fascicularis, Spirogyra spp. and Cladophora spp., and Spirogyra spp. and Spirullina spp.; and

4. **Yeast:** Saccharomyces cerevisiae and Candida utilis. Prokaryotes (bacteria and archaea) are distinguished from eukaryotes (protists, plants, fungi, and animals).

The cellular structure of eukaryotes is characterized by the presence of a nucleus and other membrane-enclosed organelles. Also, the ribosomes in prokaryotes are smaller (70S) than in eukaryotes (80S). The way in which microorganisms interact with heavy metal ions is partially dependent on whether they are eukaryotes or prokaryotes, wherein eukaryotes are more sensitive to metal toxicity than prokaryotes. The possible modes of interaction are:

(*a*) Active extrusion of metal,

(*b*) Intracellular chelation (in eukaryotes) by various metal-binding peptides, and

(*c*) Transformation into other chemical species with reduced toxicity. For bioremediation to be effective, microorganisms must enzymatically attack the pollutants and convert them to harmless products.

Bacteria and higher organisms have developed mechanisms associated with resistance to toxic metals and rendering them innocuous. Several microbes, including aerobes, anaerobes, and fungi, are involved in the enzymatic degradation process. Most of bioremediation systems are run under aerobic conditions, but anaerobic conditions make it possible microbial organisms to degrade otherwise recalcitrant molecules.

Because several different types of pollutants can be present at a contaminated site, various types of microorganisms are required for effective remediation. Some types of microorganism are able to degrade petroleum hydrocarbons and use them as a source of carbon and energy. However, the choice of the organisms employed is variable, depending on the chemical nature of the polluting agents, and needs to be selected carefully as they only survive in the presence of a limited range of chemical contaminants. The efficiency of the degradation process is related to the potential of the particular microorganism to introduce molecular oxygen into thehydrocarbon and to generate the intermediates that subsequently enter the general energy yielding metabolic pathway of the cell. Some bacteria search the contaminant and move toward it because they flexibly exhibit the potential as a chemotactic response. Numerous microorganisms can utilize oil as a source of food, and many of them produce potent surface-active compounds that can emulsify oil in water and facilitate its removal. Bacteria that can degrade petroleum products include species of Pseudomonas, Aeromonas, Moraxella, Beijerinckia, Flavobacteria, Chrobacteria, Nocardia, Corynebacteria, Modococci, Strepto myces, Bacilli, Arthrobacter, Aeromonas, and cyanobacteria and some yeast. For example, Pseudomonas putida MHF 7109 can be isolated from cow dung microbial consortia for the biodegradation of selected petroleum hydrocarbon compounds, such as benzene, toluene, and o-xylene (BTX).

Mechanisms Associated with Bioremediation by Microorganisms

Bioremediation can be separated into two categories, biosorption and bioaccumulation. Biosorption is a passive adsorption mechanism that is fast and reversible. The metals are retained by means of physicochemical interaction (e.g., ion exchange, adsorption, complexation, precipitation, and crystallization) between the metal and the functional groups present on the cell surface. Several factors can affect the biosorption of metals, such as pH, ionic strength, biomass concentration, temperature, particle size, and presence of other ions in the solution. Both living and dead biomass can occur for biosorption because it is independent of cell metabolism. On the other hand, bioaccumulation includes both intra- and extracellular processes where passive uptake plays only a limited and not very well-defined role. Therefore, living biomass can only occur for bioaccumulation.

In general, the biosorption process needs inexpensive cost because the biomass can be obtained from industrial waste, and it can be regenerated and reused in manycycles. Bioaccumulation, on the other hand, needs expensive cost because the process occursin the presence of living cells in which reuse is limited. Also, important factors to be consideredinclude selectivity of metals and the potential for regeneration. The selectivity in biosorptionis generally low because the bind only occurs by physicochemical interaction. It can be increased through modification of the biomass. Nevertheless, processes involving bioaccumulation generally perform better than those involving biosorption. The structure of the cell wall of a microorganism contains various macromolecules, such as polysaccharides and proteins, with a high number of charged functional groups, including carboxyl, imidazole, sulfydryl, thioether, phenol, carbonyl, amide, ester sulfate, amino, and hydroxyl groups. The positively charged metal present in the solution gravitates toward these functional groups and adsorption occurs. The form in which microorganisms are cultivated can influence the cell wall composition, and this can be exploited to improve the adsorption capacity of the microorganisms. Bacteria can remove heavy metals from wastewater via functional groups, such as ketones, aldehydes, and carboxyl groups present in their cell walls and thereby produce less chemical sludge. Both gram-positive and gram negative bacteria are used for the uptake of metals. Green, red, and brown algae are also used as biosorbents. Some functional presents in bacteria such as uronic acid of carboxyl groups and sulfate groups, xylans, galactans, and alginic acid are capable of performing ion exchange.

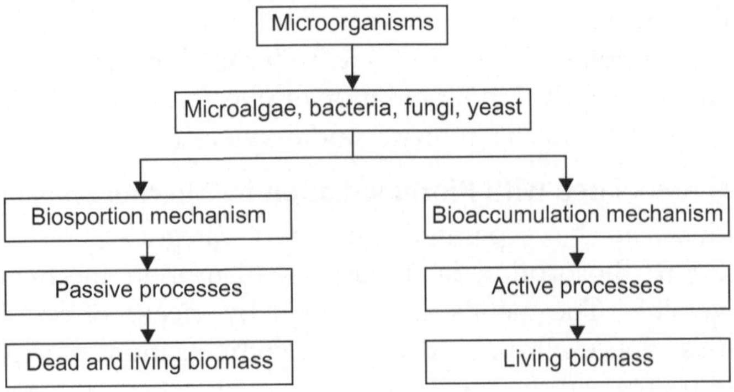

Fig. 9.4: Microorganisms employed in the bioremediation and processes/mechanisms involved in the case of dead and living biomass.

Factors Affecting Microbial Bioremediation

Bioremediation is involved in degrading, removing, altering, immobilizing, or detoxifying various chemicals and physical wastes from the environment through the action of bacteria, fungi and plants. Microorganisms are involved through their enzymatic pathways act as biocatalysts and facilitate the progress of biochemical reactions that degrade the desired pollutant. Microorganisms are act against the pollutants only when they have access to a variety of materials compounds to help them generate energy and nutrients to build more cells. The efficiency of bioremediation depends on many factors; including, the chemical nature and concentration of pollutants, the physicochemical characteristics of the environment, and their availability to microorganisms [4]. The reason for rate of degradation is affected due to bacteria and pollutants do not contact each other. In addition to this, microbes and pollutants are not uniformly spread in the environment. The controlling and optimizing of bioremediation processes is a complex system due to many factors. These factors are included here: the existence of a microbial population capable of degrading the pollutants, the availability of contaminants to the microbial population and environment factors (type of soil, temperature, pH, the presence of oxygen or other electron acceptors, and nutrients).

Biological Factors

A biotic factors are affect the degradation of organic compounds through competition between microorganisms for limited carbon sources, antagonistic interactions between microorganisms or the predation of microorganisms by protozoa and bacteriophages. The rate of contaminant degradation is often dependent on the concentration of the contaminant and the amount of "catalyst" present. In this context, the amount of "catalyst" represents the number of organisms able to metabolize the contaminant as well as the amount of enzymes(s) produced by each cell. The expression of specific enzymes by the cells can increase or decrease the rate of contaminant degradation. Furthermore, the extent to contaminant metabolism specific enzymes must be participated and their "affinity" for the contaminant and also the availability of the contaminant is largely needed. The major biological factors are included here: mutation, horizontal gene transfer, enzyme activity, interaction (competition, succession, and predation), its own growth until critical biomass is reached, population size and composition (Madhavi *et.al.*, 2012).

Environmental Factors

The metabolic characteristics of the microorganisms and physicochemical properties of the targeted contaminants determine possible interaction during the process. The actual successful interaction between the two; however, depends on the environmental conditions of the site of the interaction. Microorganism growth and activity are affected by pH, temperature, moisture, soil structure, solubility in water, nutrients, site characteristics, redox potential and oxygen content, lack of trained human resources in this field and Physico-chemical bioavailability of pollutants (contaminant concentration, type, solubility, chemical structure and toxicity). These above listed factors are determining kinetics of degradation (Adams *et.al.*, 2015). Biodegradation can occur under a wide-range of pH; however, a pH of 6.5 to 8.5 is generally optimal for biodegradation in most aquatic and terrestrial systems. Moisture influences the rate of contaminant metabolism because it influences the kind and amount of soluble materials that are available as well as the osmotic pressure and pH of terrestrial and aquatic systems (Cases *et.al.*, 2005). Most environmental factors are listed below.

Availability of Nutrients

The addition of nutrients adjusts the essential nutrient balance for microbial growth and reproduction as well as having impact on the biodegradation rate and effectiveness. Nutrient balancing especially the supply of essential nutrients such as N and P can improve the biodegradation efficiency by optimizing the bacterial C: N: P ratio. To survive and continue their microbial activities microorganisms need a number of nutrients such as carbon, nitrogen, and phosphorous. In small concentrations the extent of hydrocarbon degradation also limits. The addition of an appropriate quantity of nutrients is a favourable strategy for increasing the metabolic activity of microorganisms and thus the biodegradation rate in cold environments (Couto *et.al.*, 2014). Biodegradation in aquatic environment is limited by the availability of nutrients (Thavasi *et.al.*, 2011). Similar to the nutritional needs of other organisms, oil-eating microbes also require nutrients for optimal growth and development. These nutrients are available in the natural environment but occur in low quantities (Macaulay, 2015).

Temperature

Among the physical factors temperature is the most important one to determining the survival of microorganisms and composition of the hydrocarbons (Das, 2011). In cold environments such as the Arctic, oil degradation via natural processes is very slow and puts the microbes under more pressure to clean up the spilled petroleum. The sub-zero temperature of water in this region causes the transport channels within the microbial cells to shut down or may even freeze the entire cytoplasm, thus, rendering most oleophilic microbes metabolically inactive (Macaulay, 2015). Biological enzymes are participated in the degradation pathway have an optimum temperature and will not have the same metabolic turnover for every temperature. Moreover, the degradation process for specific compound needs specific temperature. Temperature also speed up or slow down bioremediation process because highly influence microbial physiological properties. The rate of microbial activities increases with temperature, and reaches to its maximum level at an optimum temperature. It became decline suddenly with further increase or decreases in temperature and eventually stop after reaching a specific temperature.

Concentration of Oxygen

Different organisms require oxygen others also do not require oxygen based on their requirement facilitate the biodegradation rate in a better way. Biological degradation is carried out in aerobic and anaerobic condition, because oxygen is a gaseous requirement for most living organisms. The presence of oxygen in most cases can enhance hydrocarbon metabolism (Macaulay, 2015).

Moisture Content

Microorganisms require adequate water to accomplish their growth. The soil moisture content has adverse effect in biodegradation agents.

PH

PH of compound which is acidity, basicity and alkalinity nature of compound, it has its own impact on microbial metabolic activity and also increase and decrease removal process. The measurement of pH in soil could indicate the potential for microbial growth (Enim, 2013). Higher or lower pH values showed inferior results; metabolic processes are highly susceptible to even slight changes in pH.

Site Characterization and Selection

Sufficient remedial investigation work must be performed prior to proposing a bioremediation remedy to adequately characterize the magnitude and extent of contamination. This work should at a minimum encompass the following factors: fully determine the horizontal and vertical extent of contamination, list the parameters and locations to be sample and the rationale for their choice, describe the methods to be used for sample acquisition and analysis to be performed.

Metal Ions

Metals are important in small amount for bacteria and fungus, but in high quantity inhibit the metabolic activity of the cells. Metal compounds have direct and indirect impact on rate of degradation.

Toxic Compounds

When in high concentrations of toxic nature of some contaminants can create toxic effects to microorganisms and slow down decontamination. The degree and mechanisms of toxicity vary with specific toxicants, their concentration, and the exposed microorganisms. Some organic and inorganic compounds are toxic to targeted life forms (Madhavi *et.al.*, 2012).

Bioremediation Strategies

Bioremediation coverts organic pollutants mainly to carbon dioxide, water, and biomass. Some of the pollutants can also be immobilized by binding to the humic substance fraction. Degradation may take place under aerobic, as well as under anaerobic conditions. The aerobic process is predominantly used for bioremediation and it can also be classified as ex-situ and in situ. Selection of appropriate technology among the wide range of bioremediation technologies developed to treat contaminants depends on three basic principles – the amenability of the pollutant to biological transformation, the accessibility of the contaminant to microorganisms and the opportunity for optimization of biological activity. Through appropriate selection of the technologies and adjustment of conditions, the degradation process is enhanced and the degree of degradation is improved which ultimately reduces the cost of treatment. Ex situ techniques are those that are applied to soil and groundwater at the site which has been removed from the site via excavation (soil) or pumping (water). In situ techniques are defined as those that are applied to soil and groundwater at the site with minimal disturbance. These techniques are generally the most desirable options due to lower cost and fewer disturbances since they provide the treatment in place avoiding excavation and transport of contaminants. However, in situ treatment is limited by the depth of the soil that can be effectively treated. In many soils effective oxygen diffusion for desirable rates of bioremediation extend to a range of only a few centimeters to about 30 cm into the soil, although depths of 60 cm and greater have been effectively treated in some cases.

Ex Situ Methods

Land farming

It also known as land treatment or land application is an above-ground remediation technology for soils that reduces concentrations of organic pollutants through biodegradation. This technology usually involves spreading excavated contaminated soils in a thin layer on the ground surface and stimulating aerobic microbial activity within the soils through aeration and/or the addition of minerals, nutrients, and moisture. As contaminated soil is treated in thin layers of upto 0.4 m thickness, it requires a large treatment area. To promote degradation enhancement of oxygen supply as well as mixing are done by ploughing, harrowing or milling at regular intervals. The treatment process is cost effective and can be adopted if sufficient land is available.

Composting

It is applied in bioremediation as a means of degrading toxic organic compounds and perhaps lessening the toxicity of metallic contaminants in organic residues, waste and by product. Composting is similar to those that occur biologically in soil by which organic wastes are degraded by microorganisms. Temperatures are generally higher in composts than in soils, resulting in increased solubility of contaminants and higher metabolic activity in compost. High level of substrate in composts can lead to co-metabolism of organic contaminants. Mechanical treatment by grinding, mixing, and sieving out non-degradable or unwanted materials such as metals, plastics, glass, stones gives good conditions for biological treatment of compostable materials. However, the nature of the organic contaminant, composting conditions and procedures, microbial communities, and time all affect the performance of compost mechanism.

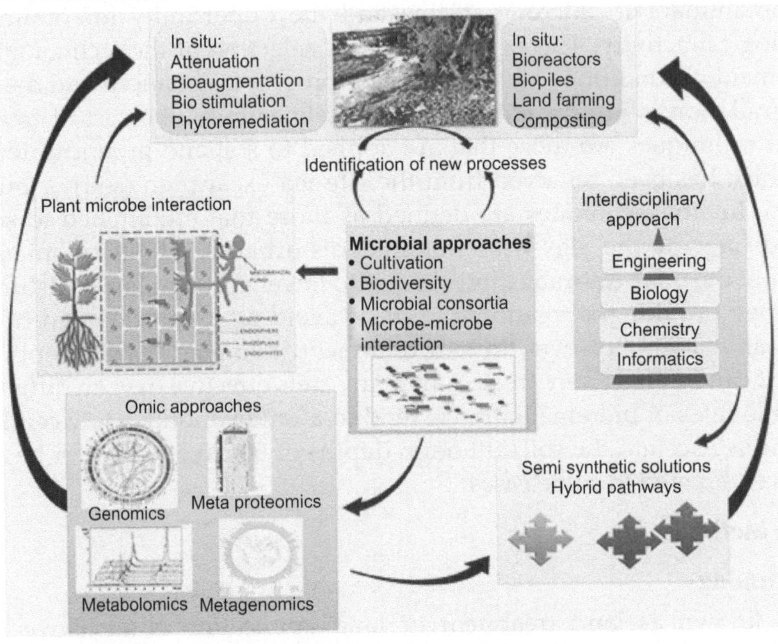

Fig. 9. 5: Techniques involved in bioremediation process.

Biopiles

It is a hybrid of land farming and composting. Excavated soils are mixed with soil amendments, placed on a treatment area, and bio-remediate using forced aeration. Contaminants are converted to carbon di-oxide and water. The basic bipile system includes a treatment bed, an aeration system, an irrigation/nutrient system and a leachate collection system. Soil piles can be up to 20 ft and may be covered with plastic to control runoff, evaporation and volatilization, and promote solar heating. If needed volatile organic compounds are treated before they entered into the air stream. Biopiles provide a favorable environment for indigenous aerobic and anaerobic microorganisms.

Bioreactors

In this process contaminated soil are treated either in solid or slurry phase. The principle of solid phase reactors is mechanical decomposition of the soil by attrition and by intensive mixture of the components in a closed container. This ensures that the contaminants, microorganisms, nutrients, water and air are brought into permanent contact. A slurry bioreactor may be defi ned as a containment vessel and apparatus used to create a three-phase (solid, liquid, and gas) mixing condition to increase the bioremediation rate of soil bound and water-soluble pollutants as a water slurry of the contaminated soil and biomass (usually indigenous microorganisms) capable of degrading target contaminants. In general, the rate and extent of biodegradation are greater in a bioreactor system than in situ or in solid-phase systems because the contained environment is more manageable and hence more controllable and predictable. However, the contaminated soil requires pre treatment (e.g., excavation) or alternatively the contaminant can be stripped from the soil via soil washing or physical extraction (e.g., vacuum extraction) before being placed in a bioreactor.

In Situ Methods

Bioventing

An in-situ remediation technology that uses indigenous microorganisms to biodegrade organic constituents adsorbed to soils in the unsaturated zone. It is based on vacuum-enhanced soil vapour extraction. The pressure differences in the sub-surface cause an inflow of atmospheric air and therefore, oxygen supply, as needed for aerobic degradation of contaminants. It is effective in remediating petroleum products, including gasoline, jet fuels, kerosene, and diesel fuel. If the contaminants to be treated are volatile, the extracted soil vapour has to be treated by adsorption of contaminants on activated carbon by biodegradation within a bio filter.

Biosparging

It exploits and stimulates indigenous microorganisms to degrade organic contaminants in saturated soil. Through boreholes, air is injected into the saturated zone (below the water table) to increase the activity of the soils indigenous microorganisms through increased oxygen dissolution. The increased oxygen enhances aerobic biodegradation of the contaminants present in the soil or groundwater. Biosparging can be used to reduce petroleum constituents that are adsorbed to soil within the capillary fringe, below the water table or dissolved in groundwater. Biosparging is commonly used at sites with mid-weight petroleum products such as diesel fuel; lighter petroleum products tend to volatilise swiftly and are removed very rapidly through sparging. Soil permeability is a key factor in the effectiveness of the technology.

Bioaugmentation

It involves the addition of microorganisms indigenous or exogenous to the contaminated sites. Two factors limit the use of added microbial cultures in a land treatment unit:

- Non-indigenous cultures rarely compete well enough with an indigenous population to develop and sustain useful population levels and
- Most soils with long-term exposure to biodegradable waste have indigenous microorganisms that are effective degrades if the land treatment unit is well managed.

The Advantage of Bioremediation

It is a natural process, it takes a little time, as an acceptable waste treatment process for contaminated material such as soil. Microbes able to degrade the contaminant and increase in numbers when the contaminant is present. When the contaminant is degraded, the biodegradative population become declines. The residues for the treatment are usually harmless product including water carbon dioxide and cell biomass.

- It requires a very less effort and can often be carried out on site, often without causing a major disruption of normal activities. This also eliminates the need to transport quantities of waste off site and the potential threats to human health and the environment that can arise during transportation.
- It is applied in a cost effective process as it lost less than the other conventional methods (technologies) that are used for clean-up of hazardous waste. Important method for the treatment of oil contaminated sites (Montagnolli. *et.al.*, 2015).
- It also helps in complete destruction of the pollutants, many of the hazardous compounds can be transformed to harmless products, and this feature also eliminates the chance of future liability associated with treatment and disposal of contaminated material.

- It does not use any dangerous chemicals. Nutrients especially fertilizers added to make active and fast microbial growth. Commonly, used on lawns and gardens. Because of bioremediation change harmful chemicals into water and harmless gases, the harmful chemicals are completely destroyed (Sharma, 2012).
- Simple, less labor intensive and cheap due to their natural role in the environment.
- Eco-friendly and sustainable.
- Contaminants are destroyed, not simply transferred to different environmental media.
- Nonintrusive, potentially allowing for continued site use.
- Relative ease of implementation.
- Effective way of remediating natural ecosystem from a number of contaminant and act as environment friendly options.

The Disadvantage of Bioremediation

- It is limited to those compounds that are biodegradable. Not all compounds are susceptible to rapid and complete degradation.
- There are some concerns that the products of biodegradation may be more persistent or toxic than the parent compound.
- Biological processes are often highly specific. Important site factors required for success include the presence of metabolically capable microbial populations, suitable environmental growth conditions, and appropriate levels of nutrients and contaminants.
- It is difficult to extrapolate from bench and pilot-scale studies to full-scale field operations.
- Research is needed to develop and engineer bioremediation technologies that are appropriate for sites with complex mixtures of contaminants that are not evenly dispersed in the environment. Contaminants may be present as solids, liquids and gases.
- It often takes longer than other treatment options, such as excavation and removal of soil or incineration.
- Regulatory uncertainty remains regarding acceptable performance criteria for bioremediation. There is no accepted definition of "clean", evaluating performance of bioremediation is difficult.
- Requires very skilled human power.

Genetic Engineering

Scientists are currently looking into certain genetically engineered micro-organisms to increase their ability to metabolize specific chemicals such as hydrocarbons and pesticides. The possibilities of using genetic engineering for improvement of bioremediation process had an early boost in the late 1980's. Recombinant DNA techniques have been studied intensively to improve the degradation of hazardous waste under laboratory condition. The genetically engineered microorganisms have higher degradative capacity and have been demonstrated successfully for the degradation of various pollutants under defined conditions. Genetic modification technology has resulted often in a wide variety of current and potential applications for use in the process of bioremediation. Bioremediation explores gene diversity and metabolic versatility of microorganisms (Fulekar, 2009). The genetic architecture of these organisms makes them valuable in biodegradation, biotransformation, biosorption and bioaccumulation. The necessary blue print of gene encoding for biodegradative enzymes is present in chromosomal and extra-chromosomal DNA of such microbes. Recombinant DNA techniques facilitate to evolve the ability of an organism to metabolize a xenobiotic by detection of such degradative genes and transforming them into appropriate host via suitable vector under the tight control of appropriate promoters. It depends on susceptibility to alteration and exchange of genetic information. The recombinant DNA technology explores PCR, anti-sense RNA technique, site directed mutagenesis, electroporation and particle bombardment techniques. The biotechnology armed with recombinant DNA technology is now fine tuning the bioremediation technology by improving pollutant– degrading microbes through strain improvement and genetic modification of specific regulatory and metabolic genes that are crucial in developing effective, safe and economical techniques for bioremediation. Bioremediation is not effective only for the degradation of pollutants but it can also be used to clean unwanted substances from air, soil, water and raw materials form industrial waste. Bioremediation is not effective only for the degradation of pollutants but it can also be used to clean unwanted substances from air, soil, water and raw materials form industrial waste.

Conclusion

Organic and inorganic contaminants deteriorated the environment on the earth because of their deliberate and accidental leakage or production and generation in the form of waste. Stimulating the natural process of Bioremediation offers an opportunity for reducing the environmental impact of various pollutants. Microbial bioremediation of these contaminations has attracted the researchers all over the world as microbes naturally offer plenty of opportunities for the cleaning-up of the polluted sites. It is the most effective management tool to manage the polluted environment and recover contaminated soil. This process involves biotransformation and biodegradation by transforming contaminants to non–hazardous or less hazardous chemicals. Often, the micro-organisms metabolize the chemicals to produce carbon dioxide or methane, water and biomass. The microorganisms with the genetic capacity to transform compounds of interest must be present in contaminant metabolism to occur in a bioremediation process. In certain cases, the addition of organisms acclimated to specific contaminants, or bioaugmentation, may decrease the duration of lag phases. Microbial bioremediation is an option that offers the possibility to destroy or render harmless various contaminants using natural biological activity.

REFERENCE

Adams GO, Fufeyin PT, Okoro SE, *et.al.* Bioremediation, Biostimulation and Bioaugmention: A Review. International Journal of Environmental Bioremediation & Biodegradation. 2015;3(1): 28-39.

Adriano, D.C. (eds) Bioavailability, Toxicity and Risk Relationships in Ecosystems, Science Publishers, Enfield, New Hampshire pp. 109–144.

Aksu Z (1998) Biosorption of Heavy Metals by Micro Algae in Batch and Continuous Systems. In: WONG, Y-S. and TAM, N.F.Y. eds. Algae for Waste Water Treatment. Germany. Springer p. 164-182.

Ayse BY, Oya I, Selin S (2005) Bioaccumulation and Toxicity of Different Copper Concentrations in Tetraselmis chuii. E.U. Journal of Fisheries and Aquatic Sciences 22(3-4): 297-304.

Carpenter A, MacGill S (2001) Charging for Port Reception Facilities in North Sea Ports: Putting Theory into Practice. Mar Pollut Bull 42: 257–266.

Cases I, de Lorenzo V. Genetically Modified Organisms for the Environment: Stories of Success and Failure and What We Have Learned from Them. International Microbiology. 2005; 8:213-22.

Cobbett C, Goldsbrough P (2002) Phytochelatin and Metallothioneins: Roles in Heavy Metal Detoxification and Homeostasis. Annu Rev Plant Biol 53:159–182.

Couto N, Fritt-Rasmussen J, Jensen PE, *et.al.* Suitability of Oil Bioremediation in an Artic Soil Using Surplus Heating from an Incineration Facility. Environmental Science and Pollution Research, 2014;21(9):6221-7.

Das N, Chandran P. Microbial Degradation of Petroleum Hydrocarbon Contaminants: An Overview. Biotechnol Res Int. 2011;1-13.

Davis T (2000) Sargassum Seaweed as Biosorbent for Heavy Metals (Davis, T., Volesky, B., Vieira, R.). Wat Res 34:4270-4278.

Dell'Anno A, Beolchini F, Rocchetti L, *et.al.* High Bacterial Biodiversity Increases Degradation Performance of Hydrocarbons During Bioremediation of Contaminated Harbor Marine Sediments. Environ Pollut. 2012;167:85-92.

Demnerova K, Mackova M, Spevakova, V, *et.al.* Two Approaches to Biological Decontamination of Groundwater and Soil Polluted by Aromatics Characterization of Microbial Populations. International Microbiology. 2005; 8:205-11.

Edgington DN, Gorden SA, Thommes MM *et.al.* (1970) The Concentration of Radium, Thorium and Uranium by Tropical Marine Algae. Limnology and Oceanography 15(1): 945-955.

El Fantroussi S, Agathos SN. Is Bioaugmentation a Feasible Strategy for Pollutant Removal and Site Remediation? Curr Opin Microbiol. 2005; 8: 268-75.

Enim AE. Factors that Determine Bioremediation of Organic Compounds in the Soil. Academic Journal of Interdisciplinary Studies. 2013;2(13):125-8.

Fulekar MH. 2009. Bioremediation of Fenvalerate by Pseudomonas Aeruginosa in a Scale up Bioreactor. Romanian Biotechnological Letters, 14(6): 4900-4905.

Gumgum B, Unlu E, Tez Z *et.al.* (1994) Heavy Metal Pollution in Water, Sediment and Fish from the Tiger River in Turkey. Chemosphere 29 (1): 111-116.

Haynes D, Johnson JE (2000) Organochlorine, Heavy Metal and Polyaromatic Hydrocarbon Pollutant Concentrations in the Great Barrier Reef (Australia) Environment: A Review. Mar Pollut Bull 41:7–12.

Inthorn D (2001) Removal of Heavy Metal by Using Microalgae. Edited by Hiroyuki Kojima and Yuan Kun Lee, Photosynthetic Microorganisms in Environmental Biotechnology. Springer, Verlag Hong Kong Ltd 310: 111-169

Jain PK, Bajpai V. Biotechnology of Bioremediation- A Review. International Journal of Environmental Sciences. 2012;3(1): 535-49.

Kobayashi H, Rittman BE (1982) Microbial Removal of Hazardous Organic Compounds. Environ Sci Technol 16: 170A- 183A.

Kumar A, Bisht BS, Joshi VD, *et.al.* Review on Bioremediation of Polluted Environment: A Management Tool. International journal of Environmental Sciences. 2011;1(6):1079-93.

Laul JC (1992) Natural Radionuclides in Ground Water. Journal of Radio analytical and Nuclear Chemistry 156(1): 235-241.

Macaulay BM. Understanding the Behavior of Oil-degrading Microorganisms to Enhance the Microbial Remediation of Spilled Petroleum. Appl Ecol Environ Res. 2015;13(1):247-62.

Madhavi GN, Mohini DD. Review Paper On – Parameters Affecting Bioremediation. International Journal of Life Science and Pharma Research. 2012; 2(3):77-80.

Megharaja M, Ragusa SR, Naidu R (2003) Metal–algae Interactions: Implication of Bioavailability. In: Naidu, R., Gupta, V.V.S.R., Rogers, S., Kookana, R.S., Bolan, N.S. and

Montagnolli RN, Matos Lopes PR, Bidoia ED. Assessing Bacillus Subtilis Biosurfactant Effects on the Biodegradation of Petroleum Products. Environ. Monit. Assess. 2015; 187 (4116): 1 17.

Pergent C, Pergent-Martini C (1999) Mercury Levels and Fluxes in Podosonia Oceanica Meadows. Environ Pollut 106: 33–7.

Phulia V, Jamwal A, Saxena N, *et.al.* Technologies in Aquatic Bioremediation. Kumar P, Zaki BMSA, Chauhan A, Editors. Freshwater Ecosystem and Xenobiotics. Discovery Publishing House.

Praepilas D, Pakawadee K (2011) Effects of Wastewater Strength and Salt Stress on Microalgal Biomass Production and Lipid Accumulation. World Academy of Science, Engineering and PVT. Ltd.: India; 2013; pp. 65-91.

Sharma S. Bioremediation: Features, Strategies and Applications. Asian Journal of Pharmacy and Life Science. 2012;2(2): 202-13.

Singh A, Kumar V, Srivastava JN. Assessment of Bioremediation of Oil and Phenol Contents in Refinery Waste Water via Bacterial Consortium. J Pet Environ Biotechnol. 2013;4(3):1-4.

Solomon KR (1996) Ecological Risk Assessment of Atrazine in North America Surface Waters. Environ Toxicol Chem 15: 31– 76

Strong PJ, Burgess JE. Treatment Methods for Wine-related ad Distillery Wastewaters: A Review. Biorem J. 2008; 12(2):70-87.

Takagi M, Karseno Yoshida T (2006) Effect of Salt Concentration on Intracellular Accumulation of Lipids and Triacylglyceride in Marine Microalgae Dunaliella Cells. J Biosci Bioeng 101: 223-226.

Tang CY, Criddle QS Fu CS, Leckie JO. Effect of Flux (Trans Membrane Pressure) and Membranes Properties on Fouling and Rejection of Reverse Osmosis and Nano Filtration Membranes Treating Perfluorooctane Sulfonate Containing Waste Water. J Enviro Sci Tech. 2007;41:2008-14.

Technology 60:1163-1168.

Thavasi R, Jayalakshmi S, Banat IM. Application of Biosurfactant Produced from Peanut Oil Cake by Lactobacillus Delbrueckii in Biodegradation of Crude Oil. Bioresour Technol. 2011; 102(3): 3366-72.

Wake H (2005) Oil Refineries: A Review of their Ecological Impacts on the Aquatic Environment. Estuar Coast Shelf Sci 62:131– 140.

Walker JD, Colwell RR, Petrakis L (1975) Degradation of Petroleum by an Algae, Prototheca Zopci. Appl Micro-biol 30:79-81.

Wang Q, Zhang S, Li Y, *et.al.* Potential Approaches to Improving Biodegradation of Hydrocarbons for Bioremediation of Crude Oil Pollution. Environ Protection J. 2011;2: 47-55.

Yang SZ, Jin HJ, Wei Z, *et.al.* Bioremediation of Oil Spills in Cold Environments: A Review. Pedosphere. 2009; 19(3): 371-81.

Soil Ecosystem and Lithosphere **Pages 120-126**
Edited by: Dr. Abhishek Swami, Dr. Prasann Kumar and Dr. Pawan Kumar 'Bharti'
ISBN: 978-93-88854-50-4
Edition: 2020
Published by: Discovery Publishing House Pvt. Ltd., New Delhi (India)

10

Salinity Stress
Daunting Face for Sustainable Growth

Priyanka Aley[1], Prasann Kumar[1, 2*]

ABSTRACT

Salinity stress is characterized as the nearness of unnecessary measure of solvent salts that block or influence the typical working of plant development. It is all around announced that, saltiness stress is where unnecessary salts in soil arrangement cause hindrance of plant development or plant demise. On a world scale, no poisonous substance limits plant development more than doe's salt. Saltiness stress shows an expanding danger to plant agribusiness. Salinization influences many flooded territories chiefly because of the utilization of bitter water (having more saltiness than freshwater, however not as much as seawater). Overall in excess of 45 million hectares of flooded land have been harmed by salts, and 1-5 million hectares are removed from generation every year because of high saltiness feelings of anxiety in the dirt. During introductory presentation to saltiness, plants experience water pressure, which thus diminishes leaf extension. During long haul introduction to saltiness, plants experience ionic pressure, which can prompt untimely senescence of grown-up leaves, and along these lines a decrease in the photosynthetic territory accessible to help proceeded with development. High saltiness influences plants in a few different ways: water pressure, particle poisonous quality, nourishing issue, oxidative pressure, adjustment of metabolic procedures, layer complication, decrease of cell division and development, genotoxicity. Together, these impacts diminish plant development, improvement and endurance. It is estimated in the term of EC (electrical conductivity), ESP (replaceable sodium rate) and Ph (capability of hydrogen). Saline soils are those that have EC of more than 4d sm-1, ESP under 15% and Ph more than 7 and beneath 8.5. Salts can happen normally inside soil and water. Salination can be brought about by normal procedures, for example, mineral enduring or by the slow withdrawal of a sea. It can likewise happen through fake procedures, for example, water system and street salt. Salt pressure majorly affects plant development and yield generation, indicating the significance of understanding the system of salt resilience in plants. Interruption of the protein

[1] Department of Agronomy, School of Agriculture, Lovely Professional University, Jalandhar, Punjab, India, 144411

[1, 2] Division of Research and Development, Lovely Professional University, Jalandhar, Punjab 144411, India

collapsing limit in the endoplasmic reticulum prompts the aggregation of unfurled protein and ER stress, which initiates an "unfolded protein reaction" (UPR).

Keywords: *Agriculture, Biotic, Crop, Density, Energy, ESP, Forage*

Introduction

There are various environmental factors that can cause problem in the growth and development of the plant. These factor can be biotic or abiotic in which one of the factor is salinity stress responsible for causing severe problems. Salt stress is the condition where excessive salt is present in the soil as a result plant face different problems i.e. inhibition of crop growth or death. Salt stress is considered an alarming condition as it decreases the agricultural productivity of soil and result in reduced crop yields (Hu *et.al.*, 2006). 20% of the agriculture land is majorly affected by salinity stress. There are various ways by which salt amount can be increased in soil like irrigated water quality, use of chemicals, and the use of brackish. If the amount of salt is high in the soil it can affect plant in various ways, such as expansion or reduction of cell division, genotoxicity, nutritional disorders, ion toxicity.

Salinity Problem

It is the accumulation of salt in land and water to a level that damages the natural and built environment. It usually occurs with other resource problems such as decreasing soil and water quality, erosion and loss of negative vegetation (Figure 10.1).

Types of salinity stress: There are different types of salinity stress.

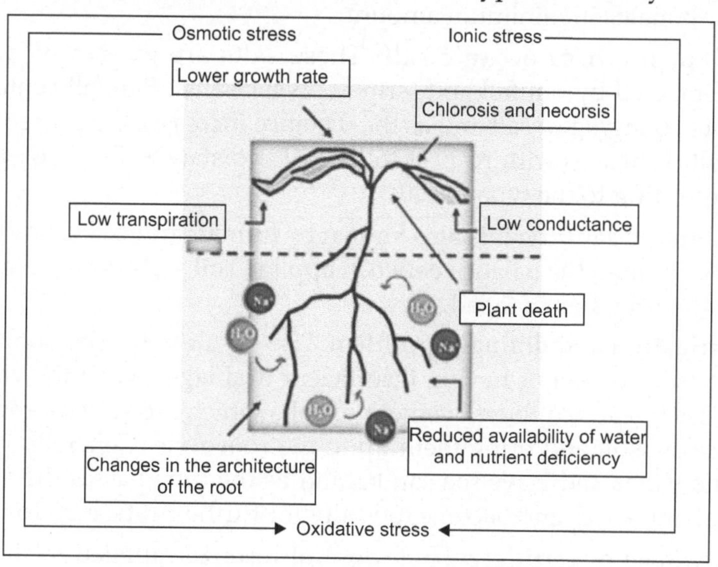

Fig. 10.1: General effects of Na^+ toxicity in plants under saline conditions

(**Source:** Based on review of literature)

- **Osmotic stress:** The osmotic stress is caused by the excess of Na^+ and Cl^- ions in the soil that decrease the osmotic potential and hampers the water uptake and nutrients.
- **Ionic stress:** Exposure to higher levels of NaCl, affects uptake of water and dissolved nutrients resulting in impaired plant water status creates ionic imbalance by means of the cellular accumulation of toxic Na^+ and Cl^- ions.
- **Oxidative stress:** High salinity induce oxidative stress in different plants and tissues (Ashraf and Harris, 2004; Chawla *et.al.*, 2013). Under salinity stress, the level of ROS (reactive oxygen species) increases in the plant tissues as a result of irregularities in the electron transport chain and accumulation of photo reducing power

Causes of Salinity

Salinity can be categorized according to the source of causes i.e. primary and secondary.

- **Primary salinity or naturally occurring salinity:** When salt accumulates for a longer period of time by natural processes in groundwater or soil it cause primary salinity. It is caused by two different natural processes.

1. **Weathering of parent material:** Parent material contain soluble salts as a result when break down of rocks occur they release soluble salt of different types mainly sodium chloride in maximum level which is the most soluble salt, calcium and magnesium, and sulphates and carbonates in minimum amount.
2. **Deposition of oceanic salt:** These salts are carried by wind and deposited by rainfall and term as 'cyclic salts'. Rainfall contains from 6 to 50 mg/kg of salt and as the distance increases the concentration of salt decreases with respect to the coast distance. The % of salt varies according to the type of soil.

- **Secondary salinity:** It is also known by human induced salinity because of the act of human the balance between applied soil water and water used by crops get disturbed or changed.

1. **Irrigation and drainage problem:** Use of salt-rich irrigation water can cause problem or having insufficient drainage. When the water table rises it leads to the movement of salts which are stored previously in the subsoil and bring them up to the root zone. Generally plant uses the water and leave the salt behind as the time passes the amount of salt increases and become too salty for further uptake by roots.
2. **Overuse of fertilizer:** High dose of fertilizer applied in the soil can cause salinity because some fertilizer contains high level of potentially harmful salts example-ammonium sulphate or potassium chloride.

When the amount of water decreases the concentration of salt increases. Continues use of these fertilizers lead to salinity buildup.

3. **Industrial effluents:** There are many industries through which saline water are discharged and through groundwater or rainfall they come in contact with soil or various effluents (waste) has been discharged into the water and get evaporated after which it came contact with the soil.

Impact of Salinity in Plant

At the point when plants are influenced with salt pressure, it causes particle irregularity and in charge of switch stream of water into the plant. Amassing of overabundance sodium and chloride in the cytoplasm happens which legitimately influence the protein capacity and pace of photosynthesis. A large portion of the agribusiness land is influenced with the dirt saltiness and in charge of corruption in soil ripeness all through the world. Over 30% of the watered land has been influenced by high soil saltiness and about 20 million hectares are being influenced each year on complete globe scale. At the point when plants are under salt pressure, stream of water into the plant is turned around and it causes particle awkwardness. Plant bites the dust as water is drawn out of the cell and aggregation of overabundance sodium (Na^+) and chloride (Cl^-) particles in the cytoplasm happens. Many effect sly affect the working of cells by influencing protein union, catalyst capacities and poor pace of photosynthesis. Salinity target different periods of development and parts of the plant-

(*a*) **On growth:** decreased rate of seed growth after an increase in soil salinity is primarily due to the osmotic effect of the salt around the roots. Increase in soil salinity causes leaf cell to loose water. Reduction in leaf elongation and also cell division lead to slower leaf appearance and smaller final size.

(*b*) **Germination:** increased osmotic pressure of the soil solution which restricts the absorption and entry of water into the seeds. Certain salt constituents are toxic to the embryo and seedlings. Anions like CO_3^-2, NO_3^-, CT^-, SO_4^-2 are more harmful to seed germination. Salt stress hampers the metabolism of stored materials.

(*c*) **Vegetative growth:** during vegetative stage salt induced water stress causes closure of stomata leads to reduction in CO_2 assimilation and transpiration. Reduction of turgor potential affects the leaf expansion. Because of reduction in leaf area, light interception is reduces, photosynthetic rate is affected which coupled with spurt in respiration, resulting into reduced biomass accumulation.

(*d*) **Photosynthesis:** accumulation of high concentration of Na^+ and Cl^- in chloroplast, photosynthesis is inhibited. Since photosynthetic electron transport appears relatively in sensitive to salts, either carbon metabolism or photophosphorylation may be affected. Photosynthetic enzyme or the enzyme responsible for carbon assimilation are very sensitive to the presence of NaCl.

(*e*) **Nitrogen metabolism:** the key enzyme, nitrate reductase is very sensitive to NaCl. One of the amino acid, glycinebetaine shows increased trend with increase in salinity in perennial halophytes and atriplex sps. Proline is a αamino acids in salt stressed plants.

(*f*) **Reproductive growth and yield:** under salt stress condition, the onset of flowering is delayed due to the limitations of source size. The no. of flowers/panicles is very much reduced. The disturbance in the normal metabolism affects the mobility of metabolites. Due to the imbalance of nutrients under salt stress, hormone synthesis is hampered leads to reduction in quantity as well as quality of crop produce.

Symptoms of Damage in Plants

Side effects are mostly regular that of soil borne or parasitic infection. In this way there are explicit test are expected to test the nearness of the salt. There are different indications

(*a*) Brown stunted root

(*b*) Slow or no growth

(*c*) Burning and dieback of young growth

(*d*) Dead and brown sections on the margins and tips of older leaves.

Sometimes white encrustations of salt can be seen on the surface of soil or potting media or around drainage holes or pots it indicates the excess amount of salt is present and taken as early warning of salinity problems.

Fig 10.2: Salt affected plants

(**Source:** Based on review of literature)

How Salinity is Measured

Excessive amount of soluble salts that hinder of affect normal functioning of the plant growth. It is measured in the terms of EC, ESP and pH (Figure 10.3).

1. **EC:** It is measured by passing an electric current between the two electrodes of a salinity meter in a sample of soil or plant. The electrical conductivity of EC of a soil or plant is influenced by the concentration and composition of dissolved salts. The salt increases the ability of a solution to conduct an electrical current, so a high EC value indicates a high salinity level.
2. **ESP:** (exchangeable sodium percentage) the extent to which the absorption complex of a soil is occupied by sodium. Amount of ESP expressed as a percentage of total exchangeable cations.it is expressed as

   ESP= exchangeable sodium (meq/100g)/cation exchange capacity (meg/100g) ×100
3. **pH:** the term ph generally refers to the concentration of hydrogen ions in a medium. Most of the plants grow best in ph values between 5.5 and 6.5. As the ph rises to 7.0 and above, boron, manganese and particularly ion may become deficient. Mostly ph is measured accurately with a ph meter containing a glass electrode.

Plants are classified into two types based on the tolerance to salt stress:

(*a*) **Halophytes:** the plants that can grow under high salt concentration. Example- spartina alterniflora, atriplex etc.

(*b*) **Glycophytes:** the plants that cannot grow under high salt concentration.

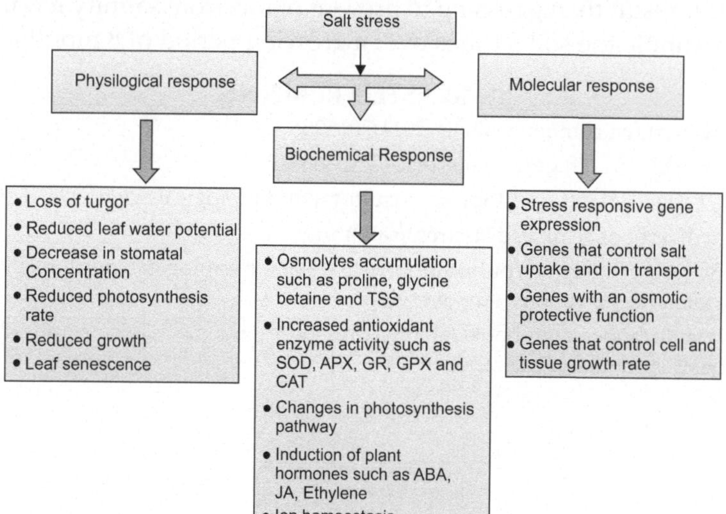

Fig. 10.3: Adaptive responses, tolerance mechanism in plants

(**Source:** based on review of literature)

How to Prevent and Manage Salinity

There are various practices that can be apply to prevent and manage the salinity:

1. **Select the crop that fits the condition in your field:** It is better to avoid planting a sensitive crop in a soil which is not well drained.
2. **Know the leaching requirement for your crop:** Apply the minimum needed flush salts from soils. This means that you always have to give a little more water than the crop consumption, to allow leaching of salts below the root zone. Heavier soils require larger amount of water than lighter soils, in order to avoid salinity build-up. the leaching requirement is expressed as-

   LR-water leached/ water applied.
3. **Keep the right intervals between irrigations:** It must be appropriate to the soil condition. Frequent and shallow applications result in salt accumulation in the root zone, while larger applications, in longer intervals will flush the salts below the root zone.
4. **Use appropriate fertilizer types:** The amount of fertilizer and there quantity should be limited as per the requirement of the crop. There are many fertilizer which contain salts which are not taken up by plants in large amounts such as chlorides. These can accumulate in the soil and can cause problems.
5. **Periodically testing of soil:** Soil analysis is majorly important and better indication of salt content in the soil. A practical approach can give more clear result than guessing to prevent plants from salinity it is important to sample the soil 5 times over a growing period of 8 months.

SUGGESTED READING

https://www.hindawi.com/journals/ijg/2014/701596/

https://www.ncbi.nlm.nih.gov/pmc/articles/PMC6384275/

https://www.sciencedirect.com/topics/agricultural-and-biological-sciences/salt-stress

https://www.liverpool.ac.uk/~sd21/stress/salt.htm

https://www.researchgate.net/publication/284837596_Physiological_mechanisms_of_salt_stress_tolerance_in_plants_An_overview

https://www.intechopen.com/books/abiotic-stress-in-plants-mechanisms-and-adaptations/salinity-stress-and-salt-tolerance

Soil Ecosystem and Lithosphere
Edited by: Dr. Abhishek Swami, Dr. Prasann Kumar and Dr. Pawan Kumar 'Bharti'
ISBN: 978-93-88854-50-4
Edition: 2020
Published by: Discovery Publishing House Pvt. Ltd., New Delhi (India)
Pages 127-165

11

Assessment of Agricultural Soil Quality with Special Reference to Heavy Metals

Pawan Kumar 'Bharti'

ABSTRACT

The rapid growth of industrialization and urbanization has created negative impacts on the environment especially in the last three decades. The industrial wastes containing organic pollutants and heavy metals in their effluents have been polluted surface and ground water. In India, the industrial effluents have contributed a major source of pollution. Textile effluent when discharged into the pond and through pond they percolated to the ground water. Thus, contaminated ground water has deteriorated immensely the drinking utilities, post agriculture irrigation and impacts on soil systems and crop productivity. The aim of this study was to emphasized on the transfer of heavy metals and extent of heavy metal contamination of soil due to irrigation with contaminated ground water affected by textile industrial effluents, on agricultural land. Metal transfer factors from effluent to ground water, from ground water to irrigated agricultural soil and from soil to vegetation are described in a simplified method in water, soil and plants.

Key words: *Heavy metals, industry, agriculture soil, transfer factor.*

Introduction

Textile effluents have consisted high concentrations of heavy metals, organic and inorganic pollutants and toxic colours, which may alter the surface water quality of the region. Toxic pollutants may percolate down via soil profile and reach in ground water, which ultimately cause the health hazards among human being and livestock after consumption as daily drinking requirements. The waste water without any treatment may cause adverse effect on the health of human, domestic animals, wildlife and environment (Sharma *et.al.*, 1999). Thus, contaminated ground water has deteriorated immensely the drinking utilities, post agriculture irrigation and impacts on soil systems and crop productivity. It is essential to know the status and functions of heavy metals discarding from textile industries in to surface, ground water, soil and crop plant vegetation for health safety of regional people, which may help in recent research in the field of soil and water pollution by industries and for advance alarming against pollution to public, NGOs and GOs. The present paper deals with the distribution and transfer of heavy metals between water and soil. Regarding human consumption and irrigation practices ground water may cause the human and livestock health hazards and reduce soil fertility and agricultural plant productivity.

Dye houses waste water of generally discharged openly into Binjhole pond water, thus polluted the surface water quality of the region (Malik *et.al.*, 2006). After delaying for a long period of time the heavy metal contents may leach down in to ground water regime through soil profile very slowly. Because the ground water movement is very slow (CPCB, 2003), so metal contents remain in ground water for a long period even in toxic form. Thus metals reach in local ground water and deteriorated the ground water quality of neighborhood area. Metals reach in agricultural soil through repeated irrigation by contaminated ground water. Some concentrations of metals again percolate in to ground water and some of them delay in soil water. Soil particles bound a huge amount of heavy metals due to adsorptive nature, which remain in capillary water and easily available for plants. Plants absorb the sufficient amount of water for their different requirements. Metals present in this available water arrive in plant tissues with water and accumulate in various parts of plant bodies (Malik *et.al.*, 2004). These metal contents may affect the plants activities and generate some physiological changes in plants sometimes (Garg and Kaushik, 2006). In other cases, accumulated amount of heavy metals may reach in livestock and human beings after continuous uptake of these crop parts.

Soil of agricultural fields requires sufficient irrigation for high production in agricultural fields. Irrigation water with poor quality can result in the alteration of physico-chemical characteristics of irrigated agricultural soil. Several minerals such as chloride, sulphate, bicarbonate, sodium, calcium and magnesium in irrigation water may change the soil quality with its continuous application on soil. These minerals contained in the irrigation water can build up the soil's trophic level and ultimately influence the agriculture productivity (Malik and Bharti, 2007; Bharti, 2007).

Historical Resume

Several researchers from India and abroad have been discussed various aspects of heavy metals pollution of water and soil in term of characteristics of water bodies, affected agricultural soils and bottom sediments from time to time. This review includes some of important contribution made in the field of industrial pollution, with references to heavy metals parameters of ground water, surface water, characterization of textile industrial effluents, contaminated agricultural irrigated soil and bottom sediment soils by different authors of country and abroad. Aggarwal and Mehrotra (1952) surveyed the soil and soil water affected by effluent in some selected regions of Uttar Pradesh. Richards (1954) evaluated the quality of saline and alkali soils and gave a technique for the improvement of these sick soil systems in the agricultural sector for good performance of agriculture productivity. Kanwar (1961) assessed the quality of irrigation water as an index of suitability for irrigation purposes.

Darra *et.al.*, (1964) evaluated the water quality of irrigation water used in Rajasthan. Saksena *et.al.*, (1966) evaluated the quality of ground waters for irrigation in Ahor developmental block, Jalore. Bhakuni and Bopardikar (1967) stated the method of recovery Zinc from the spinning bath waste of Viscos reyon factory by using ion exchange method and found it significant useful in metal removal process. Williums (1972) described the characteristics and various properties of Metals. Katz (1975) highlighted the effect of heavy metals on some environmental components and biotic organisms of aquatic environment in New York. Dowedy and Larson (1975) reported the availability of some metals in various vegetable crops in a polluted region in the vicinity of an industrial area. Dulka and Risby (1976) stated ultra trace metals in some environmental and biological systems in the vicinity of textile industrial sector. Shivakumar *et.al.*, (1977) made a geo-graphical approach for toxic trace element pollution in ground water around Patancheru and Bollaram Industrial area, A.P., India. Martin and Cougherty (1982) stated the basic monitoring techniques for detection of heavy metals pollution through the biological agents. Ireland (1983) described the heavy metals uptake and their distribution in tissues of organisms. Numberg (1984) studied on the volumetric approach in trace metal chemistry of natural waters and atmospheric precipitation. Nriagu and Pacyna (1988) carried out a study on the quantitative assessment of worldwide contamination of air, water and soil with trace metals.

Mishra *et.al.*, (1990) reported the occurrence of heavy metals in crop plants of Sanagar more than the permissible limits presence of which may cause the adverse effect on the plant/human health and may cause high mortality of fish population in affected aquatic environment. Singh *et.al.*, (1994) highlighted the degradation of water and soil quality of Parwanoo area with respect to heavy metals. Sharma and Patel (1996) determined copper in water of Raipur with the help of spectrophotometer. Prasad and Chandra (1997) studied well water quality status of Hyderabad and Khurshid and Shabeer (1997) observed water quality degradation due to heavy metal pollution. Mohan *et.al.*, (1998) observed heavy metals (Fe, Pb, Ca & Zn) in the ground water of Naini industrial area; Dist. Allahabad, U.P. Kashem and Singh (1999) had also found the decreasing concentration of Cu, Mn, Pb and Zn with increasing distance from disposal point. Stetzenbach *et.al.*, (1999) evaluated the heavy metals in ground water and used multivariate statistical analysis. Tyagi and Budhi (2000) postulated the degradation of ground water quality due to heavy metals in industrial area of India.

Kumar *et.al.*, (2001) studied on the impact of textile industry on ground water quality of Sanagar, Jaipur and found the high amount of chemicals (e.g.

sulphuric acid and acetic acid) and dyes (e.g. chrome and metal dyes) suspended solids and toxic metals in the waste which may enter in the groundwater and deteriorate its quality. Siddiqui and Pathania (2002) made some studies on heavy metals in surface and ground water of Jalandhar and Ludhiana districts of Punjab state. Shrivastava *et.al.*, (2003) collected soil samples from surface of the soil from different agriculture fields in the Khandesh region and Tapi River sediment samples were also collected from five different stations which were 7-8 km away from each other and detected the concentrations of heavy metals have been determined by ICP-AES. Khan *et.al.*, (2003) harvested some Solanum melongena plant in a laboratory experiment using five different levels of textile waste water and observed the contamination of heavy metals as 1.417 mg/g of Zn, 1.003 mg/g of Cu, 0.378 mg/g of Ni, 0.378 mg/g of Cd, 0.773 mg/g of Cr, 1.139 mg/g of Pb and 0.427 mg/g of Co in the soil of pots treated with highest ratio of distilled water and waste water. Yadav and Sumanlata (2003) indicated the heavy metal pollution in ground water in Bahadurgarh block of districts Jhajjar, Haryana. Malik *et.al.*, (2004) evaluated the accumulation of heavy metals in crop plants through irrigation of contaminated ground water in Panipat region and emphasized on bioremediation processes for combat ground water pollution. Chao *et.al.*, (2005) reported the heavy metal contaminated site in Taiwan and described the status and distribution of heavy metals in environment. It is necessary to reduce the levels of toxic metals from industrial effluents before discharging into surface waters. The general methods of treating wastewater-containing metals are coagulation, ion exchange, reverse osmosis and adsorption. Adsorption is a highly effective physico-chemical treatment for removing heavy metals for effluents.

Due to high cost of activated carbon, efforts are being directed towards finding low cost adsorbents. Recently much interest has been shown for removal of heavy metals using a large number of low cost materials. Coal fly ash, the solid waste of power plants is one of the cheapest and non-conventional adsorbents (De, 2005).

Zheng *et.al.*, (2006) assessed the heavy metals pollution of agricultural soil in Guanzhong district of China. Lokeshwari and Chandrappa (2006) evaluated the impact of heavy metals contamination of a Lake on soil and cultivated vegetation near Bangalore and found the presence of some heavy metals in rice and vegetables, beyond the limit of Indian Standards and calculated metal transfer factors from soil to vegetation are found significant for Zn, Cu, Pb and Cd. Hedge *et.al.*, (2006) revealed the provenance of heavy minerals with special reference to ilmenite of the Honnevar beach in central west coast of India and observed some trace heavy elements like Co, Cr, V and Ni in the sandy soil of the beach. Singh (2006) indicated the contamination of ground water of Ganges-Brahmaputra river basin in north east India and found the ground water unfit for direct human consumption and noticed the rice and vegetable fields irrigated by ground water received a large amount of arsenic through shallow tube wells in the affected areas of north 24 Parganas and Murshidabad, West Bangal. Malik *et.al.*, (2007) assessed the migration of heavy metals in the ground water regime of Panipat industrial area on the behalf of different spatial variations the heavy metals were found in maximum quantities at point source of pollution.

Malik and Bharti (2007) studied on soil quality of irrigated agricultural fields in a textile industrial area of Panipat city. Va´zquez, *et.al.*, (2007) monitored the heavy metal pollution in San Antonio Bay, Rı´o Negro, Argentina. Obiri (2007) determined the heavy metals in water from boreholes in Dumasi in the Wassa West District of Western Region of Republic of Ghana. Huang *et.al.*, (2007) indicated the speciation and mobility of heavy metals in mud in coastal reclamation areas in Shenzhen in China. Walker *et.al.*, (2007) identified the influence of heavy metals and mineral nutrient supply on Bituminaria bituminosa. Golia *et.al.*, (2007) measured the accumulation of metals on tobacco leaves (primings) grown in an agricultural area in relation to soil.

Mico *et.al.*, (2007) described the comparison of two digestion methods for the analysis of heavy metals by flame atomic absorption spectroscopy. Padmavathiamma and Li (2007) explained the phytoremediation technology through the hyper-accumulation metals in plants and different aspects of phytoremediation technology and the biological mechanisms underlying phyto-remediation.

Study Area

Dye houses are situated on Jatal road in industrial area, these are quite famous for handloom business in Panipat city. Textile dying industries in Panipat region consume large quantities of water and discharge it into a common effluent drain, which ends up in to a large pond situated near Binjhole village. Since last five or six years, it was noticed that ground water quality is degrading day by day of the regions and local people think that the dye waste water is the major source of heavy metal pollution in area. But these heavy metals are travelling from wastewater to ground water and ground water to soil system and from soil system to agricultural crop tissues. In this paper, the route of heavy metals in soil and water is highlighted with proper illustrations and flow diagrams.

Methodology

Metals that are naturally introduced into the waterbody come primarily from such sources as rock weathering, soil erosion, or the dissolution of water-soluble salts. Naturally occurring metals move through aquatic environments independently of human activities, usually without any detrimental effects. Humans consume metallic elements through both water and food. Some metals such as sodium, potassium, magnesium, calcium, and iron are found in living tissue and are essential to human life-biological anomalies arise when they are depleted or removed. Probably less well known is that currently no less than six other heavy metals including molybdenum, manganese, cobalt, copper, and zinc, have been linked to human growth, development, achievement, and reproduction (Vahrenkamp, 1979; Friberg *et.al.*, 1979). Even these metals, however, can become toxic or aesthetically undesirable when their concentrations are too great. Several heavy metals, like cadmium, lead, and mercury, are highly toxic at relatively low concentrations, can accumulate in body tissues over long periods of time, and are nonessential for human health.

The toxic heavy metals entering the ecosystem may lead to geo-accumulation, bioaccumulation and biomagnifications. Heavy metals like Fe, Cu, Zn, Ni and other trace elements are important for proper functioning of biological systems and their deficiency or excess could lead to a number of disorders. Food chain contamination by heavy metals has become a burning issue in recent years because of their potential accumulation in biosystems through contaminated water, soil and air. Therefore, a better understanding of heavy metal sources, their accumulation in the soil and the effect of their presence in water and soil on plant systems seem to be particularly important issues of present-day research on risk assessments (Lokeshwari and Chandrappa, 2006). Path of heavy metals in various trophic levels may be different due to the nature of heavy metals and quality of host abiotic components. Transfer rate may be evaluated by the calculation of concentrations of heavy metals between two different trophic levels. Transfer factor between plants and soil may be calculated for each metal according to the following formula-

$$TF = Ps\ (\mu g\ g{-1}\ dry\ wt)/St(\mu g\ g{-1}\ dry\ wt),$$

Where, Ps is the plant metal content originating from the soil and St is the total metal content in the soil (Lokeshwari and Chandrappa, 2006). Thus transfer factor (coefficient) may evaluate also between every two trophic levels of ecosystem.

Analysis of Metals

Collected, preserved, diluted water samples were prepared for the evaluation of metal concentrations with the help of AAS 4129. In the case of soil samples, a suspension (1:5) should be prepared in the distilled water; rest processes are like surface water and ground water samples. Metals enter in the surface, ground water and soil/ sediments through the disposing of toxic textile effluents of dye houses. For every metal a standard was required and concentration may be detected by AAS. Diluted and completely digested samples were required for metal detection by AAS 4129. Metal elements were determined with the help of Atomic absorption spectrophotometer (Model AAS 4129). Alan Walsh first developed the technique of atomic absorption spectrophotometry in 1955, and since then it has emerged as a powerful tool in quantitative analysis of more than 70 metals. The major advantages of the method are that it is free from any kind of interferences and very small concentrations are possible to be measured (De, 2002). The AAS is based on the principle that atoms of elements, which normally remain in ground state under flame condition, absorb energy when subjected to radiation of specific wavelength. The absorption of radiation is proportional to the concentration of atoms of the element. The absorption of radiation by the atoms is independent of the wavelength of absorption and temperature of the atoms. These to feature provide AAS a distinct advantage over flame spectroscopy.

Copper (Cu)

Copper in the natural waters also results in higher concentration due to pollution. It is used with sulphate as a pesticides and also separately as an algicide. Although, it passes as such through the body but there is evidence of accumulation of trace quantities in liver. The limits of it in the standards are not due to its toxic effects but are due to its taste producing capacity.

Preparation of 1000 Cu (μg/ml) standard: Dissolve 1 gm of Cu in 50 ml of 6N of HNO_3 and dilute to 1 L to give 1000 μg/ml Cu.

Cadmium (Cd)

Cadmium is fairy dense silver white malleable and most toxic metal, which melts at 320.9°C. Cadmium is used for dye and paint pigment production, batteries, ceramic industries, wooden industries and plastic production. The Cd found in a sample of Ca is likely in a inorganic form and may be relatively less toxic to plants and animals, while same amount of Cd when present in zinc or phosphates may be highly toxic to plants and animals, especially when there is calcium deficiency in soil or livestock rations.

Preparation of 1000 Cd (μg/ml) standard: Dissolve 1 gm of Cd Metal in 20 ml of 5N HCl containing 0.5 ml of concentrated HNO_3 and dilute to 1 L to give 1000 μg/ml Cd.

Iron (Fe)

Iron is one of the most abundant elements of the rocks and soil, ranking fourth by weight. All kinds of waters including ground water have appreciable quantities of iron. Iron has more solubility at acidic pH, therefore large quantities of iron are leached out from the soils by acidic waters. In the alkaline medium iron remain comparatively low in soluble phase.

Preparation of 1000 Fe (μg/ml) standard, dissolve 1.000 g of iron wire in 50 ml of (1+1) HNO_3 and dilute to 1 liter with de-ionized water to give 1000 μg/ml Fe.

Manganese (Mn)

Although not a toxic metal, Mn imparts objectionable and tenacious stains to laundry plumbing fixtures and clothing. It occurs in domestic waste water, industrial effluents, acid mine drainage and receiving strums and therby enters water bodies. Mn is relatively non-toxic to animals, but toxic to plants at higher levels.

Preparation of 1000 Mn (μg/ml) standard: Dissolve 1 gm of Mn in 50 ml of 6N of HNO_3 and dilute to 1 L to give 1000 μg/ml Mn.

Nickel (Ni)

At high concentrations, nickel has toxic properties. Aquatic organisms have varying sensitivities to nickel salts depending on the water's pH, hardness, alkalinity and type of nickel compound under consideration. Nickel as a metal is a carcinogen.

Preparation of 1000 Ni (μg/ml) standard: Dissolve 1 gm of Ni metal in 50 ml of 6N of HNO_3 and dilute to 1 L to give 1000 μg/ml Ni.

Lead (Pb)

It is a dense soft metal and is quite resistant to corrosion. It has melting point of 327°C. Major source of lead is PbS (Galena). Lead is used for pipes, solders, electrodes, batteries, newsprint, and pigments in paints. Lead is also used in insecticides, beverages, ointments and synthetic dyes. The chemical form of lead determines its solubility in water and biological fluids, the extent of its fixation on soil and type of chemical reactions occurring in atmospheric, aquatic as well as soil environment.

Preparation of 1000 Pb (μg/ml) standard: Dissolve 1 gm of Pb metal in 20 ml of 6N of HNO_3 and dilute to 1 L to give 1000 μg/ml Pb.

Zinc (Zn)

Zinc is present in high concentrations in the wastes from pharmaceuticals, paint, galvanizing, cosmetics, dyes and pigments, etc., and their discharge increases its concentration in appreciable amounts in the waters. Zinc is very essential micronutrient in human beings and only at very high concentration it may cause some toxic effects. Zinc salts produce an undesirable taste to the water and causes water to appear milky and on boiling, a greasy surface scum may also form in the water (Mani et. al., 2005).

Preparation of 1000 Zn (μg/ml) standard: Dissolve 1 gm of Zn metal in 40 ml of 5N HCl and dilute to 1 L to give 1000 μg/ml Zn.

Standards and Calibration

Possible metals and metals oxides are to be preferred in the preparation of standards. This enables the analyst to dissolve them that samples and standards will contain identical elements and hence minimizes any chemical or physical interference effects.

Only concentrated standards (above 1000 μg/ml) should be held in storage. Working standards should be diluted from standards stock solutions only when needed. At low concentrations (less than 10 μg/ml) solutions have been found to deteriorate quite quickly because of the absorption on the walls of the container. Similar standard addition solutions can be prepared containing all of the required elements. This will avoid multiple splitting of the sample for individual elements and reduce the amount of time spent in preparing standards. Before weighting, standards materials should be treated to ensure that they are in a standard state.

Metals: Wash with acetone and ether to remove any oil layers. Remove any oxide coating by abrasion with emery cloth or by acid pickling and drying.

Oxides: Dry at 110 °C for two hours. If necessary, heat to evaluated temperatures to remove bound water.

Compounds: Equilibration at constant water content, or drying at 110 °C for two hours to remove any water.

Standards of known concentrations were prepared and evaluated the concentration of metal in water/ soil digested sample. Every metal has some specific properties and atomic weight, so for every metal different condition of standard and calibration was applied for every metal (ECIL methods manual, 2004).

Observations:

Experimental site

Heavy metals in agriculture soil

Cadmium (ppm): The cadmium concentration in agricultural soil was recorded maximum 3.4 ± 0.7 in summer 2006 and minimum 0.70 ± 0.60 in monsoon 2005 ranged between 0.1 to 4.0 ppm. The highest value of cadmium in agricultural soil was found 4.0 ppm during June 2006 and lowest 0.1 ppm in August 2005.

Copper (ppm): The concentration of copper in agricultural soil was recorded maximum 36.3 ± 7.4 in summer 2005 and minimum 13.4 ± 6.0 in winter 2005-06 ranged between 5.0 to 42.5 ppm. The highest value of copper in agricultural soil was found 42.5 ppm during June 2006 and lowest 5.0 ppm in December 2005.

Iron (ppm): The concentration of iron in agricultural soil was recorded maximum 82.8 ± 18.1 in summer 2006 and minimum 26.8 ± 10.8 in monsoon 2005 ranged between 14.40 to 100.5 ppm. The highest value of iron in agricultural soil was found 100.5 ppm during May 2006 and lowest 14.40 ppm in October 2005.

Manganese (ppm): The concentration of manganese in agricultural soil was recorded maximum 13.6 ± 1.4 in summer 2005 and minimum 5.8 ± 1.7 in winter 2006-07 ranged between 2.0 to 15.0 ppm. The highest value of manganese in agricultural soil was found 15.0 ppm during June 2005 and lowest 2.0 ppm in December 2005.

Nickel (ppm): The concentration of nickel in agricultural soil was recorded maximum 10.5 ± 0.8 in summer 2005 and minimum 5.3 ± 1.1 in winter 2006-07 ranged between 3.8 to 12.1 ppm. The highest value of nickel in agricultural soil was found 12.1 ppm during May 2006 and lowest 3.8 ppm in December 2006.

Lead (ppm): The concentration of lead in agricultural soil was recorded maximum 62.4 ± 10.9 in summer 2005 and minimum 25.1 ± 6.7 in winter 2006-07 ranged between 16.0 to 73.5 ppm. The highest value of lead in agricultural soil was found 73.5 ppm during June 2006 and lowest 16.0 ppm in November 2005.

Zinc (ppm): The concentration of zinc in agricultural soil was recorded maximum 19.4 ± 4.7 in monsoon 2006 and minimum 7.7 ± 2.8 in winter 2005-06 ranged between 4.3 to 23.5 ppm. The highest value of zinc in agricultural soil was found 23.5 ppm during July 2006 and lowest 4.3 ppm in January 2006.

Control Site

Heavy metals

Cadmium (ppm) The cadmium concentration in soil on control site was recorded maximum 2.23 ± 0.31 in summer 2005 and minimum 0.225 ± 0.21 in winter 2006-07 ranged between 0.00 to 2.80 ppm. The highest value of cadmium in agricultural soil was found 2.80 ppm during June 2006 and lowest 0.00 ppm in September 2006.

Copper (ppm): The concentration of copper in soil on control site was recorded maximum 27.4 ± 5.7 in summer 2005 and minimum 10.0 ± 4.1 in winter 2005-06 ranged between 3.5 to 32.0 ppm. The highest value of copper in agricultural soil was found 32.0 ppm during May 2005 and lowest 3.5 ppm in December 2006.

Iron (ppm): The concentration of iron in soil on control site was recorded maximum 68.6 ± 17.5 in summer 2005 and minimum 18.4 ± 9.0 in winter 2006-07 ranged between 6.90 to 84.50 ppm. The highest value of iron in agricultural soil was found 84.50 ppm during April 2005 and lowest 6.90 ppm in October 2005.

Manganese (ppm): The concentration of manganese in soil on control site was recorded maximum 11.5 ± 1.1 in summer 2005 and minimum 4.8 ± 1.5 in winter 2006-07 ranged between 3.2 to 12.5 ppm. The highest value of manganese in agricultural soil was found 12.5 ppm during June 2005 and lowest 3.2 ppm in December 2006.

Nickel (ppm): The concentration of nickel in soil on control site was recorded maximum 8.43 ± 1.2 in summer 2005 and minimum 2.6 ± 1.87 in winter 2006-07 ranged between 0.00 to 9.20 ppm. The highest value of nickel in agricultural soil was found 9.20 ppm during June 2006 and lowest 0.00 ppm in November 2006.

Lead (ppm): The concentration of lead in soil on control site was recorded maximum 42.3 ± 3.1 in summer 2005 and minimum 18.25 ± 5.9 in winter 2006-07 ranged between 11.3 to 46.8 ppm. The highest value of lead in agricultural soil was found 46.8 ppm during June 2006 and lowest 11.3 ppm in November 2005.

Zinc (ppm): The concentration of zinc in soil on control site was recorded maximum 16.5 ± 3.3 in monsoon 2006 and minimum 7.3 ± 0.8 in summer 2007 ranged between 5.1 to 19.1 ppm. The highest value of zinc in agricultural soil was found 19.1 ppm during July 2006 and lowest 5.1 ppm in January 2006.

Correlation Coefficient

Correlation was found maximum 0.8421 and 0.7499 for cadmium with water holding capacity and sodium respectively. Correlation for copper was found maximum 0.9134 and 0.9454 with temperature and Electric conductivity respectively. Correlation for iron was found maximum 0.8736 and 0.8436 with water holding capacity and sodium respectively. Correlation for manganese was found maximum 0.8162 and 0.9076 with temperature and Electric conductivity respectively. Correlation for nickel was found maximum 0.7798 and 0.8286 with water holding capacity and Electric conductivity respectively. Correlation for lead was found maximum 0.8483 and 0.8596 with water holding capacity and Electric conductivity respectively. Correlation for zinc was found maximum 0.8513 and 0.7586 with temperature and Electric conductivity respectively.

For cadmium correlation was found maximum 0.8706 and 0.7532 with water holding capacity and Electric conductivity respectively. Correlation for copper was found maximum 0.9142 and 0.8290 with temperature and chloride respectively. Correlation for iron was found maximum 0.8397 and 0.8795 with water holding capacity and sodium respectively. Correlation for manganese was found maximum 0.8814 and 0.7925 with temperature and chloride respectively. Correlation for nickel was found maximum 0.7267 and 0.6699 with temperature and water holding capacity respectively. Correlation for lead was found maximum 0.8608 and 0.8055 with water holding capacity and Electric conductivity respectively. Correlation for zinc was found maximum 0.8704 and 0.7613 with temperature and chloride respectively. For cadmium correlation was found maximum 0.7611 and 0.6466 with cadmium and lead respectively. Correlation for copper was found maximum 0.9733 and 0.9121 with iron and nickel respectively. Correlation for iron was found maximum

0.8074 and 0.8628 with manganese and lead respectively. Correlation for manganese was found maximum 0.9279 and 0.9548 with nickel and zinc respectively. Correlation for nickel was found maximum 0.9458 and 0.9475 with manganese and nickel respectively. Correlation for lead was found maximum 0.9482 and 0.9664 with copper and manganese respectively. Correlation for zinc was found maximum 0.8065 and 0.5301 with iron and nickel respectively. For cadmium correlation was found maximum 0.7650 and 0.7646 with copper and manganese respectively. Correlation for copper was found maximum 0.2703 and 0.2542 with cadmium and iron respectively. Correlation for iron was found maximum 0.2989 with cadmium. Correlation for manganese was found maximum 0.7224 and 0.5619 with cadmium and iron respectively. Correlation for nickel was found maximum 0.8617 and 0.8799 with cadmium and iron respectively. Correlation for lead was found maximum 0.8432 and 0.7390 with copper and manganese respectively. Correlation for zinc was found maximum 0.7216 and 0.8553 with manganese and lead respectively.

Metals Accumulation Factor

Metal accumulation factor for cadmium was found maximum 8.56 in winter 2006-07 and minimum 0.91 in monsoon 2005. For copper metal accumulation factor was found maximum 3.15 in summer 2005 and minimum 1.31 in monsoon 2005. Metal accumulation factor for iron was maximum 1.49 in winter 2006-07 and minimum 1.12 in summer 2005. For manganese metal accumulation factor was maximum 1.31 in summer 2007 and minimum 1.11 in monsoon 2005. Metal accumulation factor for nickel was found maximum 2.05 in winter 2006-07 and minimum 1.17 in monsoon 2005. For lead metal accumulation factor was found maximum 1.48 in summer 2005 and minimum 1.28 in monsoon 2005. Metal accumulation factor for zinc was maximum 1.20 in monsoon 2005 and minimum 1.02 in winter 2006-07.

Discussion

Waste waters from textile industries have the high amount of the heavy metals entering them most hazardous for soil plant and other organisms including human beings (Sial *et.al.,* 2006). Many effects of Cd action results from interactions of various micro and macro elements as it antagonizes to Cu, Zn and Fe and also interferes with Ca absorption. Cadmium found in a sample of Ca is likely in an inorganic form and may be relatively less toxic to flora and fauna, while same amount of Cd when present in zinc or phosphates may be highly toxic to plants and animals, especially in calcium deficiency in soil. The use of contaminated water into irrigation may be increase the cadmium status in agricultural soil (Mani *et.al.,* 2005). An increasing number of ground water wells were found to be contaminated by chemical waste from point sources and also widespread known point source pollution from fertilizers was threatening the water resources in extensive areas (Lagas *et.al.*, 1989 and Meier and Mull, 1989).

Cadmium concentrations in textile industrial effluent (0.005-0.052 ppm), pond water (0.001-0.012 ppm) and agricultural soil (0.7-3.4 ppm) turn down in rainy season due to the dilution factor, while in the ground water system its impact seems after monsoon and cadmium concentration reduces. Cadmium slightly fluctuated and remains mostly constant in pond sediment (4.0-5.7 ppm) and drain sediment (4.2-5.8 ppm). Transfer factor for cadmium (0.12-1.5) from textile industrial effluent to ground water was recorded high in winter months (after monsoon). In geo-accumulation index cadmium (3.77-3.81) laid in between 3 to 4 mean strongly polluted by cadmium. Metal accumulation factor for ground water (57.1-250.0) was found mostly very high or infinite for cadmium, because in most samples of control sites cadmium was absent.

Transfer factor of cadmium from ground water to agricultural soil on control site was found infinite, because cadmium was almost absent in ground water and agricultural soil at control site. So, any correlation between ground water and agricultural soil was not noticed. Cadmium transfer is due to some other non-point sources of cadmium pollution. Figure-5.4.6 showing the transfer factor of cadmium from ground water to agricultural soil clearly indicated the transfer level of metal. During the last decade, the industrial use of Cd has increased and can create both acute and chronic cases of clinically identifiable toxicity in humans. In human, absorption of dietary Cd is limited up to 15 % and that of inhaled Cd is high 40 % and not absorbed from skin (Mani *et.al.*, 2005). When the animal kept on contaminated feed along with the industrial polluted environment for long time, they suffer from its toxicity symptoms which may be sub clinical or clinical. The retention time of Cd is quite high, half life being 40 years. Cadmium is produced as inevitable by-product of zinc (or occasionally lead) refining (lenntech.com). Cd was found slightly high in ground water for drinking purposes, because it should not be more than 0.003 mg/l for health views, while it should be less than 1 μg/l generally in drinking water (WHO, 2006). Helena (1999), Umar and Ahmad (2000), Kumar *et.al.*,(2001) and Yadav *et.al.*,(2002) observed the high Cd concentrations in industrial area like the present study of ground water, while Krebs *et.al.*, (1999), Singh *et.al.*,(1994) and Fakayode and Oniyawa (2002) in soil and Bordas and Bourg (1998), Vazquez *et.al.*, (2007) and Korfali and Davies (2004) in sediment.

During the last decade, the industrial use of Cd has increased and can create both acute and chronic cases of clinically identifiable toxicity in humans. In human, absorption of dietary Cd is limited up to 15 % and that of inhaled Cd is high 40 % and not absorbed from skin (Mani *et.al.*, 2005). When the animal kept on contaminated feed along with the industrial polluted environment for long time, they suffer from its toxicity symptoms which may be sub clinical or clinical. The retention time of Cd is quite high, half life being 40 years. Cadmium is produced as inevitable by-product of zinc (or occasionally lead) refining (lenntech.com). Cd was found slightly high in ground water for drinking purposes, because it should not be more than 0.003 mg/l for health views, while it should be less than 1 μg/l generally in drinking water (WHO, 2006). Helena (1999), Umar and Ahmad (2000), Kumar *et.al.*,(2001) and Yadav *et.al.*,(2002) observed the high Cd concentrations in industrial area like the present study of ground water, while Krebs *et.al.*, (1999), Singh *et.al.*,(1994) and Fakayode and Oniyawa (2002) in soil and Bordas and Bourg (1998), Vazquez *et.al.*, (2007) and Korfali and Davies (2004) in sediment.

Concentrations of copper in textile industrial effluent are due to the residues of some dyes especially used for blue or green colours. Copper concentrations in textile industrial effluent (0.16-0.44 ppm) were found parallel or sometimes higher than iron. Most of the part of copper content reach in pond water (0.25-0.43 ppm) and rest settle down on drain sediment (45.8-54.8 ppm). Copper in pond sediment (38.6-52.4 ppm) also settled down after some time. Transfer factor of copper from pond water to ground water (0.97-1.17) and ground water to agricultural soil (0.45-0.82) was found higher than other microelement except cadmium. In geo-accumulation index copper was not recorded in polluted condition. Metal accumulation factor for copper was recorded high in winter season (3.28) for ground water; while in agricultural soil high metal accumulation factor was found in summer months (1.20).

Copper is sometimes found in insufficient quantity in soil (Miller and Turk, 2002) but it may be added in to soil system by some anthropogenic activities. Copper may accumulate in living organisms and their various body parts (Kudesia, 1992). High amount if heavy metals like cu and Zn may harm to living organism of existing ecosystem (Aslam *et.al.*, 2004).

However, Cu concentration was not detected high in ground water samples as described by WHO (2006) in drinking water i.e. 2.0 mg/l. The Cu concentrations level in study area have compared with those observed by Yusus and Sonibare (2004), Aslam *et.al.*, (2004), Helena (1999), Umar and Ahmad (2000), Kumar *et.al.*,(2001) and Yadav *et.al.*,(2002) in ground water; Krebs *et.al.*, (1999), Singh *et.al.*,(1994) and Fakayode and Oniyawa (2002) in soil and Bordas and Bourg (1998), Nasr *et.al.*,(2006), Vazquez *et.al.*, (2007) and Korfali and Davies (2004) in sediments. Ather and Vohra (1985) reported that heavy metal enters in water system by various ways in natural resources like erosion, weathering, volcanic activities and anthropogenic activities that include direct emissions of heavy metal by different industries.

Iron is one of the most abundant elements of the rocks and soil, ranking fourth by weight. All kinds of waters including ground water have appreciable quantities of iron. Iron has more solubility at acidic pH, therefore large quantities of iron are leached out from the soils by acidic waters. In the alkaline medium iron remain comparatively low in soluble phase. Excess calcium can reduced the activity of iron in soil and soil aeration may influence the availability of iron to plants (Miller and Turk, 2002).

In ground waters most of the iron remains in ferrous state due to general lack of oxygen. In alkaline conditions in ground waters, the iron is mostly ferrous bicarbonate, which is a colourless substance. When the ground water with higher concentrations of iron is tapped, it quickly oxidizes to ferric state in the form of insoluble ferric hydroxide, a brown substance. If appreciable quantities of ferrous bicarbonates are present in ground water, and they come in contact with oxygen at surface, the hydroxides are formed, CO_2 is released and hence it increases the pH, facilitating the oxidation processes (Minhas and Gupta, 1992). Generally, movement of iron compounds take place downward through the soil profile and reach in to ground water table (Miller and Turk, 2002). However, iron was not found in high concentration in textile industrial effluents (0.24-0.54 ppm), but the high concentrations of iron were observed in effluent drain sediment (5656.0-8467.7 ppm) due to the continuous settlement and abundantly natural occurrence in earth crust materials. Iron in shallow ground water samples (1.5-3.8 ppm) was found higher to textile effluents, while iron in deep ground water (0.48-1.05 ppm) and control ground water (0.363-0.868 mg/l) was not detected in high concentrations. Iron was present in high quantity in pond sediment (3803.5-6013.4 ppm) and effluent drain sediment (5656.0-8467.7 ppm). Iron concentration in agricultural soil was analyzed comparatively higher than other metals.

Iron's transfer factors were found very high from textile industrial effluent to ground water (5.93-9.64), from textile industrial effluent to pond water up to 25.00, while iron was transferred from pond water to ground water with highest 0.40 coefficient. However, transfer factor of iron was noticed low in comparison to other metals from shallow ground water to agricultural soil. Metal enrichment factor in all seasons and in all sediment samples was calculated 1000.0 due to the comparative parameter for other metals for determination metals enrichment factor. In geo-accumulation index for drain sediment and pond sediment iron was not indexed at very high rank, it was found very low because the natural occurrence of iron in earth crust shale was very high, so iron was not a pollution causing agent in industrial area during the present study. Metal accumulation factor of iron was found from 2-4 for ground water in Panipat region. Iron was detected in ground water with 2-4 times high quantities in comparison to control site's ground water. Iron in textile industrial effluent and pond water was found very high, while in ground water samples it was also found very high for drinking purposes (WHO, 2006) Helena (1999), Yusus and Sonibare (2004), Umar and Ahmad (2000), Kumar *et.al.*,(2001) and Yadav *et.al.*,(2002) observed the similar trends of iron concentrations in ground water and Singh *et.al.*,(1994) in agricultural soil of industrial area.

Manganese was found as a second abundant element in the effluent drain and pond sediment after iron. However, manganese was comparatively low in textile industrial effluent (0.11-0.31 ppm) and very low in ground water samples (0.28-0.55 ppm). In ground water samples manganese remains below 1.0 during the study even in shallow aquifer. In agricultural soil, manganese was comparatively low in concentrations (5.8-13.6 ppm) regarding other metals. Manganese was third most enriched element in ground water samples. Mn was found slightly high at experimental sites in the case of soil samples. Manganese has positive relationship with all the physico-chemical parameters of ground water as correlated with temperature (0.6892), total solids (0.8508) electric conductivity (0.8544), total alkalinity (0.7074) except dissolved oxygen.

Transfer factor of Mn from textile industrial effluent to pond water was noticed from 1to 4 almost in all seasons, while below 1 in winter season. Transfer factor was calculated near 1 in all seasons from pond water to ground water. Transfer factor from ground water to agricultural soil was noticed very low at experimental sites as well as at control site. Enrichment factor of Mn was found around 100-200, highest after Fe in drain sediment, while enrichment factor was noticed higher in pond sediment. The value of Mn in geo-accumulation index was noticed always below 1 with negative rank even highest value in drain sediment as well as pond sediment due to the high natural shale value of Mn in earth crust. Metal accumulation factor of Mn in ground water was high and ranged between 2 to 4, while in soil environment it was found below 2 always. Mn was found slightly high in ground water for drinking purposes, because it should not be more than 0.5 mg/l for health views in drinking water (WHO, 2006).

Mathess (1974) reported that fresh ground water constitutes 0.00-0.007 ppm cadmium, WHO (1984) recommended Cd concentration should not exceed maximum of 0.01 ppm in raw drinking water supply, 0.5 ppm in irrigation water. USEPA (1990) recommended maximum permissible Cd concentration as 0.04 and 0.02 ppm to protect aquatic life including fish. Hart (1982) reported a concentration range of Pb 0.0003-0.03 ppm in natural fresh water, while Frostner and Wittman (1979) the likely level as 0.002 ppm. Siddiqui and Pathania (2002) reported that the high value of Pb, Cr and other trace metals in ground water in Jalandhar and Ludiana industrial area.

Manganese, Iron and potassium may deficient in alkaline soil (Miller and Turk, 2002), while manganese and iron is soluble in acidic soil (Brady, 1995). Manganese usually is present in sufficient quantity in most soils and need not be added for plant growth (Miller and Turk, 2002). Yusus and Sonibare (2004), Umar and Ahmad (2000), Kumar *et.al.*,(2001) and Yadav *et.al.*,(2002) gave a report of Mn status in ground water, Fakayode and Oniyawa (2002) in soil system and Nasr *et.al.*,(2006) in sediments of aquatic system affected by industrial pollution.

Nickel is one of the second trace elements of the present study after cadmium. As it is very toxic to plants and animals in low concentrations and has a tendency to accumulate in body parts. However Ni was presented in very minor concentrations in textile industrial effluent (0.007-0.067 ppm), and pond water (0.047-0.13 ppm), it was found comparatively high due to the regular input. Ni concentrations in pond were noticed higher during the summer season due to the loss of water by vaporization from pond system. About similar conditions were observed in ground water samples. In deep ground water, Ni was almost absent like cadmium. In agricultural soil all metals were found higher than ground water so, nickel was also found high (5.3-10.5 ppm). Ni was found very high like other metals due to the settling of metals on bottom beds in pond sediment (49.0-63.7 ppm) and drain sediment (58.0-75.0 ppm). Nickel has no positive correlations with any physico-chemical parameter of soil and water except total alkalinity, Calcium, electric conductivity and water holding capacity. Highest transfer factor of Ni from textile industrial effluent to pond water and ground water (14.14) was found in monsoon seasons. However, transfer factor from pond water to ground water (0.83-1.29) was not found effective comparative to transfer factor of other metals from ground water to agricultural soil at control site. Like cadmium, Ni was sometimes found infinitive in winter seasons.

Enrichment factor of Ni (7.35-11.7) was not effective in comparison to iron in drain sediment, but in pond sediment (8.38-14.85) it was slightly high due to the high retention time of wastewater in pond. The observations of present study reveals that Ni never reflected the pollution load in drain or pond sediment through the geo-accumulation index because it was found always below than 1. Metal accumulation factor in agricultural soil was recorded around 1-2, while in ground water it was found slightly high or sometimes infinitive. Ni was found high in ground water for drinking purposes, because it should not be more than 0.07 mg/l for health views, while it should be less than 0.02 mg/l generally in drinking water (WHO, 2006). Nickel may accumulate in aquatic life but its presence is not magnified along food chains (lenntech. com). So, there is not so big fear of nickel toxicity to higher animals including human beings, but agricultural plant health will be affected in contaminated agricultural soil. This trend of Ni concentrations in present study have been supported on the basis of recommendation of Kumar *et.al.*, (2001) and Yadav *et.al.*,(2002) in ground water, Kasem and Singh (1999), Singh *et.al.*,(1994) and Fakayode and Oniyawa (2002) in soil and Nasr *et.al.*, (2006) in sediment. Jayabaskeran and Sree Ramulu (1996) observed a great heavy metal movement in sewage irrigating light textured soil than in heavy textured soil. It may be pointed out that the builds up of heavy metal like Cr, Pb, Ni warrant toward continuous monitoring and suitable measures are needed before these become toxic.

Lead was found highest in textile industrial effluent, but it accumulated in drain sediment in comparatively less quantity. Lead mostly remained in effluent (0.25-0.50 ppm) and fluctuated in pond (0.5-1.8 ppm). Rest quantity of lead settled down on bed sediment of drain and pond, so, the lead concentration was found low in pond sediment (44.0-69.0 ppm) and high in drain sediment (47.2-70.0 ppm). Lead was the second most abundant metal species after iron. Lead was found in high concentrations in shallow ground water (0.85-1.84 ppm) in comparison to deep ground water (0.28-0.41 ppm). Pb was also second most enriched element after iron in agricultural soil (25.1-62.4 ppm) due to the high distribution of these metals in earth crust. Lead is deposited mostly in bones and some soft tissues. High concentrations of lead may create toxicity in human (Kudesia, 1992).

Pb was found slightly high in ground water (0.85-1.84 ppm) for drinking purposes and also in pond water (0.50-1.8 ppm), because it should not be more than 0.01 mg/l for health views, while it should be less than 0.1 mg/l generally in drinking water (WHO, 2006). Helena (1999), Umar and Ahmad (2000), Kumar *et.al.*,(2001) and Yadav *et.al.*,(2002) were observed the same trend of occurrence of Pb concentrations in ground water, Fakayode and Oniyawa (2002), Krebs *et.al.*, (1999) and Singh *et.al.*,(1994) in soil environment and Bordas and Bourg (1998), Nasr *et.al.*,(2006) and Vazquez *et.al.*, (2007) in sediment.

However, zinc was not found so high in textile industrial effluent (0.11-0.34 ppm) in comparison to lead, but it was found in very high concentrations in drain sediment (143.5-260.0 ppm). Similarly, it was found in less quantity in pond water (0.11-0.2 ppm) and accumulated in very high quantity in bed sediment (116.2-240.0 ppm) of pond. Zinc concentration was fluctuated in pond sediment (116.2-240.0 ppm) season to season, while in drain sediment (143.5-260.0 ppm) the fluctuation of zinc concentrations was not observed in high concentration. Zinc concentration (0.13-0.22 ppm) was found at fifth position in ground water samples among the all seven metals, while zinc concentration was found at fourth position in agricultural soil (7.7-19.4 ppm) among all metals studied. However, the concentrations of zinc in agricultural soil was found manifold than ground water, pond water and textile industrial effluent due to the natural occurrence of zinc in soil profile. During the study, in all experimental soils zinc concentration was found slightly higher than those at control soil (7.3-16.5 ppm). Positive correlations were found between zinc and temperature (0.8704), electric conductivity (0.2569), Cl (0.7613), pH (0.4955) in agricultural soil. Positive relationship was noticed between heavy metals of ground water with Zn. Transfer factor of zinc from textile industrial effluent to pond water was not found more than 1. However, transfer factor of Zn was found more than 1 from pond water to ground water during almost all seasons.

Transfer factor of Zn from ground water to agricultural soil was found slightly higher than 1 at experimental sites, while it was also found higher even more than 2 at control site. Enrichment factor of zinc in drain sediment was ranked at third position, while it was noticed slightly high in pond sediment due to the long retention time. In geo-accumulation index, the value of zinc was found more than 1.0 in all seasons, and ranked below 1 in geo-accumulation index in drain sediment.

Metal accumulation factor of Zn was calculated between 2 to 3 in ground water samples, while metal accumulation factor was found near 1 in the case of agricultural soil and always remain below 2. Zn was found low in ground water and in pond water for drinking purposes, because it should not be more than 3.0 mg/l for health views, while it should be less than 5.0 mg/l generally in drinking water (WHO, 2006).

Zinc is sometimes found in insufficient quantity in soil (Miller and Turk, 2002). Zinc salts are relatively non-toxic, but high concentrations may cause health problems like vomiting, renal damage, etc. (Kudesia, 1992). High amount of Zn may harm to living organism of that ecosystem (Aslam *et.al.*, 2004). Helena (1999), Umar and Ahmad (2000), Kumar *et.al.*,(2001), Yadav *et.al.*,(2002), Yusus and Sonibare (2004) and Aslam *et.al.*, (2004) reported the same fluctuations of Zn concentrations in ground water, Singh *et.al.*,(1994), Krebs *et.al.*, (1999) and Fakayode and Oniyawa (2002) in soil and Bordas and Bourg (1998), Nasr *et.al.*,(2006), Vazquez *et.al.*, (2007) and Korfali and Davies (2004) in sediment.

Heavy metals added to the soil in the field strongly absorbed by first component of upper part of undisturbed soil horizons. Subsequent redistribution to lower soil layers probably takes a very long time due to slow adsorption and heavy metals in upper layer tend to increase with time (Alumaa *et.al.*, 2001). The trace heavy metal ions activities, depends on the solubility in the soil and often a much better indicator of heavy metal in soil solution reflected the soil metal fraction, that is most directly available for plants uptake, absorption by soil biota or leaching to ground water (McBride etal., 1997; Cances *et.al.*, 2003 and Lofts *et.al.*, 2004).

Minor or secondary elements such as magnesium, manganese, calcium, zinc, copper, boron, iron, and perhaps others are essential but except in certain specific cases either they are injurious to crop and soil in large quantity. If any element is lacking in soil or it is present in improper proportions normal plant growth will not occur (Miller and Turk, 2002). It is urgently required that industries should continuously monitor textile effluent and take necessary actions to properly treat waste water prior their disposal to water bodies and save already depleting natural water resources (Aslam *et.al.*, 2004).

Transfer of Heavy Metals

In the recent years there has been a growing concern with environmental protection. This can be achieved either by decreasing the afflux of pollutants to the environment or by their removal from contaminated media. The former is a feasible choice only for pollutants of anthropogenic origin, whereas, the latter is unavoidable for those of natural origin (Gomez-Serrano *et.al.*, 1998). The presence of heavy metals in the aquatic environment has been of great concern to scientists and engineers because of their increased discharge, toxic nature, and other adverse effects on receiving waters (Singh, 2006).

In heavy metals analysis, the total concentrations of the metals are often determined (Okonwo *et.al.*, 1999, 2001; Castro Dentros *et.al.*, 2003). However, total concentration of trace metals provides no information concerning the fate of the metal in the terms of its interaction with sediments, its mobility, bioavailability, or resultant toxicity (Christie, 1995). It is now widely accepted that measuring total metal concentrations cannot fully assess the role of aquatic sediments as a sink or as a source of pollutants. In addition, determination of total elements does not given an accurate estimate of the likely environmental impact. Instead, it is desirable to have information on the potential availability of metals (whether toxic or essential) to biota under various environmental conditions. Since the mobility of heavy metals, as well as their bioavailability and related eco-toxicity to plants, critically depends upon chemical forms in which, a metal is present in the sediment, considerable interest exists in trace element speciation (Davidson *et.al.*, 1994).

Heavy metals are introduced into aquatic system from various anthropogenic sources. Heavy metals constitute a special group of contaminants of aquatic systems and deserve special attention. Since metals are not removed by natural degradation processes, they may become enriched in sediments over time. Metal contamination of sediments is an issue of growing concerns worldwide (NRC, 1989). Both natural processes and anthropogenic activities are responsible for introducing metals in to the aquatic system (Nriagu, 1989). Many contaminants discharged into surface waters rapidly become associated with the particulate matter and incorporated in sediments. Metals in aquatic systems become part of the water-sediment system and their distribution is controlled by a dynamic set of physical-chemical interactions and equilibrium, largely governed by pH and type of legends and chelating agents, oxidation state of the mineral components and the redox conditions of the system. Metal contaminated sediments may release heavy metals back to the overlying water column and, thus, pose risk to aquatic life and ecosystems. Due to their particle reactivity, heavy metals tend to accumulate in sediment as a result may persist in the environment long after their primary sources have been removed (Forstner and Wittman, 1981).

Heavy metals travel from one level to another in the ecological system due to the accumulation in abiotic and biotic components. In the study area, basically anthropogenic source of heavy metals are the dye houses in textile industrial area. Heavy metals reach in effluent drain and also its bottom sediment and further into pond and bed sediment of pond near village Binjhole adjoining to textile industrial area of Panipat. Heavy metals percolate slowly from the bed sediment of Binjhole pond towards the ground water table and there may be a threat to deep aquifers also by leaching process of metals. As the ground water was mostly used in irrigation and drinking purposes in most rural parts of Haryana, which have affected the agricultural soil health after irrigation by contaminated ground water and ultimately influence on the agricultural productivity, vegetation health and grain quality also. The use of ground water for drinking purposes of human and cattle in contaminated conditions, a threat of various health hazards and diseases have occurred to public at present. Some of the diseases caused by toxic heavy metals have been lethal to living organisms.

Accumulation of Heavy Metals

Due to the industrialization, a huge quantity of waste materials discarded outside from the industries, in which various toxic substances including heavy metals are present. These large quantities of discarded heavy metals have been created havoc in the environmental ecosystem and affected all biotic components of the surrounding water and agricultural system. The accumulating processes of run-off derived metals from the point and non-point pollution sources and their significant accumulation in the sediment of drain and pond with furthermore retention in agricultural soil has been observed by many investigators (Harper *et.al.*, 1984; Nightangle, 1987 and Yusuf *et.al.*, 1986). The extent of contamination due to heavy metal deposition in different industrial sites in relation to quite vulnerable metal toxicity among soil biota and plants have been investigated by Moon *et.al.*, (1991) and recorded Cd, Cu, Pb, Zn level in the industrial drain and top soil of agricultural fields.

Heavy metals have a tendency to accumulate and store in a component or trophic levels. The storage of heavy metals has created harmful effects for biotic components. The heavy metals accumulated in sediment and percolated down in to ground water known as bio-accumulation of metal. From ground water, heavy metals may turn into two ways; one is though irrigation and second is through drinking by human beings. The accumulation of heavy metals through the food chain is called the biomagnifications. The concentrations of metal increased at every next trophic level, whereas metals can cause various harmful effects on irrigated agricultural soil, human beings and livestock by alteration in some biochemical reaction in body cells (De, 2002).

In the present study, heavy metals in pond water were observed slightly lower than textile industrial effluents, whereas the heavy metal concentrations in effluent drain were higher than pond sediment. Shallow ground water of about 40 ft depth was highly polluted in comparison to increasing depth of water table. Although the effect of spatial variation was also found in the study, when the heavy metals concentrations in ground water and soils at control site were presented comparatively in less or very less quantities. Some metals like cadmium and nickel were not detected in ground water at control site. After all, if the conditions will be same in textile industrial area then definitely there is a fear to contamination of ground water into horizontal direction also and this will affect the ground water of surroundings and deep aquifers with the time.

Table 11.1: Seasonal Variation of Heavy Metals in Agricultural Irrigated Soil

Heavy metals	Unit	Summer2005		Monsoon2005		Winter2005-06		Summer2006		Monsoon2006		Winter2006-07		Summer 2007	
		Mean	SD	Mean	SD	Mean	SD	Mean	SD	Mean	SD	Mean	SD	Mean	SD
Cadmium (Cd)	ppm	3.333	0.611	0.667	0.551	1.780	0.444	3.350	0.686	1.200	1.153	1.925	0.350	2.650	0.212
Copper (Cu)	ppm	36.300	7.422	30.200	5.345	13.400	5.968	34.875	9.309	32.333	5.498	14.350	4.916	20.850	3.748
Iron (Fe)	ppm	76.667	16.805	26.767	10.772	28.800	13.221	82.825	18.097	30.400	12.375	27.450	10.051	62.100	13.859
Manganese (Mn)	ppm	13.567	1.401	10.233	2.380	5.900	2.799	13.075	1.910	11.033	1.960	5.775	1.676	10.450	1.768
Nickel (Ni)	ppm	10.467	0.757	7.633	1.137	5.780	1.244	10.525	1.812	8.067	1.504	5.325	1.056	9.050	1.061
Lead (Pb)	ppm	62.400	10.922	39.333	11.675	25.340	9.226	61.300	11.385	44.933	15.791	25.100	6.733	46.150	4.738
Zinc (Zn)	ppm	13.167	3.911	18.533	5.150	7.680	2.805	13.025	3.471	19.400	4.747	9.150	3.101	8.000	1.697

Table 11.2: Seasonal Variation of Heavy Metals in Soil at Control Site

Heavy metals	Unit	Summer 2005		Monsoon 2005		Winter 2005-06		Summer 2006		Monsoon 2006		Winter 2006-07		Summer 2007	
		Mean	SD	Mean	SD	Mean	SD	Mean	SD	Mean	SD	Mean	SD	Mean	SD
Cadmium (Cd)	ppm	2.233	0.306	0.733	0.473	0.460	0.351	2.000	0.770	1.233	0.451	0.225	0.206	1.400	0.141
Copper (Cu)	ppm	11.533	15.396	23.000	4.036	9.980	4.141	20.525	13.495	22.733	4.966	10.250	5.637	15.800	4.667
Iron (Fe)	ppm	68.633	17.539	19.000	11.207	20.940	12.563	66.450	15.315	21.133	11.208	18.400	9.038	48.250	9.263
Manganese (Mn)	ppm	11.500	1.114	9.200	1.833	4.962	2.028	10.775	1.791	9.533	2.159	4.800	1.490	7.950	1.202
Nickel (Ni)	ppm	8.433	1.172	6.533	1.026	3.380	1.846	8.050	1.313	6.767	1.026	2.600	1.867	6.300	0.283
Lead (Pb)	ppm	42.267	3.121	30.633	8.999	19.000	7.316	41.925	3.677	31.400	7.602	18.275	5.934	34.600	4.101
Zinc (Zn)	ppm	12.100	1.500	15.400	3.830	7.460	2.475	11.700	2.655	16.467	3.275	8.950	2.885	7.250	0.778

Table 11.3: Mean Values (±SD) of Heavy Metals in Soil at Control and Experiment Sites

Heavy metals	Unit	2005-06				2006-07			
		Control Site	SD	Experi-mental sites	SD	Control Site	SD	Experi-mental sites	SD
Cadmium (Cd)	ppm	1.033	0.819	1.950	1.098	1.183	0.893	2.292	1.099
Copper (Cu)	ppm	14.317	9.218	24.100	11.451	17.050	9.744	26.075	11.391
Iron (Fe)	ppm	35.267	25.354	43.150	25.433	36.975	24.866	49.417	29.212
Manga-nese (Mn)	ppm	7.984	3.215	9.283	3.850	8.158	3.086	9.908	3.601
Nickel (Ni)	ppm	5.675	2.527	7.608	2.161	5.767	2.731	8.133	2.611
Lead (Pb)	ppm	29.317	11.729	39.967	17.818	30.508	11.188	43.750	18.264
Zinc (Zn)	ppm	10.667	4.148	11.867	5.640	11.525	4.195	12.833	5.460

Table 11.4: Correlation Between Heavy Metals and Physico-chemical Parameters of Agricultural Soil

Param-eters	Temper-ature	WHC	Bulk density	Soil mois-ture	pH	EC	Cl	Na	K
Cadmium (Cd)	0.2211	0.8421	-0.5639	-0.8066	-0.2848	0.3965	0.3654	0.7499	0.6852
Copper (Cu)	0.9134	0.5300	-0.0815	0.0914	0.3754	0.9454	0.8479	0.0853	-0.1689
Iron (Fe)	0.3455	0.8736	-0.6445	-0.6449	-0.4051	0.4198	0.3249	0.8436	0.7116
Manganese (Mn)	0.8162	0.6657	-0.2403	-0.0712	0.2034	0.9076	0.7254	0.3169	0.0611
Nickel (Ni)	0.7218	0.7798	-0.3816	-0.2585	0.0187	0.8286	0.6603	0.4813	0.2623
Lead (Pb)	0.7091	0.8483	-0.4542	-0.2607	0.0462	0.8596	0.6972	0.4876	0.2369
Zinc (Zn)	0.8513	0.0750	0.3246	0.5031	0.6535	0.7586	0.7744	-0.4581	-0.6269

Table 11.5: Correlation Between Heavy Metals of Agricultural Soil

	Cadmi-um (Cd)	Copper (Cu)	Iron (Fe)	Man-ganese (Mn)	Nickel (Ni)	Lead (Pb)	Zinc (Zn)
Cadmium (Cd)	1						
Copper (Cu)	0.3719	1					
Iron (Fe)	0.7981	0.5348	1				
Manganese (Mn)	0.4834	0.9502	0.6730	1			
Nickel (Ni)	0.6368	0.8904	0.8093	0.9581	1		

Lead (Pb)	0.6911	0.8811	0.7809	0.9274	0.9566	1	
Zinc (Zn)	-0.1615	0.7484	-0.0190	0.5876	0.4374	0.466065186	1

Table 11.6: Metal Accumulation Factor for the Agricultural soil of Panipat Region

	Summer 2005	Mon-soon 2005	Winter 2005-06	Summer 2006	Monsoon 2006	Winter 2006-07	Summer 2007
Cadmium (Cd)	1.49	0.91	3.87	1.68	0.97	8.56	1.89
Copper (Cu)	3.15	1.31	1.34	1.70	1.42	1.40	1.32
Iron (Fe)	1.12	1.41	1.38	1.25	1.44	1.49	1.29
Manganese (Mn)	1.18	1.11	1.19	1.21	1.16	1.20	1.31
Nickel (Ni)	1.24	1.17	1.71	1.31	1.19	2.05	1.44
Lead (Pb)	1.48	1.28	1.33	1.46	1.43	1.37	1.33
Zinc (Zn)	1.09	1.20	1.03	1.11	1.18	1.02	1.10

Conclusion

The study indicates that there was heavy metals pollution in pond water and sediment, which affected the ground water of the industrial area of Panipat region. Beside this, the bottom sediment of common effluent drain stored the heavy metals in high quantities, which have no secure or pre-managed future. Thus, textile industrial effluents discharging from dye houses contaminated the surface water, drain sediment, pond sediment and ground water also. Furthermore, the impact of heavy metals reflected negative impacts on agricultural soil after irrigation by contaminated ground water. Heavy metals remained in upper part of soil horizons mostly but moved in to lower soil layers probably after a long time due to slow adsorption (Alumaa *et.al.*, 2001). Heavy metals strongly absorbed by first component to which they make contact and plants uptake them. So there is a fear to accumulate the heavy metals in different body parts of vegetation. High quantity of heavy metals accumulated in organisms may be harmful for health of organisms and create various diseases, which may magnify through food web of the water and agricultural ecosystems.

Heavy metals from textile industries affected the shallow ground water quality in shallow badly, while deep ground water affected slightly. Vertically, heavy metals contamination decreased with the increasing depth of water table. In the case of horizontal distribution, the heavy metal concentrations decrease with increasing distance from pollution source. In the circle of 1 Km from pollution source almost heavy metals level was found higher than the outer wide circle in the industrial area. Heavy metals contamination was found to be low in soil at control site and also in outer circle of textile industrial

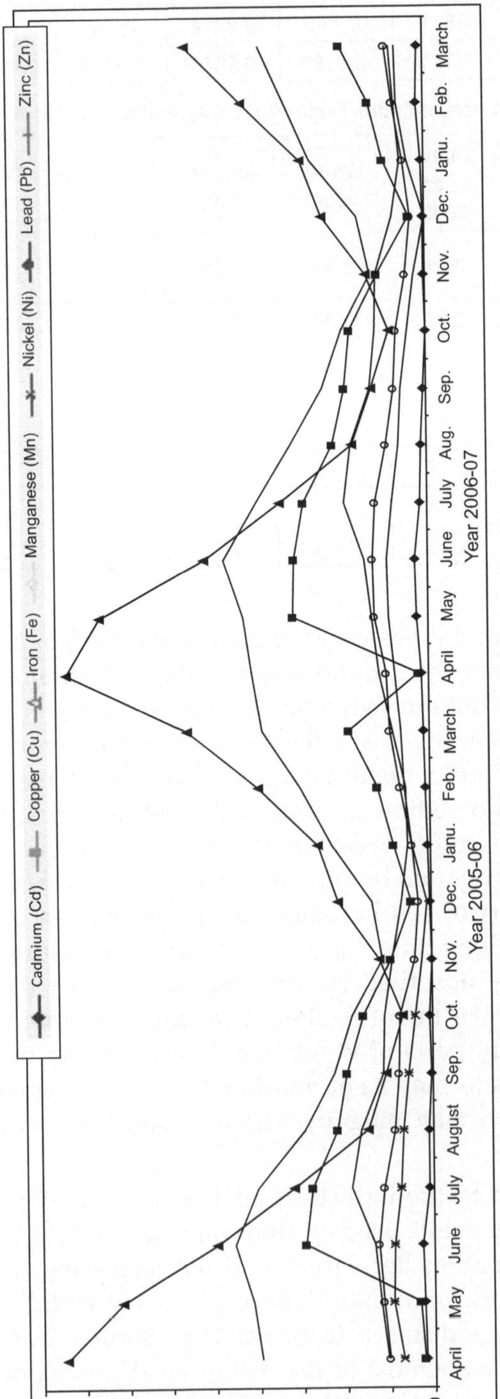

Fig. 11.1: Heavy metals fluctuation in agricultural soil

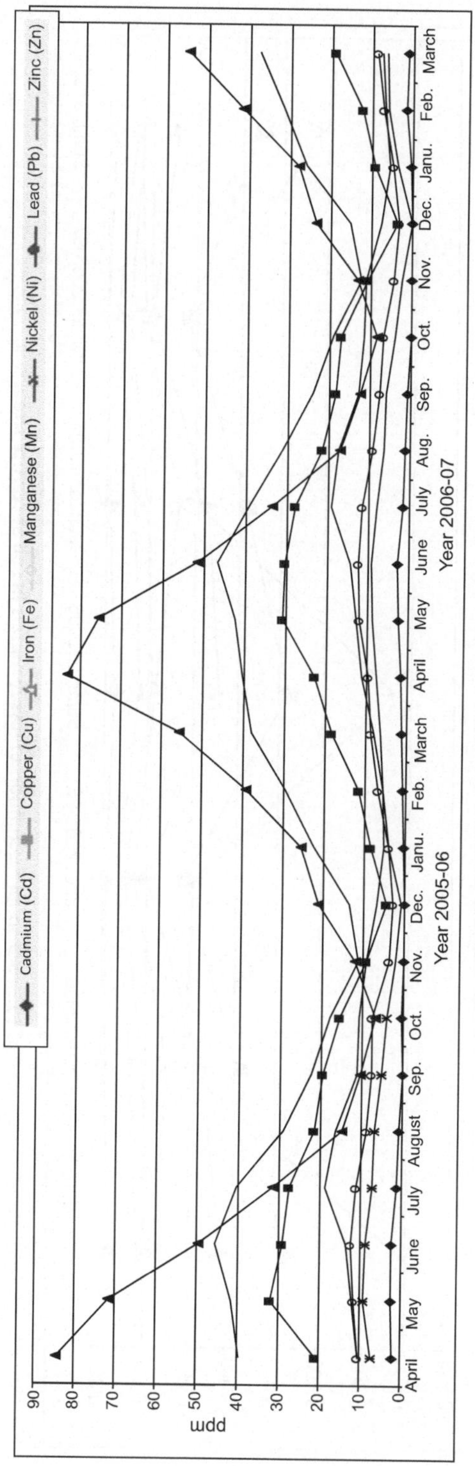

Fig. 11.2: Heavy metals fluctuation in soil at control site

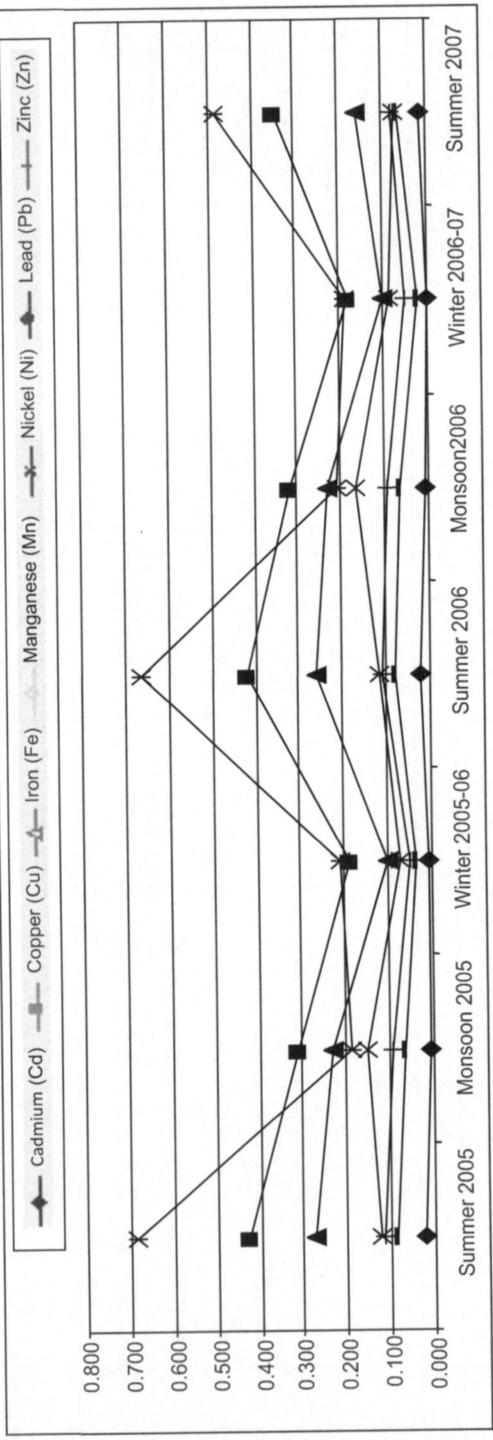

Fig. 11.3: Seasonal fluctuation of heavy metals in soil at control site

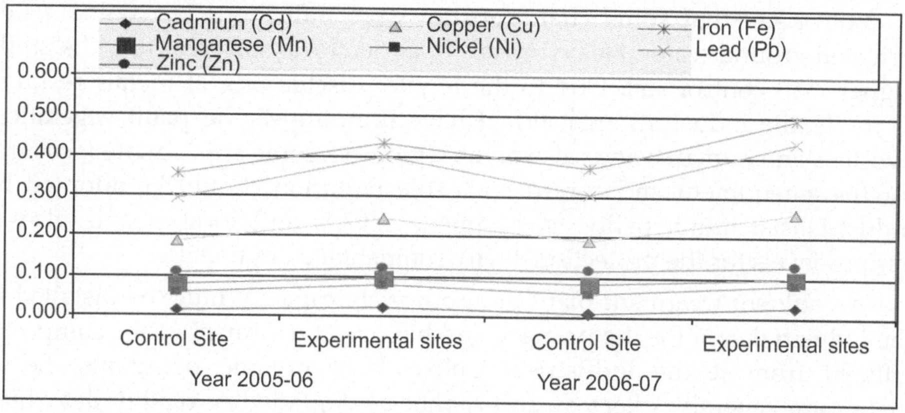

Fig. 11.4: Mean values of heavy metals in soil at control and experimental sites

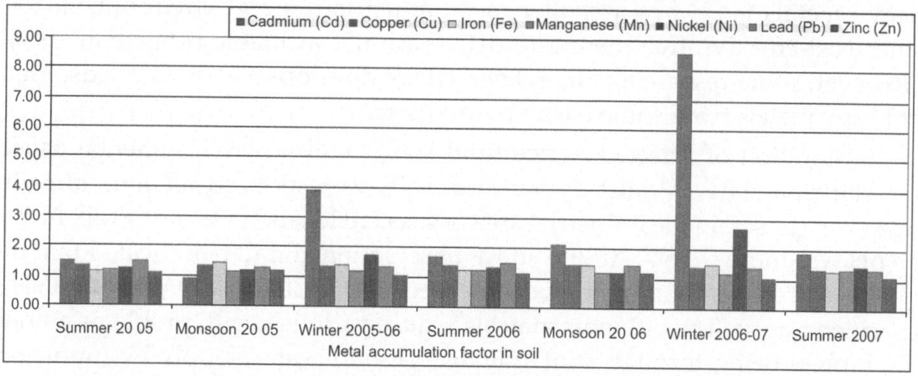

Fig. 11.5: Accumulation factor for various metals in agricultural soil of Panipat region

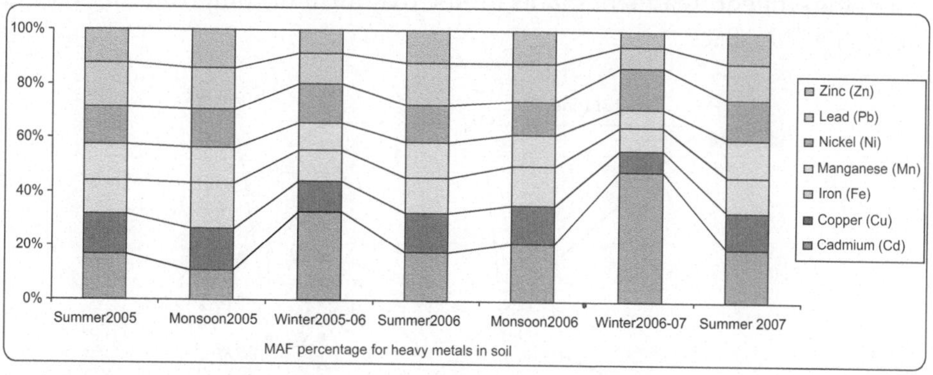

Fig. 11.6: Percentage MAF for various metals in agricultural soil of Panipat region

area. However, the area of around 1 km from textile industrial area was found highly affected by heavy metals in Panipat region. Textile industrial effluent or contaminated ground water has been altered the physico-chemical parameters of agricultural soil. It was indicated that the comparison of agricultural soil to control soil that some characteristics were influenced by contaminated irrigated ground water. Heavy metals in agricultural soil were found slightly higher than control soil. Due to the regular discharging of metals residues in the textile industrial area, threat have been appear on plant vegetation, livestock and human beings also of the region. So, some appropriate measures for the amendment and control of textile pollution should be adopted by industrialists, municipality, government, NGOs and local people also at various levels for the protection of environmental components.

An effluent treatment plant of appropriate capacity must be installed in the industrial area for the primary and biological treatment of for composite effluent from textile industries. Unlike most organic pollutants, heavy metals are generally refectory and cannot be degraded or readily detoxified biologically. Hence the safe and effective disposal of wastewater containing heavy metals is always a challenge to industrialists and environmentalists, since cost-effective treatment alternative are not available (Manahan, 1984). However, some researchers like Singh (2006) developed a low cost adsorbent of heavy metals from some cheap byproducts.

Restoration of affected agricultural soil is still an environmental aspect for Haryana state. Almost agricultural soils were noticed alkaline already, however, the soil in the industrial area of selected location was not so alkali, but its pH was more than 7. All the above observation and data indicated that the qualities of effluents sometimes do not meet the CPCB, BIS, MINAS and WHO specified norms. The effluents may also cause various health problems among the human being through contaminated ground water supply by municipal tube wells water scheme. In order to achieve the standards it is suggested to install the effluent treatment plants for the treatment of composite effluents of the textile industries.

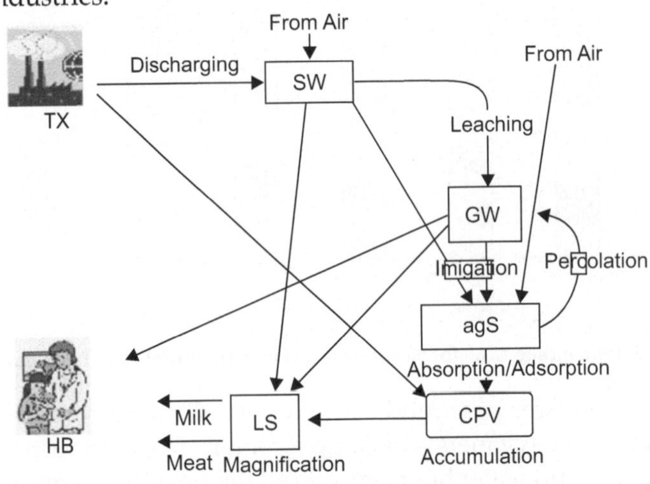

Fig. 11.7: Basic mechanism of heavy metal transfer between water and soil

On the basis of all above given facts, formula and functions related to water, soil, plants and heavy metals, it is concluded that heavy metals travel among all the abiotic environmental components and ultimately reach in livestock and human beings. Available figure may also express the movement of heavy metals from textile industrial waste to surface water, from surface water to ground water, from ground water to agricultural soil, then in crop plants and at last to livestock and human beings. In nature, every element has a natural cycle in the environment but these heavy metals have not any appropriate recycle way in industrial environment, which may be hazardous to all living and non-living components of ecosystem.

REFERENCES

Aboulhassan, M.A.; Souabi, S.; Yaacoubi, A. and Baudu, M. (2005): Treatment of Textile Wastewater Using a Natural Flocculants, Environmental Technology. 26: 705-711.

Abson, J.N.; Furness, C.D. and Howe, C. (1967): Development of the Simicar Resipirometer and Its Application to Waste Treatment, Waste Poll. Control, 66: 607.

Aggarwal, R.R. and Mehrotra, R.R. (1952): Soil Survey and Soil Water in Uttar Pradesh, Suptd. Printing and Stationery, Aallahabad, pp: 361-372.

Ajmal, M. and Khan, A.U. (1985): Effects of a Textile Factory Effluent on Soil and Crop Plants, J. Env. Poll., 37(2): 131-137.

Al-Degs, Y.; Khraisheh, M.A.M.; Allen, S.J. and Ahmed, M.N. (2000): Effect of Carbon Surface Chemistry on the Removal of Reactive Dyes from Textile Effluent, Water Research, 34(3): 927-935.

Alumaa, P.; Steinnes, E.; Kirso, U. and Petersell, V. (2001): Heavy Metal Sorption by Different Estonian Soil Types at Low Equilibrium solution Concentrations, Proc. Estonian Acad. Sci. Chem., 50(2): 104–115.

Ameta Suresh C., Punjabi Pinki Bala, Kothari Shilpa, Sancheti Anjali (2003): Effect of Untreated and Photocatalytically Treated Dyeing Industry Effluent on Growth and Biochemical Parameters of Allium Cepa (Onion), Poll. Res., 22(3): 389-392

Annadurai, G.; Juang, R.S. and Lee, D.J. (2002): Use of Cellulose Based Wastes for Adsorption of Dyes from Aqueous Solutions, J. Haz. Mat., B92: 263-274.

APHA (2005): Standard Methods for the Examination of Water and Waste Water, American Public Health Association, 21st edition, 1015, Fifteenth Street, NW, pp: 1170.

Aslam, M.M.; Baig, M.A.; Hassan, I.; Qazi, I.A.; Malik, M. and Saeed, H. (2004): Textile Wastewater Characterization and Reduction of Its COD and BOD by Oxidation, Electron. J. Environ. Agri. Food Chem., 3(6): 804-811.

Ather, M. and Vohra, S.B. (1985): Heavy Metals and Environment, New Age International Publisher Limited, Wiley Eastern Limited, New Delhi, pp: 635.

Aurangabadkar, K.; Swaminathan, K.; Sandhya, S; Uma, T.S.; Jothikumar, N. and Paramasivam, R. (2001): Ground Water Quality Around a Municipality Solid Waste Dumping Site at Chennai, IJEP, 21(4): 323-327.

Bachmat, Y. (1994): Ground Water as Part of the Water System. In: Ground Water Contamination and Control, ed. V. Zoller. Marcel Dekker, Inc, New York, pp: 1-560.

Bae, W.; S.H. Lee; and G.B. Ko (2004): Evaluation of Predominant Reaction Mechanisms for the Fenton Process in Textile Dyeing Waste. Water Sc. and Tech. 49 (4): 91-96.

Baruah N.K.; Kotoki, P.; Bhattacharya, K.G. and Borah, G.C. (1996): Metal Speciation in Jhanjhi River Sediments. Sci. Total Environ., 193: 1-12.

Basu, A.K.; Rao, C.G.S.; Dhaneshwar, G; Mukharjee, M.K.A.; Kutty, D. Ray and Trivedi, R.C. (1973): Study on Hooghly Estuaries Pollution in the Vicinity of Tissue Mill, Proc. Symp. on Environ. Poll., pp: 24-26.

Beven, K. (2000): On the Future of Distributed Modeling in Hydrology, Hydrological Processes, 14: 3183-3184.

Bhakuni, T.S. and Bopardikar, M.V. (1967): Method of Recovery Zinc from Spinning Bath Waste of Viscos Reyon Factory by Ion Exchange Process, Env. Health, 9(4): 327-338.

Bhargava, G.P.; Singhla, S.K. and Abrol, I.P. (1972): Characteristics of Some Typical Saline Sodic Soils Occurring in Karnal District Haryana state, Report No. 2, Division of Soils and Agronomy; CSSRI, Karnal, pp: 35.

Bharti, P.K. (2007): Effect of Textile Industrial Effluents on Groundwater and Soil Quality of Panipat (Hariyana), Thesis Submitted to Gurukula Kangri University, Haridwar, pp: 192.

Bhat, R. and Kulkarni, R. (2005): COD Reduction of Dye Industry Effluent, J. Ind. Poll. Control, 21 (1): 147-150.

Bordas, S, and Bourg, C.M. (1998): A Critical Evaluation of Sample Pretreatment of Contaminated Sediments to be Investigated for the Potential Mobility of their Heavy Metal Load, Water, Air and Soil Pollution, 103: 137-149.

Bousselmi, L.; Gelsson S.V. and H. Schroeder (2004): Textile Wastewater Treatment and Reuse by Solar Catalysis: Results from a Pilot Plant in Tunisia, Water Sc. & Tech., 49(4): 331-337.

Brady, N.C. (1995): The Nature and Properties of Soils, Prentice Hall of India Pvt. Ltd., New Delhi, pp: 621.

Cances, B.; Ponthieu, M.; Castrec-Rouelle, M.; Aubry, E. and Benedatty, M.F. (2003): Metal Ion Speciation in a Soil and Its Solution: Experimental Data and Modal Results, Geoderma, 113: 341-355.

Canter, L.W. (1987): Ground Water Quality Protection, Lewis Publications. Inc., Chelsea, MI, pp: 1-650.

Castro Dentros, T.S. Dentos Neto, A.A. Moura, M.C., P.A. Barros Neto, E$.I., Forte K.R., Leite, R.H.L. (2003): Heavy Metals Extraction by Micromulsion, Wat. Res., 37: 2709-2717.

Chao, Keh-Ping; Tsai, Ching-Tsan; Wang, John H.C.; Lin, Shaw-Tao and Chiang, Chow-Feng (2005) Health Risk Assessment of a Heavy Metal Contaminated site in Taiwan. Jr. Practice Periodical of Hazardous, Toxic, and Radioactive Waste Management, pp: 167-171.

Christie, S.L. (1995): Speciation, In: Fitfield, F.W., Haines. P.J. (Eds). Environmental Analytical Chemistry, Chapman and Hall, UK, pp: 245-273.

Chung, K.T. (1983): The Significance of Azo-reduction in the Mutagenesis and Carcinogenesis of Azo Dyes, Mutation Research, 114: 269-279.

Considine, D.M. (1974): Chemical and Process Technology Encyclopedia, McGraw Hill Book Co., New York, pp: 655.

CPCB (2003): Ground Water, Central Pollution Control Board, Parivesh Bhawan, Delhi, pp: 56.

CPCB (2003): Parivesh: Ground Water, Central Pollution Control Board, Delhi-32, July, pp: 40.

Darra, B.L.; Mehta, K.M. and Pareek, B.L. (1964): Quality of Irrigation Water in Rajasthan, J. Indian Soc, Soil Sc., 12: 121-130.

Dash, S.K. and Sahoo, H.K. (1998): Quality Assessment of Groundwater in a Part of Sundargarh District, Indian J. Environmental Protection, 19(4): 273-278.

Davidson, C.M., Thomas R.P., McVey, S.E., Perala, R., Littlejohn, D. and Ure, A.M. (1994): Evaluation of a Sequential Extraction Procedure for the Speciation of Heavy Metals in Sediments. Anal.Chim. Acta., 291: 277-286.

Dayama, O.P. (1987): Influence of Dyeing and Textile Water Pollution on Nodulation and Germination of Gram, J. Acta. Ecol., 9(1-2): 34-37.

De, A.K. (2002): Environmental Chemistry, New Age International (P) Limited Publishers, pp: 392.

De, A.K. (2005): Adsorption of Cadmium and Zinc on Coal Fly Ash, J. Ind. Poll. Control, 21 (1): 27-30.

Desh, D. (1981): Activated Sludge Treatment of Liquid Waste- A Review, J. IAWPC Tech., Vol-VII, pp: 69-72.

Dhar, N.R.; Khoda, A.K.M.B.; Khan, A.H.; Bala, P. and Karim, M.F. (2005) A Study of Effect of Acid Activated Saw Dust on the Removal of Different Dissolved Tannery Dyes (Acid dye) from Aqueous Solutions. Journal of Environ. Sci. & Engg. 47 (2): 103-108.

Doneen, L.D. (1954): Stalinization of Soils of Salts in Irrigation Waters, Trans. Geophys. Union, 35: 943-952.

Dowedy, R.H. and Larson, W.E. (1975): The Availability of Sludge Borne Metals in Various Vegetable Crops, J. Env. Qual., 4: 278-282.

Dulka, J.J. and Risby, T.H. (1976): Ultra Trace Metals in Some Environmental and Biological Systems, Analytical Chemistry, 48(8): 640-653.

Dutta, P.S. (1999): Ground Water Situation in Delhi- Red Alert, Nuclear Research Laboratory, IARI, New Delhi, pp: 39.

Dutta, P.S. (2005): Ground Water Ethics for Its Sustainability, Current Science, 89 (5): 812-817.

Dwivedi, A.K.; Shashi and Singh, J. (2005): Water Pollution and Ground Water Recharging, Current Science, 91 (4): 407-408.

Eaton, F.M. (1950): Significance of Carbonates in Irrigation Waters, Soil Sc., 39: 123-133.

ECIL Methods Manual (2004) Methods Manual, Atomic Absorption Spectrophotometer, AAS 4129, Electronic Corporation of India Limited, Hyderabad-500062, pp: 85.

Eckenfelder, W.W. and Bornad, J.L. (1971): Treatment Cost Relationship for Industrial Waste, Chemical Engg. Progress, 67(9): 76.

Fakayode, S.O. and Onianwa, P.C. (2002): Heavy Metal Contamination of Soil, and Bioaccumulation in Guinea grass (Panicum maximum) Around Ikeja Industrial Estate, Lagos, Nigeria, Environmental Geology, 43: 145-150.

Fetter, C.W. (1994): Applied Hydrology, 3rd edition, Macmillan, New York.

Florence, T.M. (1982): The Speciation of Trace Elements in Waters, Talanta, 29: 345-369.

Forstner, U. (1985): Chemical Forms and Reactivities of Metals in Sediments in Chemical Methods for Assessing Bioavailable Metals in Sludge and Soils, In: Leschber, R., Davies, R.D. and Hermite, L.P. (Eds), Elsevier, London, pp: 1-30.

Forstner, U. and Wittman, G.T.W. (1981): Metal Pollution in the Aquatic Environment, Second ed. Springer, Berlin, pp: 486.

Forstner, U.; Ahlf, W.; Calmano, W.; Kersten, M. and Schoer, J. (1990): Assessment of Metal Mobility in Sludge and Soild Wastes, In: Metal Speciation in the Environment (Eds.- Broeckaert, J.A.C; Gucer, S. and Adams, F.) Springer, Berlin, pp: 1-41.

Fransson, Åsa (2007): A Case Study to Verify Methods for Estimating Transmissivity Distributions Along Boreholes, Hydrogeology Journal, 15: 307–313,

Fraser, B.G. and Williams, D.D. (1998): Seasonal Boundary Dynamics of a Ground Water/ Surface-Water Ecotone, Ecology, 79(6): 2019-2031.

Frostner, U., and Wittman, G.T.W. (1979) Metal Pollution in the Aquatic Environment, Berlin Germany, Springer-Verlag., pp: 545.

Gardner, W.R. (1957): Some Steady State Solutions of the Unsaturated Moisture Flow Equation with Application to Evaporation from a Water Table, Soil Sci., 85: 228-232.

Garg, V. K; Sharma, I.S. and Bishnoi, M.S. (1998): Fluoride in Under Ground Water of Uklana Town, District Hisar, Haryana, Poll. Res. 17(2): 149-152.

Garg, V.K. and Kaushik, P. (2006): Influence of Short-term Irrigation of Textile Mill Wastewater on the Growth of Chickpea Cultivars, Chemistry and Ecology, 22(3): 193-200.

Garg, V.K.; Chaudhary, A.; Deepshikha and Dahiya, S. (1998): An Appraisal of Ground Water Quality in Some Villages of District Jind, Indian J. Environmental Protection, 19(4): 267-272.

Gharaibeh, M.A.; Eltaif, N.I. and Bayan Al-Abdullah (2007): Impact of Field Application of Treated Wastewater on Hydraulic Properties of Vertisols, Water Air Soil Pollut, DOI-10.1007/s11270-007-9423-z.

Golia, E.E.; Dimirkou, A. and Mitsios, I.K. (2007): Accumulation of Metals on Tobacco Leaves (Primings) Grown in an Agricultural Area in Relation to Soil, Bul.l Environ. Contam. Toxicol., DOI 10.1007/s00128-007-9111-0.

Goltenboth, F. (1994): Impact of Textile Factory in Salatiga on Ledok River System, Central Java, J. Environ. Toxicol., South East Asia, pp: 301-317.

Gomez-Serrano, Garcia-Macias, A., Espinosa-Mansilla, A. and Valenzuela-Calahorro (1998): Adsorption of Mercury, Cadmium and Lead from Aquoes Solution on Heat Treated and Sulphurized Activated Carbon. Wat. Res., 32:1-4.

GoogleEarth (2006): Software for Satellite Imagery, available at http://www.google.com.

Gopal, B. (1994): Conservation of Inland Water in India: An Overview. Verh. Internet. Verein. Hydrobiologia, 384: 267.

Govindan, V.S. and Sundarlingam, V.S. (1979) Studies on Treatment of Textile Mill Waste Water by Stabilization Pond Method. J. Pollution Control, 5 (2):137-145.

Gray, C. W. and Mclaren, R. G. (2006): Soil Factors Affecting Heavy Metal Solubility in Some New Zealand Soils, Water, Air and Soil Pollution, 175: 3-14.

Groff, K.A. (1993): Textile Waste, Environmental Research. 65: 421.

Gupta, R.K., Singh, R.R. and Abrol, I.P. (1989): Influence of Simultaneous Changes in Sodicity and pH on Hydraulic Conditions of an Alkali Soil, Soil Science, 147: 28-33.

Harper, H.H.; Yusuf, Y.A. and Wanielista, M.P. (1984): Fate of Heavy Metals in Stromwater Management System, In: Lake and Reservoir Management, USEPA, Washington, pp: 329-334.

Hart, B.T. (1982): Trace Metals in Natural Waters, Speciation Chem. Australian, 49: 260-265.

Hedge, V.S.; Shalini, G. and Kanchanagouri, D.G. (2006): Provenance of Heavy Minerals with Special Reference to Ilmenite of the Honnevar Beach, Central West Coast of India, Current Science, 91 (5): 644-648.

Helena, B.A.; Vega, M.; Barrado, E.; Parado, R. and Fernandez, L. (1999): A Case of Hydro-Chemical Characterization of an Alluvial Aquifer Influenced by Human Activities, Water, Air and Soil Pollution, 112: 365-387.

Hesse, P.R. (1994): A Textbook of Soil Chemical Analysis, CBS Publishers and Distributors, 485, Bholanathnagar, Shahdhra, Delhi-110032, pp: 520.

Hitz, H.R.; Huber, W and Rud, R.H. (1978): The Absorption of Dyes on Activated Sludge, Journal of Society of Dyers and Colorists, February: 71-76.

Horing, R.H. (1976): Characterization and Treatment of Textile Dyeing Wastewaters, In: Proceedings of National Technical Conference, American Association of Textile Chemists and Colorist, pp: 100-104.

Hoston, A.K. (1965): An Index Number System for Rating Water Quality, J. Wat. Poll. Cont. Fed., 37(3): 300-306.

http//:www.engg.ksu.edu as access on 16 November, 2006

Huang, J.; Huang, R.; Jiao, J.J. and Chen, K. (2007): Speciation and Mobility of Heavy Metals in Mud in Coastal Reclamation Areas in Shenzhen, China, Environ. Geol., DOI 10.1007/s00254-007-0636-7.

Hynes, H.B.N. (1970): The Ecology of Running Waters, Liverpool University Press, Liverpool, 4th Impression: 1-555.

Ireland, M.P. (1983): Heavy Metals Uptake and Tissue Distribution, In: Earthworm Ecology-from Darwin to Vermiculture (Ed.- Satchell, J.E., Chapman and Hall), pp: 135-147.

IUPAC (1994): Atomic Weights of the Elements, 1993, International Union of Pure and Applied Chemistry, Pure Appl. Chem., 66: 2423.

Jain, C.K. (2004): Metal Fractionation Study on Bed Sediments of River Yamuna, India, Wat. Res. 38: 569-578.

Jayabaskeran, K. J. Sree Ramulu U. S. (1996): Distribution of Heavy Metals in Soil of Various Sewage Farms in Tamil Nadu, J. Indian Soc. Soil. Sci., 44: 401-404.

Jha, M.N. and Pandey, P. (1984): Impact of Growing Eucalyptus and Soil Monocultures on Soil in Natural Sal Area of Doon Valley, Ind. For., 110: 16-18.

Judlins, J.F. and Hornsby, J.S. (1978): Color Removal from Textile Dye Waste Using Magnesium Carbonate, Journal of Water Pollution Control Federation, 50: 2446-2456.

Kalra, Y.P. and Maynarol, D.G. (1991): Methods Manual for Forest Soil and Plant Analysis. For. Can., Northwest Reg. North. For. Cent. Edmonton, Alberta. Inf. Rep. Nor. X-319, pp: 1-65.

Kanwar, J.S. (1961): Quality of Irrigation Water as an Index of Suitability for Irrigation Purposes, Potash Review, 13: 1-13.

Karle, K.K.; Bhusal, S.S.; Gunjal, P.S. and Kuchekar, S.R. (1992): Studied on Ground Water Quality in Pravaranagar Area of Ahmednagar District, Poll. Res. 11(2): 65-68.

Kashem, M.A. and Singh, B.R. (1999): Heavy Metal Contamination of Soil and Vegetation in the Vicinity of Industries in Bangladesh, Water, Air and Soil Pollution, 115: 347-361.

Kataria, H.C. (1996): BOD and COD Contents in Bore Well Water of Bhopal (M.P.), Natcon, 8(1): 69-72.

Kataria, H.C.; Gupta, S.S. and Jain, O.P. (1995): Water Quality of Bore Wells in B.H.E.L. Area of Bhopal, Poll. Res. 14 (4): 455-462.

Katz, M. (1975): The Effect of Heavy Metals on Fish and Aquatic Environment. (Ed.- Krenkel, P.A.), Pregamon Press, New York, pp: 637-645.

Kaushik, M.P. (2006): Vanaspati Vigyan, Prakash Prakashan, Muzaffarnagar, 834.

Khan T.I., Marwari Richa, Singh N. (2003): Impact of Textile Wastewater on Solanum Melongena var-FI- Hybrid Kanhaiya in Pot Experiment with Special Emphasis on Analysis of Heavy Metals. Dimensions Polln, 2: 108-116.

Khurshid, Zaheeruddin and Mohd. Usman Shabeer (1997): Degradation of Water Quality Due to Heavy Metals Pollution in Faridabad district, Haryana, India, Poll. Res. 16(1): 41-43.

Korfali, S.I. and Davies, B.D.E. (2004): The Relationship of Metals in River Sediments (Nahr-Ibrahim, Lebanon) and Adjacent Floodplain Soil, the CIGR J. of Scientific Research and Development, Manuscript LW 04 010, 6: 1-22.

Krebs, R.; Gupta, S.K.; Furrer, G. and Schulin, R. (1999): Gravel Sludge as an Immobilizing Agent in Soils Contaminated by Heavy Metals: A Field Study, Water, Air and Soil Pollution, 115: 465-479.

Krishna, A. K. and Govil, P. K. (2004) Heavy Metal Contamination of Soil Around Pali Industrial Area, Rajasthan, India, Environmental Geology, 47: 38-44.

Krull, R. and E. Dopkens (2004): Recycling of Dye House Effluents by Biological and Chemical Treatment, Water Sc. And Tech. 49(4): 311-317.

Kudesia, V.P. (1992): Water Pollution, Pragati Prakashan, Meerut, pp: 407.

Lofts, S.; Spurgeon, D.J.; Svendsen, C. and Tipping, E. (2004): Deriving Soil Critical Limits for Cu, Zn, Cd, and pH: A Method Based on Free Ion Concentration, Environ. Sci. Tech., 38: 3623-3631.

Lokeshwari, H. and Chandrappa, G.T. (2006): Impact of Heavy Metal Contamination of Bellandur Lake on Soil and Cultivated Vegetation, Current Science, 91(9): 622-627.

Lokeshwari, H. and Chandrappa, G.T. (2006): Impact of Heavy Metal Contamination of Bellandur Lake on Soil and Cultivated Vegetation, Current Science, 91(9): 622-627.

Loska, K. and Wiechula, D. (2002): Speciation of Cadmium in the Bottom Sediment of Rybnik Reservoir, Water, Air Soil Pollut., 141: 73-89.

Lung, W. (1990): Speciation Analysis – Why and How? Fresenius J. Anal. Chem. 337: 557-564.

Malik, D.S. and Bharti, P. K. (2007): Soil Quality of Irrigated Agricultural Fields in Textile Industrial Area of Panipat city, Asian Journal of Experimental Sciences, 21 (2): 445-451.

Malik, D.S.; Bharti, P.K. and Grover, S. (2006): Alteration in Surface Water Quality Near Textile Industries at Panipat (Haryana), Environment Conservation J., 7(2): 65-68.

Malik, D.S.; Bharti, P.K; Kamboj, N. and Yadav, R. (2007): Quantification of Heavy Metals Migration in Ground Water Regime Due to Discharge of Textile Industrial Effluents in Panipat area, Haryana, Pollution Research, 26 (4): 123-125.

Malik, D.S.; Yadav, R. and Bharti, P.K. (2004) Accumulation of Heavy Metals in Crop Plants Through Irrigation of Contaminated Ground Water in Panipat Region, Environmental Conservation Journal 5 (3): 101-104.

Manahan, S. (1984): Environmental Chemistry, Brooks/Colei, CA, USA, pp: 638.

Manchanda, H.R. (1990): Significance of the Type of Salinity for Growing Pulses Under Saline Conditions, Indo-Pak Workshop on Soil Salinity and Water Management, Feb, 10-14, pp: 2-3.

Mani, V.; Kaur, H. and Mohini, M. (2005): Toxic Metals and Environmental Pollution, J. Ind. Poll. Cont., 21(1): 101-107.

Martin, J.M. and Whitfield, M. (1983): The Significance of the River input of Chemical Elements to the Ocean, In: Wong, C.S.; Boyle, E.; Bruland, K.W.; Burton, J.D. and Goldburg, E.D. (Eds.), Trace Metals in Sea Water, Plenum Press, New York, pp: 324-331.

Martin, M.H. and Cougherty, P.J. (1982): Biological Monitoring of Heavy Metals Pollution, Applied Science Publishers, pp: 463.

Masters, G.M. (1998): Introduction to Environmental Engineering and Science, Prentice-Hall India, pp: 460.

Mathess, G. (1974): Heavy Metals as Trace Constituents in Natural and Polluted Ground Water, Goel Mijnbouw, New Jersy, USA, 53: 149-155.

McBride, M., Sauve, S. and Hendershot, W. (1997): Solubility Control of Cu, Zn, Cd, and Pb, in Contaminated Soils, Euro. J. Soil Science, 48: 337-346.

Mico, C; Recatal, L.; Peris, M. And Sanchez, J. (2007): A Comparison of Two Digestion Methods for the Analysis of Heavy Metals by Flame Atomic Absorption Spectroscopy, Spectroscopy Europe, 19 (1): 23-26.

Mido, Y. and Satake, M, (1995): Chemicals in the Environment, Discovery Publishing House, New Delhi, pp: 491.

Millar, C.E. and Turk, L.M. (2002): Fundamentals of Soil Science, Biotech Books, Delhi-35, pp: 462.

Minhas, P.S. and Khosla, B.K. (1986): Solute Displacement in a Silt Loam Soil as Affected by the Method of Water Application under Different Evaporation Rates, Agric. Wat. Mgmt, 12: 63-75.

Mohan, R.; Chopra, N. and Chowdhary, G.C. (1998): Heavy Metals (Fe, Pb, Cd, Zn) in the Ground Water of Naini Industrial Area, Dist. Allahabad, U.P., Poll. Res. 17(2): 167-168.

MPCA (2001): Effects of Land Use on Ground Water Quality, St. Cloud Area, Minnesota – Short Report, Minnesota Pollution Control Agency, Ground Water Monitoring and Assessment Program, pp: 1-29.

Muller, G. (1979): Schwermetalle in Den Sedimenten des Rheinsveranderungen Seit, Umschau, 79: 778-783.

Nasr, S.M.; Okbah, M.A. and Kasem, S.M. (2006): Environmental Assessment of Heavy Metal Pollution in Bottom Sediments of Aden port, Yemen, International Journal of Oceans and Oceanography, 1(1): 99-109

National Research Council (NRC) (1989): Contaminated Marine Systems-assessment and Remediation, National Academy Press, Washington, D.C. pp: 185.

Navarro, A. and Font, X. (1993): Discriminating Different Sources of Ground Water Contamination Caused by Industrial Waste in the Besos River Basin, Barcelona, Spain, J. Applied Biochemistry, APPGEY, 8: 277.

Nedunuri, K.V.; Govindaraju, R.S.; Erickson, L.E. and Schwab, A.P. (1995): Modeling of Heavy Metal Movement in Vegetated, Unsaturated Soils with Emphasis on Geochemistry, In: Proceedings of the 10th Annual Conference on Hazardous Waste Research, pp: 57-66.

Nongkynrih, P.; Dkhar, P.S. and Khathing, D.T. (1996): Micronutrients Elements in Acid Alfisols of Meghalaya Under Rice Cultivation, J. Soil Si., 44(3): 455-457.

Nriagu, J.O. and Pacyna, J.M. (1988): Quantitative Assessment of Worldwide Contamination of Air, Water and Soil with Trace Metals, Nature, 333: 134-139.

Numberg, H.W. (1984): The Volumetric Approach in Trace Metal Chemistry of Natural Waters and Atmospheric Precipitation, Analyst. Chim. Acta, 164: 1-21.

Obiri, Samuel (2007): Determination of Heavy Metals in Water from Boreholes in Dumasi in the Wassa West District of Western Region of Republic of Ghana, Environ Monit Assess, 130: 455–463.

Padmavathiamma, P.K. and Li, L.Y. (2007): Phytoremediation Technology: Hyper-Accumulation Metals in Plants, Water Air Soil Pollut., DOI- 10.1007/s11270-007-9401-5.

Palanivelu, K.; Priya, M.N.; Selvan, A.M. and Natesan,U. (2006): Water Quality Assessment in the Tsunami Affected Coastal Areas of Chennai, Current Science, 91 (5): 583-584.

Prasad, S. (2003): Fundamentals of Biostatistics (biometry), Emkey Publication, Delhi-51, pp: 168.

Pujari, G.K. and Sinha, B.K. (1999): Studies on the Water and Soil Quality of Some Villages of Attabira Area Irrigated by Bargarg Main Canal Originated from Hirakund Reservoir of Orissa, J. of Env. and Poll., 6(1): 71-76.

Rao, K.V.G.K.; Gupta R.K. and Kamra, S.K. (1987): Reclamation of Waterlogged High SAR Saline Soil, CSSRI, Karnal, A Feasibility Report for CIRB, Hissar, CSSRI, Karnal, pp: 21.

Rhoades, J.D. (1987): Use of Saline Water for Irrigation, Wat. Qual. Bull., 12: 14-20.

Richards, L.A. (1954): Diagnosis and Improvement of Saline and Alkali Soils, US Deptt. Agri., Edited Handbook, No. 60: 160.

Saxena, M.M. (1994): In: Environmental Analysis Water, Soil and Air, Agro Botanical Publishers. pp: 1-180.

Schroeder, W.H. (1989): Development in the Speciation of Mercury in Natural Waters, Trends Anal. Chem. 8: 339-342.

Sharma, D.R. (1978): Testing of a Model for Prediction Sodium Hazards of Irrigation Waters, J. Indian Soc. Soil Sci., 27: 204-208.

Sharma, D.R. and Parihar, S.S. (1973): Effect of Depth and Salinity of Ground Water on Evaporation and Soil Salinization, Indian J. Agric. Sci., 43: 582-586.

Shrivastava V.S. and Patil B.H. (2003): Metallic and Some Physico-chemical Studies of Soil and Aquatic Sediments, Eco Env Conserv, 9(1): 75-77

Singh, B. and Bhumbla, D.R. (1968): Effect of Quality of Irrigation Water on Soil Properties, J. Res. (Punjab Agri. Univ.), 5: 166-171.

Singh, B. Rana, D.S. and Bajwa, M.S. (1977): Salinity and Sodium Hazards of Underground Irrigation Waters of Bhatinda District (Punjab), Indian J. Ecol., 4: 32-41.

Singh, K.N.; Bains, S.S. and Dayanand (1969): Salinity Problem in High Water Table Areas-An appraisal, Indian J, Agron., 14: 31-34.

Singh, K.S. and Sharma, R.P. (1971): Studies on the Effects of Saline Irrigation Waters on Physico-chemical Properties of Some Soils of Rajasthan, J. Indian Soc. Soil Sci., 18: 345-356.

Singh, T.B.; Jadon, S.P.S. and Mishra, G.J. (1994): Degradation of Water and Soil Quality of Parwanoo Area with Respect to Heavy Metals, IJEP, 14 (4): 282-287.

Srinivasan, M. and Murali, M. (1996): Some Studies on Effect Pollutants on Properties of Soils, IJEP, 16(7): 522-523.

Tan, K.H. and Nopamornbodi, O. (1981): Electron Microbeam Analysis and Scanning Electron Microscopy of Soil-root interfaces, Soil Sci., 131: 100-106.

Taylor, S.R. (1964): Abundance of Chemical Elements in the Continental Crust – A New Table, Geochim. Cosmochim. Acta. 28: 1273-1275.

Trevors, J.T. and Saier Jr., M.H. (2007): Regulation of Pollution, Water Air Soil Pollut, DOI 10.1007/s11270-007-9344-x.

Trivedi, R.K. and Goel, P.K. (1984): Chemical and Biological Methods for Water Pollution Studies Karad, Environmental publication, pp: 1-251.

USEPA (1990): Operation and Quality Control Manual, Environmental Protection Agency (EPA), Athens, GA 30613.

Va´zquez, N.N.; Gil, M.A.; Esteves, J. L. and Narvarte, M. A. (2007): Monitoring Heavy Metal Pollution in San Antonio Bay, Rı´o Negro, Argentina, Bull. Environ. Contam. Toxicol., DOI 10.1007/s00128-007-9084-z.

Walker, D.J.; Bernal, M.P. and Correal, E. (2007): The Influence of Heavy Metals and Mineral Nutrient Supply on Bituminaria bituminosa, Water Air Soil Pollut, DOI 10.1007/s11270-007-9422-0.

Walker, R. (1970): The Metabolism of Azo Compounds: A Review of the Literature, Food Cosmetics Toxicology, 8: 659-661.

WHO (2006) Standards for Drinking Water, available at http//:www.lenntech.com

Williums, D.R. (1972): Metals, Ligands and Cancer, Chemical Review, 72 (3): 203-213.

Wint, A. (1981): The Disposal of Toxic Wastes, In: Industrial Effluent Treatment Vol-I (Eds.- Watler, J.K. and Wint, M.), pp: 1-19.

Yadav, R.K.; Goyal, B.; Sharma, R.K.; Dubey, S.K. and Minhas, P.S. (2002): Post-irrigation Impact of Domestic Sewage Effluent on Composition of Soils, Crops and Ground Water- A Case Study, Environment International, 28: 481-486.

Yuandong, Z.; Shirong, L. and Jiangming, M. (2006): Water-holding Capacity of Ground Covers and Soil in Alpine and Sub-alpine Shrubs in Western Sichuan, China, ACTA Ecologica Sinica, 26(9): 2775-2782.

Zheng, G.; Yue, L.; Li, Z and Chen, C. (2006): Assessment on Heavy Metals Pollution of Agricultural Soil in Guanzhong District, J Geographical Sciences, 16, (1): 105-113.

Index